Charles Conrad Abbott

Upland and meadow:

A Poaetquissings chronicle

Charles Conrad Abbott

Upland and meadow:
A Poaetquissings chronicle

ISBN/EAN: 9783337731687

Printed in Europe, USA, Canada, Australia, Japan

Cover: Foto ©ninafisch / pixelio.de

More available books at **www.hansebooks.com**

UPLAND AND MEADOW,

A Poaetquissings Chronicle

BY

CHARLES C. ABBOTT, M.D.

AUTHOR OF
"PRIMITIVE INDUSTRY" "A NATURALIST'S RAMBLES ABOUT HOME" ETC.

NEW YORK
HARPER & BROTHERS, FRANKLIN SQUARE

PREFACE.

A CRITICAL friend told me I must write a preface, and when he saw that my despair became a serious matter, suggested that it might properly consist of a few words with reference to the supplementary title of the book.

Following Campanius, who, in his "History of New Sweden," mentions a stream, I presume to be in this neighborhood, as Poaetquissings Creek, I have followed his spelling of the name. It is not euphonious, I admit, yet quite pronounceable, and therefore has been freely mentioned. But so occupied have I been with the features of the stream itself, that not until recently, when the book was completed, did it occur to me to either determine the meaning of the word or how near to the Indian pronunciation the spelling adopted by Campanius might be.

I have learned both facts, and should certainly deem the result disastrous were I necessitated to frequently struggle over the proper pronunciation.

My learned friend, Dr. Daniel G. Brinton, informs

me that "the word has suffered considerable mutilation. It has certainly lost its first syllable, which is a common occurrence with Anglicized native words. I take it to be a synthesis of *ach-poan*, corn-bread, and *ach-gussen*, to roast or cook, with the locative termination *nk*. Hence the full form would be *achpoachgussink*, and would mean 'the place of corn-bread baking.'"

Says good Thomas Campanius, of Stockholm, " Poaetquissings Creek is by nature provided with everything that man can desire;" but where is Poaetquissings Creek?

The map of the Delaware River made by Peter Lindstrom in 1654, and described by Campanius in his quaint little "History of New Sweden," has been a source of amusement to me ever since I dared venture alone in a boat. I have been trying, whenever opportunity offered, to determine to what points he referred in his brief descriptions, and have never felt discouraged, even though the more accurate Acrelius, writing some years later, remarks, " Aquikonasra, Warentapecka, Trakonick, Poaetquessing, Mencieck, etc., etc., are forgotten places."

Wandering on the river from point to point, I find, even now, many curious features, as I explore the little inflowing creeks, or pause at the mouth of some pretentious stream, as it empties into the river, and say, "Perhaps this is Aquikonasra;" or, chancing in winter upon some open water, ask, "Can this be Warentapecka?" Campanius says of the latter, it is a spot where the water never freezes, and swans abound at all seasons. If the half-hidden stream that I enter is choked with wild weeds, and I am stopped by the absence of a defined channel, I recall what our author says of Trakonick, "It is difficult to navigate through this part."

Now, as a matter of fact, there are not so many creeks, on the Jersey side, emptying into the Delaware between the falls and the capes, as Lindstrom mentions or Campanius describes in detail, and we can only conclude that two or more names refer, in some cases, to the same stream, or the creek and the land it drained were known by different names. In either case, we have left us no alternative but to guess which is which, and, so doing, I conclude that the little stream near by, which I have at times called Popihacka and Mencieck, as fancy suggested, may, after all, be that which our author mentions in so striking a manner when he says, "At Poaetquissings Creek . . . is everything that man can desire."

The tangible little stream to which I refer, whatever name it possessed in Indian times, is the second below the rapids of the river, or where the Assunpink empties into the Delaware, and is very near, if not quite, within the region mentioned by Campanius when he says, "From Trakonick, and farther up on the east side of the river, the soil is fine, and bears black maize of the color of tar; the Indians have planted it there for many years. It is difficult to navigate through this part. It is inhabited on this side by the *Manteese* Indians; that nation considers itself entitled to these shores by the right of possession; their numbers are now much diminished by wars. The land within is very rich in animal productions. There are beavers, otters, elks, bears, wolves, and lions, with every other kind of wild beasts; also, a great quantity of swans, geese, turkeys, pigeons, and other wild fowl."

This description can be verified to a great extent. Whether we call them Manteese or Lenâpè or Delawares, certain it is that Indians were here in days gone by, and here for many centuries. As a proof of this, we have only to land at any point, and wander a few rods from the bank of the creek. Wherever the sod is broken, whether by the plough or gullied by summer showers, we are sure to find broken pebbles, splinters of flinty rock, and battered stones, which of themselves tell the story of Indian times; but not so readily can we read their history as when we find a little arrowhead, a carved stone ornament, an axe, or broken pot. These are sufficient to satisfy even the most incredulous, and from such scattered relics a more trustworthy history of the past can be reconstructed than from such prejudiced mention of the Indians as is made by the short-sighted missionaries who, in questionable efforts to elevate them, destroyed every good quality, and gave them nothing of lasting value in return. What splendid opportunities had the early Quakers to preserve to us a much-desired knowledge of the aboriginal people of the Delaware valley, and what trivial facts have they left on record! Later, such men as the Brainerds might have taught us much; they have left us only the record of their own laborious but fruitless lives. Such pitiful incidents of the past are now well-nigh forgotten, and well they may be.

The Indians, to whom Aryan civilization proved a curse, and whose last days here were embittered by the bigotry that beset them, have left imperishable traces on every acre of the Delaware valley, which now afford to him who loves to ramble a ceaseless round of pleasure in gathering their weapons, ornaments, domestic implements, and even the toys of their children.

From these, indeed, we can reconstruct fairly well the story of their lives; perhaps better than could those who, desirous of bettering them temporally and eternally, only succeeded in depriving them of their lands and embittering their lives; and, of this long river valley, perhaps no spot is more profusely supplied with the relics of the Indians than what I believe to be the Trakonick neighborhood mentioned by Campanius, and particularly the shores of the little creek I assume to be Poaetquissings.

So much, at least for the present, of the people who dwelt here in pre-European times. The stream as it is to-day will now command our attention.

I have been told by a lady, a former resident of Chicago, that, during the great fire in that city, she was bidden by her parents, when the house was about to be burned, to remove from her room such valuables as she could conveniently carry. She retired for that purpose, and, forgetting all her jewelry, returned to her parents with a cake of soap.

I trust that, having been out of doors nearly every day of the year, either in the uplands or the meadows, it has not proved to so little purpose. The jewels were there, and free to him who would select; may what I offer, as the gatherings of many rambles, prove something better than *a cake of soap.*

C. C. A.

PROSPECT HILL, TRENTON, N. J.

CONTENTS.

CHAPTER	PAGE
I. AT THE OUTSET	1
II. POAETQUISSINGS IN WINTER	18
III. 'TWIXT COLD AND HEAT	61
IV. MARSH-WRENS	88
V. A COLONY OF GRAKLES	101
VI. FOUR RED BIRDS	114
VII. THE SPADE-FOOT TOAD	132
VIII. TRUMPET-CREEPERS AND THE RUBY-THROATS	142
IX. THE DRAWING OF THE SEINE	147
X. A SUMMER AT HOME	189
XI. SEPTEMBER SUNSHINE	247
XII. AN OCTOBER DIARY	264
XIII. AN OCTOBER DIARY—CONTINUED	308
XIV. AN OCTOBER DIARY—CONCLUDED	348
INDEX	391

UPLAND AND MEADOW.

A Poaetquissings Chronicle.

CHAPTER I.

AT THE OUTSET.

BETTER repeat the twelve labors of Hercules than attempt to catalogue the varied forms of life found in the area of an average ramble. Indeed, I have seldom seen a half-acre that was not a "Zoo" which the study of a lifetime would fail to exhaust; but, if this is the sole incentive to take a recreative stroll in the upland or meadow, it were better to stay at home.

On the other hand, to feel that whatever creature we may meet will prove companionable—that it is no stranger, but rather an amusing and instructive friend—assures us both pleasure and profit whenever we chance abroad.

He who has this interest in the life about him can never be lonely, wander wheresoever he will, nor return from a contemplative ramble other than a wiser and happier man.

When I talked, years ago, to the old men of the neighborhood—there is not one of them left—I invariably wished that I had been my grandfather. I felt fully a century too late.

If half the tales they told me were true, nothing of to-day equals that which was found here when they were young. If this had been an old man's fancy it would have only provoked a smile; but, alas! it was so far true as to cause me at the time endless regret. It was by no means a sugar-coated pill that I was forced to swallow when one of these gray-beards quietly remarked, "You seem to know something about animals, but we had the critters themselves."

This was not cheering to one who was ambitious of seeing something of wild life, but I had one consolation; my old friend had not seen the country in its best days, as judged from his point of view. As proof of this, compare his remarks with the following, from an old diary:

"Ninth mo., 1734. Father reports Friend Stacy as saying that formerly ducks and geese were more abundant than they now are. He thinks the use of great noisy guns has reduced their numbers. How they could be more abundant than of late puzzleth me to comprehend. Watson's Creek is often truly black with them, and gatherings of fowl of many kinds do now pass up the Crossweeksen, such as take several minutes to pass by. The geese are always in wedge-shaped companies, and are never so numerous as in the smaller sorts. I do seldom see the great swans, but father says they are not unusual in the wide stretches of the Delaware. The Indians that lately tarried by the great spring on our hillside did shoot several near where the creek joins the river. . . . Father allowed me to accompany Oconio, my Indian friend, to Watson's Creek, that we might gather wild fowl, after the Indian manner. With great eagerness I accompanied Oconio, and thus happened it. We did reach the widest part of that creek early in the morning. I think the sun was scarcely an half-hour high. Oconio straightway hid himself in the tall grass by the water, while I was bidden to lie in the tall grass at a little distance. With his bow and arrows, Oconio quickly shot a duck that came near by, swimming within a short space from him. I marvelled much with what skill he shot, for his arrow pierced the head of the duck, which gave no alarming cry. Then, with a second arrow, he struck down another, but not so quickly, at which the great company of fowl flew away, with great clamor. Very many returned quickly, much to our pleasure. Oconio did now fashion a circlet of green boughs, and so placed them about his head and shoulders that I saw not his face, and, thus arrayed, he otherwise disrobed and walked into the stream. He held in one hand a shotten duck, so that it swam lustily, and, so equipped, was in the midst of a cluster of fowl, of which he deftly seized several so quickly that its fellows took no alarm. These he strangled beneath the water, and, when he had three of them, came back, with caution, to where the thick bushes concealed him. He desired that I should do the same, and with much hesitation I disrobed and assumed the disguise Oconio had fashioned; then I put forth boldly towards the gathered fowl, at which they did rise with a great clamor, and were gone.

I marvel much why this should have been, but Oconio did not make it clear, and I forbore, through foolish pride, to ask of him. And let it not be borne against me that, when I reached my home, I wandered to the barn, and writing an ugly word upon the door, sat long and gazed at it. Chagrin doth make one feel very weak, I find, but I set no one an example by speech or act, in thus soothing my feelings in so worldly a manner.

"While I do yet write of our wild beestes of this country, let me here remark, that while we rejoice that great bears have mostly gone far towards the unsettled mountains, still a few do linger with us; and Oconio recently did assure me that he knoweth of a small one that liveth in a great chestnut-tree, not far within the great east woods.... With much misgiving that we were to go without my parents' knowledge, but hoping success would secure forgiveness—for a longing heart offers tid-bits to our scruples—we set out, while it was yet dark, on third day; and it was frostful and stingy for so early in the ninth month. As we passed the growth of dwarf chestnuts bordering the common road, I marvelled at the great companies of squirrels that were then gathering the harvest of nuts; but Oconio chided me for lingering, and, following chiefly his footsteps, we strode straightway and silently through the wood. There was yet a proper pathway that was readily to be seen, which, as I have learned, was that used by the Indians when they passed to Amboy, where they gathered the bounty of the sea. When we had gone so far as an hour's walk taketh one, suddenly Oconio turned into a dense and trackless thicket; first looking at his gunne, and the flint and priming thereof. I could not readily keep to him in the midst of the bushes, and labored much to force my way where he moved silently. But it rejoiced me to know we had but a short distance to go, for suddenly he turned about and pointed to a great tree. It was the greatest of all trees that I have seen. I confess to being puzzled to know what Oconio was to do, that a bear should come from the tree and be shotten. I ventured a question, but it was only answered by an impatient 'See,' so I remained standing, eager to know, yet doubtful of my safety should there be even a small bear in the great tree. Oconio directly gathered a bundle of sticks and of crisp leaves, and the store thereof he placed at the foot of the tree, where I saw was a hole that even he could have entered. With his tinder and flint in a moment he added fire to the leaves, and with a great roaring the smoke rushed through the trunk of that tree. This was answered by a louder murmur, which I took to be the voice of the enraged bear, and Oconio stood bravely with his gunne should it appear. Account it not against me that I desired to flee, and I should have turned had I known just where to seek safety; and then came a greater terror as the enraged bear growled with fiercer anger. I turned, and Oconio exclaimed 'Ugh!' as I did so. The bear was upon us—not as one creature, but as thousands; for we had driven from the tree a hiving of bees. I turned so quickly that I fell, and the maddened bees were quickly covering me, as I thought; but I regained my feet, and was soon fleeing from their torment. Whether Oconio did lead or follow I knew not, but we met at a brook, where I bathed my smarting flesh.

"We walked home in silence; and to this day I feel chagrined when my father talketh of bears; nor is honey a sweet morsel to me."

Almost my last conversation with my venerable friend was much the longest. He seemed far more disposed to talk than walk, and, while sitting in the dense shade of my three beeches, he remarked, "There was a spice in livin' when the country was younger you don't get now that all the big critters are about gone;" and, pointing to a little woodpecker near by, asked, "Do you see that sapsucker? I can remember when the big log-cocks were about as plenty as those are nowadays. Back towards the great Cattail Swamp, where there was yaller-pine woods, the log-cocks used to run up and down the trees like mad, and the way they sent the bark flyin' was a caution. If they thought there was a bug or grub under the bark, they'd lift it out, and, to get it, sometimes ripped a bit of bark off big as a dinner-plate. Now you see nothin' of all this, but have come down to little sapsuckers."

"Not quite," I replied; "there are flickers and red-heads left us."

"That's so, but they're not much better, nor many of 'em, and who livin,' but me, ever heard a wolf growl or a painter screech?"

"Did you ever see a panther about here?" I asked.

"Didn't I as much as say so just now? See one, yes, once, and that was enough."

"Tell me the circumstance, please," I requested, with much pleasurable anticipation.

"Tell you the circumstance? If you mean the main p'ints of the matter, I can give 'em to you. It was during a January thaw, and a big fresh on the lowlands. It's such times, you know, when all the fun comes in round here. Well, I'd lost a new boat, and found it in the woods near the mouth of Crosswicks Creek. It was left up in the bushes after the water had gone down a bit. I scrambled out of my skiff to reach to it, when the critter looked up and grinned right in my face. He'd been curled up in the boat, and didn't show any notion of leavin'; but I did, and, makin' one big jump for my skiff, the critter follered suit, and made for the woods. I didn't look behind, thinkin' he was comin' for me; but it seems he wasn't, and that was the last of him."

"Is that all?" I asked, with a show of disappointment.

"All? Yes, and if you'd been in my place half the facts would have satisfied you. Critters like painters might go, and bears weren't always pleasant to meet with, but all the others were good in their way, and, along with the miles of big woods, made it a pleasant country. I don't say it to tease you none, but you've got now to take up with small fry, and only think about them that's gone for good. When I hear the tap-tap of the sapsuckers I think of the log-cocks, and when there's a bayin' hound in the fields I can hear the wolves, which, 'long late as '95, used to keep me 'wake o' nights. Things have littled down since I was a boy, sure enough. What you call trees we'd say were saplins', and such trees as I've cut are too scarce to count. Afore you're fairly in a woods now you're on t'other side of 'em."

But, in spite of the changes wrought by the deforesting of the country and the increased population, even in these later days unfrequented corners can be found, and one may have a bit of adventure if one chooses.

The average farmer is eminently practical, and quite properly so, but if an acre cannot be reclaimed for cultivation, or if its wood be not worth cutting for fuel, it is pretty sure to be abandoned to the few who love to see nature free from all artificiality. I know of an island in a creek, *planted* with swamp-sumac, where I can roam at will, because this tree does not poison me, and all my neighbors have to give it a wide berth, or suffer the consequences; and here I can sit as much alone as though in the deepest cañon of the Colorado River of the West. But, while I have outgrown the feeling of disappointment that I live in so tame a country, and now prefer a mouse to a muskrat for a playfellow, very often finding my interest in animal life to be inversely to the bulk of its body, still an occasional exciting episode is not distasteful, as a recent occurrence proved.

Bitter cold though it happened to be, Miles Overfield moved with deliberation across the snow-clad fields, and even stopped at times to look backward and meadowward, as though he feared something he had left behind him might disappear in his absence.

I saw him before he reached the yard, for I had been out for a ramble on homemade snow-shoes—my first and last experience of the kind—and we met at the garden gate.

"St!" he hissed, in a half-whisper, and raised his forefinger as he spoke, to suggest that I should stand still and hear him through, though why all this mystery on his part, is to this day a mystery to me.

"Nobody knows, I guess," Miles continued, "for they're in a mean quicksandy tangle in the three-corner meadow. All snug in a hollow tree, and all briers and stuff about. 'Spose we're in for a hunt; go along?"

"Please tell me, first, what are in the hollow tree?" I replied.

"Why, a couple of big 'coons. I just got a glimpse of one, but I know there's two of 'em."

"How do you know?" I asked.

"Can't say; but I know it, and I'm in for a hunt to-night; so can't you go?" Miles asked, somewhat impatiently.

"If you know where they are, it won't be much of a hunt, Miles, for you've simply to go to the tree and take them out, provided they don't give you the slip. Where will the fun come in, such a cold night as this will be?"

"All right, if you don't want to go; I can get 'em alone, I guess. I wouldn't have hurried over here, but I thought you would like the fun;" and he turned about with a look of mingled disappointment and disgust. Seeing this, after a moment's reflection I concluded to go, and called to him to that effect.

He turned about, but did not approach, and said, "All right, and, as my house is nearer than yours to the meadow, come down by eight o'clock. Put on boots, and, if the clouds threaten, whistle to 'em on your way over to keep off the moon;" and again Miles started for his home, walking with a brisker step than when he came, because the meadows and the 'coon tree were now in full view before him.

Before eight o'clock I was ready, and duly reported at Miles's cottage. In a few minutes we were under way, he carrying a gun and axe, and I leading a snarling cur, which Miles thought might be useful.

The full moon made the wintry night a perfect one; not a breath of wind sighed through the bare trees; the whole earth seemed silent and motionless under the firm white crust we trod upon. There was merit enough and beauty enough in the night alone to warrant a moonlight walk, even though I went home empty-handed.

"The critters are in there," said Miles, pointing to a big maple.

"Suppose they are, how are you going to get them out? Wait for them?" I asked.

"Root 'em out. The tree hasn't any holler so we can smoke 'em; but you get up there and punch 'em out with a stick, and when they crawl out on the branches shake 'em down to me and the dog."

"Oh!" I exclaimed, drawing a long breath, "that's your plan. Why didn't you tell me before?"

"Because you might have thought best not to come. Now you're here, you won't mind the job, will you?" he asked, with a grin, that explained the disappointment I had noticed when I half declined his invitation.

"Your theory, Miles, about punched 'coons coming out of their holes, and all that, is no doubt good, but suppose I can't punch them?" I asked, and, somehow, my doubts increased as I thought of the bear proving to be bees, as in my great-great grandfather's case.

While Miles started a little fire at a short distance from the tree, I considered the matter, and concluded to fall in with his plans as soon as my fingers were sufficiently warmed to enable me to climb. Of course, Miles wouldn't climb the tree and let me catch the falling 'coon. He always took advantage of his years, and had that convenient form of rheumatism which prevented his doing anything he could get others to do. It was much the same as the boy's nine-o'clock fever, which secures to him an occasional holiday, when the outside of the schoolhouse is more attractive than the inside.

While we were crouching before a few flickering flames, a low growl was heard by both of us, and the curious antics of the dog at the same time called us at once to our feet, to discover the precise whereabouts of the 'coons. Miles stepped back a few paces, and, gazing intently at the main crotch of the maple, cried out, after a few seconds, "There it is!" I looked in the direction indicated by him, and, sure enough, there was the animal. From where it sat no amount of shaking could dislodge it, and to climb the tree would be to put your hand on the animal before you could secure a firm footing. I thought we were baffled, unless we shot it, which Miles was averse to doing, as he did not wish to have it known he was able to hunt, or work would be expected of him.

"What shall we do?" I asked, impatiently, for the whole affair was growing monotonous.

"Do?" remarked Miles, "why, I mean to snowball the critter till it climbs out on a limb, and then you climb up."

A dozen big snowballs induced the 'coon to move, and we got a better view of him. "He's got no tail," I remarked, as the animal crept out a short distance on a nearly horizontal branch.

"Yes, he has; it's the moonlight blinds you," Miles replied; and so, accepting the decision that it was a 'coon, I commenced to climb. Securing, at last, a firm foothold where the 'coon had been, I took a general survey of the situation. The bright moonlight rendered every object distinct, and I had a full view of the "critter." There it sat, staring me full in the face, and with as wicked a countenance as I ever met; but it was no ordinary 'coon. Its broad, blunt face, its gray fur, arched back, and short tail, told quite another story. I was facing a wildcat!

There are occasions when a man's thoughts outspeed the lightning, and this was one of them; but my actions could not keep pace. I had a thousand plans, and followed none. An angry scream is all I remember now, as it seemed to hurl me headlong to the ground. Down into the snow I plunged, burying my arms and legs far below the frozen crust, and there, for the moment, I lay helpless. My next remembered thought was that Miles was attacked, as his rapid ejaculations, mingled with the yelping of the dog, seemed to indicate. It acted as a restorative, and, struggling to my feet, I was astonished to find that the cat had disappeared, and that Miles was some distance off, rapidly pursuing a homeward course. I hurried after, but he was safely housed before I could overtake him. Entering the door he had so recently slammed behind him, I found the man, pale as a ghost, and shivering before the empty andirons. It was a long time before he could speak intelligibly, but at last he calmed down sufficiently to tell me his story.

"While I was waitin' to see what you were goin' to do, I saw you sail out into the air; and such a yell as that critter gave! It took me all aback, and 'fore I knew what was comin' the thing struck me on the head. I jumped clear o' my hat, and put for home, but the critter held on. I cleared fence, ditch, and snowbank without touchin' 'em, so it seemed, and not till I teched the garden-gate did the critter let up. Where it's gone, I don't know."

"Here it is," I replied, and from Miles's coat-collar I took half a yard of green brier that had been scratching him at every leap.

Miles looked at the thorny branch a moment in silence, and then found courage to whisper,

"Suppose we don't say anything about this 'coon-hunt?"

"Suppose we don't?" I replied, and went home.

To realize what a wealth of animal and vegetable life is ever at hand for him who chooses to study it, let a specialist visit you for a few days. Do not have more than one at a time, or you may be bewildered by their enthusiasm.

I have had them come in turn—botanists, conchologists, entomologists, microscopists, and even archæologists. What an array of names to strike terror to the breasts of the timid; yet they were all human, and talked plain English, and, better than all, were both instructive and amusing.

The botanist came. He minded no paths, but darted from point to point with that delightful uncertainty that made it a nice study for me to keep at his heels. What cared he? Indeed, the cholera may come, and he will not fret. Has he not found a plant not previously known to grow in New Jersey? He was a bit indignant that I took the whole matter quietly. He shouted until hoarse, and all because of a little vine which not one man in a thousand would notice, in spite of its pretty flowers.

And he of the shells! How eagerly was the dip-net thrust into the mud of every little pool in search of a diminutive bivalve, with a name long enough and high-sounding enough for the largest mollusk of the ocean. I may as well admit it now and here; I had never before seen or heard of these baby-clams, as I called them, although the mud that harbored them was before me year in and year out. I am thankful that the conchologist came. If another visits me, how Pisidium and Sphærium will figure as old acquaintances of mine.

My friend's enthusiastic search for still smaller shells—*pupæ* he called them—was an excellent illustration of how earnest a naturalist can and should be. Dirt, sticks, and stones were carefully passed through his fingers, and scrutinized with a lens. The naked eye cannot readily detect these shells, and so a long summer afternoon passed, and not one pupa rewarded his laborious search. Was he discouraged? Not a bit of it. He searched for a week, *and found them.* This, too, was but the beginning of his work. The tongues of those pupæ were to be taken out, and the teeth thereupon counted. To become an accomplished naturalist is certainly no child's play.

The insect-men are more substantial fellows, for much depends upon their muscle. Although armed only with a gauze net, it was a matter of business when they were afield. A beetle can fly fast, and a dragon-fly dart erratically, but the entomologist is equal to the task, and skims over the meadow on the tips of his toes. One that I know could safely board the lightning-express when under way, and all through practice in gathering tiger-beetles along the sandy river-shore.

He always had something to show at the end of the day, and always forced from me the admission that I had never seen such and such insects before.

The microscopist is a favorite of the few that come. He has so easy a time of it that a lazy man naturally envies him. A pint jar, tied up in a newspaper, that the public may not see the contents, and a tin dipper on a stick, are the sum of his equipments when he ventures abroad. Watching the clouds, that he may be sure of pleasant weather, he leisurely takes a stroll to some wayside pool, dips up a half-pint of muddy water, and, lo! his work is done. He has but to go home, enter his den, and look at that water when the spirit moves him. There must be an attraction in this apparently monotonous procedure, but it is not one to be shared by an outsider. He announces new infusoria, novel forms of imperceptible life, and gives to them startling names. We stand by in astonishment, and shudder, as the enlarged portraits of these monsters are held up to our gaze, and, later, start in our slumbers, when a nightmare recalls them. His ill-shaped creatures afford him endless joy; our nightmare recollections of them murder sleep. But the microscopist himself is so good a fellow that we welcome him whenever he comes, although his portfolio is daily filled with a new budget of horrors.

The archæologist must not be overlooked. His work, if rightly pursued, is not easy; but, unfortunately, it is made a pastime to collect relics, and so the student finds too often an unfruitful field.

Away back in the indefinite past men who called themselves Lenâpè wandered all the way from the St. Lawrence to the Delaware River. Why they did so it is vain to conjecture, but come they did, and tarried long; centuries too many to number, it would seem, as judged from their handiwork in stone, which, scarcely two centuries ago, they discarded for metal weapons supplied by outsiders. And now these worked flints are the quest of the archæologist. He comes, he gathers, he advises me to continue in his footsteps, but after his departure his excellent advice is soon forgotten. Relic-hunting has its advantages, to be sure. There is no danger of bite, sting, or poison; but then the excitement is uncertain, for a half-day's tramp may result in no finds; and many a mound is nothing, after all, but dirt from top to bottom; but when my friend comes home with a half-hundred of chipped flints, or some novelty, then I wish I had been a student of the subject; and there it ends. In turn, I resolve to be a botanist, a conchologist, a student of insect life, a microscopist, an archæologist; and then, when each has gone, very naturally relapse to my normal condition of procrastination and dream-life, lulled by the singing of the birds that I do love.

CHAPTER II.

POAETQUISSINGS IN WINTER.

WHILE bound in icy fetters, and free of the dense shade that in summer is cast by the overhanging branches of the towering trees that hide the headwaters of the creek, this quiet nook is by no means lifeless; it is never forsaken. However severe the winter, and whatever the time of day, I am always a little later than some other visitor. The brave kinglets find it a pleasant resting-place, and clamber about the grapevine that has now reached to the topmost branches of the great elm. The song-sparrows know the spot of old, and, cheered by fitful glimmerings of winter sunshine, sing a few liquid notes that are sweetly accompanied by the rippling waters that, issuing from a cavern beneath the elm-tree roots, glide smoothly over a few glistening pebbles, and are lost in a mat of evergreen grasses. I take it that about every spring there remains a trace of the past summer; just enough to recall the glories of the dead year, and to keep alive our faith that another such good time will come again. Does not this, of itself, warrant our wandering about Poaetquissings' headwaters even in winter?

Bluebirds, too, that now remain with us all the year, whatever they may have done in years past, are always coming and going at the elm-spring, however dull or stormy the day, finding food in or near its waters, I doubt not, and flitting among the drooping branches of the trees, they warble suggestively of spring. Although the ground may be snow-clad, and ice may cover all the creek beyond, the bluebird's warble so warms one's blood and banishes the nippings of Jack Frost, that, half-forgetful of the time of year, we glance about for pink arbutus or blue houstonia. Recently, although the air was thick with snow, I rambled hitherward in search of saw-whet owls that I thought were hiding in the dense cedars that dot the hillside. Perhaps they were there, but I could not find them, and, weary with my tramp, I paused by the spring, as usual, and found good company, as I expected.

A song-sparrow near by twittered, "Good-morning;" a pair of bluebirds whistled, and repeated comments on the weather, or what I accepted as such, but I, rather uncivilly, took but little notice of their greetings, and centred my attention upon a winter-wren, that stood upon a projecting pebble in the basin of the spring. My sudden presence startled the bird, and it flew to a neighboring spring a few yards distant. As it seemed so partial to the water, I was induced to follow, as I did, cautiously, and to observe the bird closely, remaining myself unseen by it.

This second spring, near which the wren was now sitting, differs from the other, in that it issues from a slightly higher level, and, passing over a broad slab of iron-cemented pebbles, falls, as a sheet of water a foot in height, and twice that measurement in breadth. Behind this pretty little cataract is a mossy, dripping cave, a cubic yard in extent, and a great rendezvous for many forms of semi-aquatic life. Over the floor creep insect larvæ, in their tubular homes of cemented sticks and pebbles; scores of a small black spider hide in the moss on the sides, and, wherever there is even partial cover, little salamanders may be found. How the existence of this cave was known to the wren I cannot imagine, for I am sure the bird could not see into it through the falling water. But the wren knew of it, for, after a moment's tarrying in the storm, with a chirp it folded its wings, and, diving, passed out of sight. Immediately stooping before the spring, and leading the waters to one side by a cedar branch held obliquely against them, I peered into the recess. There, sure enough, was the restless bird, moving swiftly over the mossy patches on the sides of the cave, engaged, I suppose, in spider-hunting.

I have seen swallows dart through the spray of a mill-dam, and watched wagtails dart about rapid waters in ways suggestive of the water-ouzel, but never have seen either deliberately dive, as did the wren, or pass entirely through an unbroken sheet of water, however thin. The movement of the winter-wren, just mentioned, was so ouzel-like that it was of great interest, as illustrating how readily a slight change of habit may take place, these changes, of course, sooner or later, leading to corresponding ones in anatomical structure. The ouzel not only dives, but can remain for a long time under water, and can walk "about on the pebbles or gravel at the bottoms of streams or pools, in search of larvæ and aquatic insects, just as a man in a diving-dress seeks for lost treasure round the hull of a sunken ship." The late John Keast Lord, from whose charming "Naturalist in British Columbia" I have quoted the above, further says of this bird, "I once found the nest of the American dipper built among the roots of a large cedar-tree that had floated down the stream and got jammed against the mill-dam. . . . The water, rushing over a jutting ledge of rocks, formed a small cascade, that fell like a veil of water before the dipper's nest, and it was most curious to see the birds dash through the waterfall rather than go in at the sides, and in that way get behind it."

In the case of our winter-wren, which is by no means an aquatic bird, we have an instance of the same thing, so far as water proving no obstacle before the entrance of a place guarded and, indeed, concealed by it.

The uniform temperature of spring water and of the atmosphere immediately in contact therewith is sure to keep green the rank growth of hardy grasses that mark the spot, and in this there are many forms of active life to be found, even in the depths of winter. The day of my adventure with the winter-wren was marked, also, by another interesting phase of bird-life. Scarcely a rod from the spring proper, in such green grass as I have mentioned, I found a yellow rail, which, by its vigorous flight and readiness to start on being disturbed, was evidently not a wounded bird, that had been unable to join in the usual autumnal migration of these and the other species of rail-birds that, from May to October, are so abundant in our meadows.

The occurrence of migratory birds under such circumstances is by no means uncommon; and there are probably few birds, if they so willed it, but could stand the severest winters, so far as temperature alone is concerned, and but little ingenuity would be required to enable them to find a sufficiency of food. The wrens, as a family, illustrate this. There are three species that may be said to be strictly migratory, and two which are resident, and winter visitants. The food, in all cases, is the same. The common house-wren finds insects enough from April to November, and from November to April the winter-wren replaces the former species, and probably never goes hungry for a day. If the plucky house-wren could but be made to believe it, it could comfortably live in its summer haunts from the falling of the leaves to the bursting of the buds. Some of our delicate summer warblers have found this out, and one species, in particular, has become as hardy as a snow-bird, and sings merrily, be it ever so cold.

It is not until we get fifty yards away from the terrace from which gush the springs that, collectively, go to make up the stream proper, that a boat can be floated, and even here the water is too shallow and the banks too near each other to allow the use of a paddle. "Only a decent ditch" has been said of it by a travelled companion, who could see nothing attractive about it. Only a decent ditch, indeed! Thank the powers that be that such decent ditches are accessible to a lover of nature. What with its patches of water-plants, hiding innumerable fishes; its burrowed banks, harboring muskrats, shrews, and star-nosed moles; its banks, thick-set with birches, that tempt the red-wing blackbirds in February, and the stretches of level meadow that, even in winter, may be studied to advantage — this "decent ditch" may well tempt any one abroad, and, if not a wholly unreasonable person, such a doubtfully complimentary name will be dropped forthwith, and my favorite rambling-ground will, with due respect, be called Poaetquissings henceforth and forever.

My friend, the microscopist, takes Poaetquissings home by the tumblerful, and has recorded species and genera of strange animals that, until then, were unknown to science. He holds it a very respectable ditch, I am sure. My well-read friend, who supposed all life to hibernate with mathematical precision, if it hibernated at all, found, in January, under ice a foot thick, the majority of the fishes that he had seen with delight during his summer vacation. I coaxed a lover of spring birds to take a winter walk along the banks of the stream, and a boyish romp of run and slide over its frozen surface, and how puzzled, yet pleased, was he to hear the song-sparrows, the pine-finches, linnets, crossbills, foxy sparrows, and a cardinal grosbeak all singing at once. How quickly he forgot where the thermometer was ranging as he bared his muffled ears, that he might catch the clear notes that came so crisply through the keen air from the birches hard by. Poaetquissings is something more than a "decent ditch" to him.

Pushing through the shallows for a hundred rods or more, the creek suddenly widens to a respectable extent, and the canoeist at last feels that he is fairly afloat.

But now, in midwinter, the water is not sufficiently open to navigate, even in the line of the "bottom springs," which, bubbling up with much force, prevent the ice from wholly covering them. A good substitute, however, is now available. We can walk on the creek, and have the banks in full view. This is a great advantage. To ramble along the shore of a stream, in summer or winter, is never satisfactory to the naturalist. Do what he will, he is always unable to see much that is going on, and is himself seen and shunned by every creature that he most wishes to observe. From the middle of the stream the familiar banks present an unusual aspect; it is like visiting a new locality; and, as every creature living on the bank of a stream has the entrance to its home facing the water, we can now, being on the creek, look into their front doors. The pleasant path on shore may be the roofs of innumerable homes of cunning creatures, whose presence we do not suspect while walking over them.

During the memorably cold and snowy winter of 1883–84 I was much struck with the abundance of hawks that congregated in the meadows drained by the Poaetquissings Creek.

The red-tailed buzzard, the rough-legged falcon, the broad-winged buzzard, the peregrine, the goshawk, the merlin, the winter falcon, and a stray eagle were all here, and their various screams, as they circled the air, when the weather was clear, were attractive, if not exactly musical. There can be no doubt but that the abundance of meadow-mice was the one great attraction to most of them; and I could not but comment on the unreasonableness of the farmers who so relentlessly persecute hawks. Here, for weeks, these birds had poultry in abundance in full view, yet I doubt if a single pullet was destroyed; and I do know that these same hawks were busy, while daylight lasted, in capturing the mice, creatures many fold more destructive to grass and grain than all the hawks in New Jersey are to poultry. Even when the snow was too deep to enable them to find mice, I saw no evidence that the poultry was molested. The thousands of snow-birds supplied the hawks, at such times, with all needed food.

I will not discuss the matter at this time, but venture to dogmatically assert that all birds are useful, including the owls, hawks, and crows. Even if they were not, I would be willing to share the expense with my neighbors, and pay in poultry, in the case of the hawks, for the satisfaction of watching them soaring in wide circles over the meadows; of hearing their wild cries, that restore to us a bit of the wildness that was once a feature of even these tame lands; and for the pleasure of puzzling over the mystery of their flight, as with unmoved wings they sail upward, or hover for seconds, motionless as statues.

The several species of hawks that I mentioned are very different in their dispositions, and merit consideration in this respect. I believe I can always recognize the several species by their manner, both when on the wing and when at rest. Not that their methods of flight vary a great deal—they do to some extent—but there are peculiarities which are very uniform. Collectively considered, the eight species that I have mentioned may be called "meditative" hawks, in contradistinction to the three small falcons, which may be classed as "impetuous." The latter, to which reference will be made hereafter, are visitors only to the banks of Poaetquissings Creek, but the meditative hawks are characteristic winter features of the stream. Many of these birds are migratory, and those that are resident are busy with their nests, and haunt the thick woods, except from November to March, and it is then only that we find them perched in the tall trees along the creek, or sailing for hours over the broad expanse of meadows far beneath them.

As I walk along the frozen creek I mark them as they appear in the course of my progress down the stream, and generally recognize the several species by the positions they assume. A "red-tail" sits with more extended neck, and is more alert, than the less common broad-winged buzzard; which hawk sits in what my son calls a "scrouged-up" manner. As I draw near, these birds become alarmed and take flight, the red-tailed hawk when I am within a hundred yards of it; but its broad-winged cousin is willing to take a somewhat greater risk, and I can cover half the distance before it, too, sails away, usually with an impatient scream. Quite differently, too, do these birds start from their perches. The wary "red-tail" tumbles off the limb, and flaps in a hurried and evidently frightened manner, while the other, with deliberation, literally sails away, moving the wings as little as possible.

Thus we see that the broad-winged hawk is not only

meditative but deliberate. Like a wise man, it relishes seasonable fun, but permits no nonsense. The crows, quick-witted as they are, have not yet learned this fact, and often suffer, therefore, for want of knowledge. Recently I saw excellent evidence of this. A troop of wandering crows came lazily along the creek, just skimming the tree-tops. They discovered the broad-winged hawk that was sitting directly in the course of their flight. With a shrill $k\breve{a}\ \overline{kaw}\ k\breve{e}\ k\breve{e}$ the leader announced the hawk's presence, and the whole troop, twenty or more, halted in their flight. One, more eager or less experienced than the rest, boldly dashed at the hawk, and pecked it, for aught I know. At all events, a second onset was more than the quiet hawk would suffer, and, meeting his boasting, noisy assailant in mid-air, he gave it one stroke with his talons and a nip with his beak that sent the impudent crow reeling earthwards, and screaming, I presume for help. The hawk straightway resumed its perch, while the astonished crows reversed their tactics and fled in dismay, wholly unmindful of their afflicted companion, which could barely keep itself in the air.

What I have said of these two hawks may be repeated of the others. Some are quick to suspect danger; others are less timid, or, at least, are slower to perceive the approach of a suspicious object. The black hawk, or rough-legged falcon, is, perhaps, of our larger species, the very laziest. It does not even hold up its wings when sitting in the birches, but lets them hang so loosely that the bird looks like a wet skin hung out to dry; nevertheless, it is not often that you catch it napping.

Sitting, as these large hawks do, often for hours at a time, what is passing through their minds the while? They can scarcely be supposed to be sleeping, and are not weakened from hunger at any time. I have called them meditative because they appear to be thinking while they sit on their elevated perches. Perhaps, Micawber-like, they are waiting for something to turn up. But they cannot even do this without thought. There is nothing simply "instinctive," whatever that may be, in the meditative hawks that I watch, as they sit in the trees along Poaetquissings Creek. Still, I am forced to confess that the matter of their thoughts is past finding out.

When the black hawk acquires its black plumage— when, save a bit of white on the tail, it is jet black, then it is less timid than the blotchy-brown, rough-legged hawks that so largely represent this family. Why it should be for a long time puzzled me, but I am inclined now to believe that it passes itself off for a crow, and so considers itself in less danger than its browny-white brother. I recently saw a fine specimen, black as the ace of spades, quietly walking through the tangled dead grass on the banks of Poaetquissings. It even waddled like a crow, and appeared to be industriously in search of mice. Halting behind a convenient birch, I watched the hawk for some minutes. Presently it came to where a net had been recently drawn from the water, and where a few small fish were lying, left by the fisherman. These it ate greedily. Placing one foot upon the fish to hold it down, the head was seized, and swallowed in good-sized pieces. Not a morsel was discarded. Three fishes were thus eaten, when I suddenly appeared upon the scene. With a hurried grasp the startled hawk, with a fish in its talons, flew off, uttering a tri-syllabic scream that evidently meant, "You be—hanged!"

How different from all this is the method and manner of the three little hawks that I have referred to as impetuous—the sharp-shinned, Cooper's, and the sparrowhawk. The first of these is feathered lightning. He ceases to be before you realize that he is, and Cooper's hawk is almost his equal. The smallest of all, the sparrowhawk, *par excellence*, is quick enough in all conscience, but you can follow his movements, nevertheless. These three hawks are not common at Poaetquissings. They come and go. At least, certain blue streaks that flash in mid-air are supposed to be sharp-shinned hawks. The little sparrowhawk knows that tree sparrows, by hundreds, roost in the shelter afforded by Poaetquissings' clustered cedars, and, suddenly appearing at the day's close, picks up an unlucky sparrow, as it is settling down for the night—picks it up, and is gone. One need but pass a single afternoon on the creek bank to witness this and be sure of the little hawk's identity, but the blue streaks are a matter of doubt. That they are hawks is eminently probable, but none dare make a positive assertion to that effect.

The creek cuts through a long, artificial bank in its riverward course, and the bisected ridge is now partially covered with a vigorous growth of cedars. The junction of the creek and cedar-grown knoll is a pleasant spot at all times, but is peculiarly so during those bright, sunny December days of which we occasionally can boast. Frequent visits have shown that it, then, is a great haunt for winter birds, and then it was, during the past winter, that I happened upon a flock of crossbills.

Any bird of pluck, if wounded, will be found to be cross-billed, when carelessly handled. Even a hen, with young chickens, may be classed as a crossbill. Faithful retrievers have learned, to their sorrow, that a wounded bittern is a veritable crossbill. Spaniels have been stabbed to death by them. None such were the little birds I saw last December. On the contrary, they were the gentlest wild birds I have ever met, and their "crossness" lay only in the twist of their beaks. There were hundreds of them, and their black and red plumage showed admirably against the deep blue of the cloudless sky, or the wide-spread whiteness of the snow-clad meadows. These birds did not confine themselves to the cedars, but wandered to the scattered birches as well, and clambered, in a curiously parrot-like manner, over every limb and twig. They were as much at ease, when head down and tail up, as in the normal position, and were never still for a second. I walked directly up to them, and they simply kept a little beyond arm's length. With a butterfly net I could have caught a dozen. When on the trees they scarcely uttered a sound. Possibly a faint chirp now and then, but of this I cannot be positive; when fairly upon the wing, however, they warbled with much animation. Later, when, with common consent, they formed a dense flock, and flew away, the united songs of the happy company were clear, loud, and melodious.

Crossbills cannot be said to be rare winter visitors, and yet a winter or two may pass without our seeing them. This signifies nothing, however. These birds are eminently social, and always, I believe, live in flocks during the winter. This being true, how natural that when you chance to go out of your front door, crossbills may be clambering over the pines in the back yard; and if you chance to go out by the rear entrance, these birds may be seed-hunting in the evergreens in front.

"I saw horned larks, as I came down the lane," remarked a friend to me, some years ago.

"That's odd," I replied, "I've been looking for them all winter."

I know now that there was nothing strange about it. Luck simply had favored my friend and had not favored me. Never, I advise, venture to say a bird is rare, or absolutely wanting to the fauna of your neighborhood, because you have failed to find it.

An old farmer once assured me that there were no skunks in the neighborhood. That same winter, his next-door neighbor trapped seven, and spoke of others who had had even better luck. The fact is, that as crossbills are generally seen every winter, it is merely by chance that they occasionally escape notice. Their visits are probably as regular as the ceaseless round of the seasons.

Another arctic bird that lends a charm to our meadows and Poaetquissings-Creek bank, is the diminutive lesser red-poll linnet. Too long a name for so small a bird; but they are so full of glee, and sing so merrily, that we lose sight of the fact that they are such midgets. Like the crossbills, the linnets are social, and are seen only in flocks, when here. A peculiarity, too, is the great elevation at which they fly, when passing to any point at a considerable distance. They usually, it would seem, fly at a height beyond the range of our vision, and so, when they suddenly appear, it is not from some adjacent tree, or around a corner. They appear rather to drop from the clouds. More than once, while watching the crows on their way to their roosts, I have detected minute black dots in the sky, which, as I watched them, grew rapidly larger and more abundant. Down, down, down they came, and, reaching the top of some tall tree, spread over it, and reminded me of the emptying of a feather pillow in the wind.

Unlike the crossbills, the linnets keep up a continual chatter when they alight, and all the time that they tarry in the trees. While apparently without a leader, they act much as though they were regularly drilled by a strict disciplinarian. I suppose, in this case, that it is mutually agreed that whoever, for the time, takes the lead, that all will follow. At all events, by some subtle telegraphy, the like impulse moves them all at the same second, and as suddenly as they appeared, so they depart.

Poaetquissings Creek is not an aviary. Let us look at something belonging to it that is not feathered and flighty. There are still some noble trees upon its banks; but, alas! far nobler ones have been gathered for firewood. What a pity there are not forests in the moon, and that from thence we might derive our supplies of fuel. Prominent among the big trees still remaining is an enormous buttonwood or sycamore, that towers nearly one hundred feet above the creek. Much, I take it, to the satisfaction of every passing bird, this tree is dead at the top. There is one twisted and nearly horizontal branch that reaches beyond the uppermost leaf-bearing twig, which is now worn smooth by the feet of thousands of travel-weary birds, that halt here on their journeys. All birds that deign to leave the ground at all love such grand outlooks as this mighty tree affords. Even diminutive fly-catchers sing with greater unction when perched upon it; and there are migratory warblers that, settling there, sing to the clouds, but never vouchsafe a twitter to the earth-bound creatures below.

Whenever the lightning strikes a tall tree, I believe there is rejoicing in the hearts of the birds. They cannot build observatories, but give them credit for thankfulness that Nature provides them with very many. I confess to envying the birds that can sit on the topmost twig of a tall tree, which the lightning has bared of all foliage and superfluous branches. What a prospect lies before them! Be it even a crow or a blackbird, it is all the same. They cry out in unmistakable terms, *see! see! see!* Only the meditative hawks enjoy the ontlook in silence. Perhaps, were I living in a hilly country, my enthusiasm would be less pronounced. My mountain experiences are limited to the garret windows, and an occasional climb to the cupola of the barn.

To return to the trees; if we cannot say of any tracts of woodland still remaining, "This is the forest primeval," it is some satisfaction to know that we can still stand in the shade of single trees and say of such, "This is a remnant of the primeval woods." Such a tree, it may be, is this lone buttonwood on Poaetquissings' bank. It measures nearly seven feet in diameter at the base; and so long ago as 1750 was the "big buttonwood" of the neighborhood. There are others still standing which are even larger, but none of equal height and general massiveness. Poaetquissings' buttonwood is the tree, according to local tradition, which was used by the Lenâpè Indians as a stake, when they tortured Iroquois prisoners. They bound the victim to the creek side of the tree, so that the sight of the water would increase his agony, while the flames licked his limbs. There is even a slight hollow or dent in the trunk at its base, which, it is said, was burned out gradually, as prisoners were tortured. This is nonsense, I believe, for so long ago as the Indian days, when such things occurred, the tree was too small for any such purpose, and stakes, in the centres of villages, were used. Still, such a tale, once heard, invests a tree with an unusual interest, and every black speck at the roots we imagine is charcoal or burned bones, while, at the same time, we laugh at the absurdity of such an idea. Stories of this tree, in connection with the Indians, were told me nearly forty years ago, and to me it must remain an "Indian tree," while I know that the possibilities are, to say the least, that no Indian was ever aware of its existence.

The trunk of the tree, for a distance of thirty or forty feet, is now half hidden with grape-vines, green-brier, and Virginia creeper, and in winter it looks like a ship's mast, covered with broken and tangled rigging. This, in one sense, forlorn appearance has its charm for nesting birds, and the tree and its covering often shelters a half-dozen broods of as many different kinds of birds.

Squirrels, strangely enough, do not frequent this buttonwood. I have thought that possibly the shelly bark caused them too often to lose their foothold, and, therefore, they kept aloof. I recall the fact that a pair of red squirrels, that for a season tenanted a hollow locust in the yard, seemed to avoid the one small sycamore that stood near by.

Seeing birds, and particularly the hawks, on the top of the big buttonwood so frequently, during the winter, roused in me the desire to see the surrounding country from so advantageous a point, and at last I was able to gratify the whim. It is true

"We have not wings, we cannot soar.
But we have feet to scale and climb,"

and, aided by cross-slats that I nailed upon the tree as I proceeded, I finally reached as near the top as I deemed it prudent to go. What a jolly spot was that cross-limb whereon I rested, seventy feet or more from the ground. I could take in, at one glance, a wide range of familiar country, known heretofore only by sections. Poaetquissings' springs, the straight ditch, the old bank, the great-spring meadow, the floodgates, the main creek, the pasture-lands, and the river—all that goes to make up my little world—was visible at once. Such experiences are red-letter days to a rambler, and tree-climbing I have since held should be more cultivated. Little wonder is it to me now that the meditative hawks love to sit by the hour in just such places. At the time of my first visit to the tree-top, I put myself in the place of a hawk, and hunted, from where I sat, for a mouse in the dead grass seventy feet below me. Did I see one? Emphatically, No! and I have my doubts as to the ability of any hawk to see at that distance so small an object; and I say this, bearing in mind that Mr. Romanes, in his invaluable work on "Mental Evolution in Animals," has remarked, "The eye of a hawk . . . is able to distinguish from a great height a protectively colored animal from the surface of the ground which it so closely imitates." Perhaps, if a mouse ventured over the snow, or even moved slowly over bare ground, it would be seen, but when we consider how seldom the running mouse is really exposed, and how closely it hugs the ground, and creeps under or among the grass and weeds, rather than on them, it becomes far more probable that a perched hawk is not on the lookout for prey, but is either asleep or absorbed in contemplation. Certainly there is no better place in which to pass a meditative half-hour than when perched in a high tree. There is much to be gained, sometimes, in being even fifty feet above the common level of your fellow-mortals. To see what your neighbor fails to discover gives you the advantage over him that you can tell him something that he did not know, and so pass for a bit of a philosopher, although, in fact, you may be much nearer a fool than he is. We all know how the village ladies look only to the dominie for information on every subject, yet how frequently are these very men profoundly ignorant of natural history.

There are several pin-oaks growing on the banks of Poaetquissings, some of which were more than saplings when Penn juggled the Delawares out of their lands. The largest of them was fortunate enough to get an ugly twist in its sapling days, and being too crooked for timber, has been spared by the greedy wood-choppers of the past century. This tree is on the decline now— standing on a sloping bank, it always was—and only a small portion of its branches now bear leaves. Better than all, it has a great, cavernous interior; a hollow that one approaches with caution, as though it contained a hibernating bear, or sheltered a crouching panther. The happy days when such things were possible are gone forever; but during one winter ramble over the frozen creek I stopped, as usual, to peep into the hollow tree —I never before had seen so much as a mouse in it— and in the uncertain light I caught a glimpse of two bright eyes that glared most wildly at me. The surprise was great, and the withdrawal of my head instantaneous. I doubt not, but what little hair I have was visibly affected, and I am sure my scalp wrinkled with innumerable ridges. What could it be? Opossum, 'coon, cat, or my imagination? I listened, but no sound could be detected. I thumped upon the hollow trunk, but it caused no commotion within. I thrust a long stick into the tree and whirled it around as best I could. It disturbed the mysterious creature, but did not bring him out. Finally I tried smoke, and, in time, my efforts were partially successful. With a faint squeak, out sprang my neighbor's Maltese cat, and its rate of speed, as it bounded homeward, was indeed astonishing. I have never seen any animal, not even a frightened fox, that ran as this persecuted cat did, upon this occasion. The occurrence was not simply an amusing incident. I learned soon after that this cat had partly returned to a feral state, and was often gone from home for weeks at a time. It was known by its owner to live along the creek, and prey upon the snow-birds and wild mice; and when it did deign to return to its former home it was quite unsocial, and finally became dangerously savage. Since my adventure with tabby, I have found a lazy and indifferent 'coon in the same tree. On being forced to show itself, it started for the creek and trotted across the ice-bound surface at a rattling rate. Once across, it climbed a maple-tree with great ease, and so snugly ensconced itself where several branches met that I had much difficulty in finding it while standing at the foot of the tree. Probably a hundred times, since then, I have halted by this old tree to see if some animal was occupying it, but never have I found anything larger than a mouse. A common house-mouse I took this creature to be, but it may have been a different species. It did not show its teeth, nor give me the chance to measure its tail; so I cannot be certain. Still, is it not true that *mus musculus* is truly wild, and at home far away from any house? The impression among housewives is, that after harvest the mice become more numerous and troublesome; that they leave the house in June, or earlier, and return in October. This is very probably true, for certainly a mouse no way distinguishable from the semi-domesticated species is all too common in our corn-fields. That another mouse, generically distinct, is also to be found in the fields, I have recently been led to believe. It is one of more active habits, an excellent climber, and nests in the corn-shocks, instead of on the ground. It is probably the Southern harvest mouse, but may be different; perhaps a "geographical variety."

A curious tree is the crooked maple near the first bend in the creek. It is the first object to strike one's attention, as we pass the splendid elms on the "fourteen acre" piece, of which more hereafter. As a boy I knew it best as the N tree, and I still call it by that name. The thrifty sapling has evidently met with an accident in early life, and the main stem has been bent, if not broken, until it fell forward and downward towards the water. Bent or broken, it was not beyond partial recovery, and the wound has healed after a fashion, and growth continued. The top, now growing waterwards, at last has met the surface of the stream, and, checked in this direction, has turned again and made a vigorous skyward growth. The result is a trunk that has acquired the shape of a letter N—hence the local and expressive name. As in the case of the twisted pin-oak, the unusual shape has proved the salvation of the tree, and the shivering fuel-cutters of past generations have spared it. Growing over the creek, too, added to its chances; for so crooked a tree would have been troublesome to fish out of the deep waters that flow beneath it. It is, I am sure, a relic of the preceding century; and now is not only old, but past its maturity, and partly decayed. Near the upper or first acute angle in its trunk there is a hollow of small diameter but considerable depth, and here an escaped swarm of bees from some neighbor's garden have been making honey on their own account, in blissful ignorance of patent combs, imported queens, or fumes of burning sulphur. Having escaped the attentions of man, these bees have not been allowed to go scot free nevertheless. Honey is a toothsome morsel to many quadrupeds as well as bipeds, and a family of flying squirrels, that live in a hollow tree hard by, are constant visitors during autumn, and, for aught I know, in winter, unless the weather is unusually severe.

When I found the bees' nest, in November, the squirrels had been for some time raiding upon it, and, cunning creatures that they were—I had heretofore looked upon them as rather stupid—they did not waste the precious store of food, or publish its whereabouts by dropping morsels of it, as they passed to and fro. They came and went with proper circumspection, and perhaps surveyed the ground about their nest-tree before each visit, to see that no spy was near them. Before Christmas the hive was empty, and now the foolishness of the squirrels was as evident as was their cunning of a short time before. By too great greediness they had killed the goose that laid the golden egg; they had not only eaten the honey, but the bees. Is it not strange that the idea does not dawn upon them, to leave so much of the hive intact as to secure a supply of honey each succeeding winter? We have harvesting ants, and food-hoarding mammals; so why should not these flying squirrels, in time, become more provident? Squirrels have been robbing bee-hives so far back in time, that the years cannot be numbered, yet it does not appear that they have gained one whit of wisdom in this important direction. It is a matter of feast and famine, so far as honey is concerned, and this checkered experience has yet to give that additional twist to their cerebral convolutions that shall make them wiser. This is no fanciful matter. The storing of nuts by gray squirrels, of small grains by white-footed mice, and of seeds by ants, had its commencement, and was the ultimate result of a protracted series of experiences; the habit grew, and was not established at the outset, by creative fiat. Considered in this light, the thoughtlessness, if we may call it such, of the flying squirrels is much to be wondered at.

The sheltering bluff near by will tempt a botanist to linger here, when elsewhere, for miles around, there is nothing but the frost-blackened bloom of the past summer spread before him. Here, even in January, the witch-hazel, a thrifty shrub ten feet high or more, is starred with yellow blossoms that laugh at the north winds shrieking in the tops of the towering oaks. A veritable witch, it hides in sheltered nooks that no frosty breath can reach, and from November until February invites its flowering friends to be less timid, and seems to assure them that here, at least, winter is no great drawback after all. Usually this is quite true, but if the season of '84–'85 was not discouraging to the witch-hazel, it has, indeed, a brave heart. It may have been blooming lately, but, if so, I overlooked it.

Bent twigs of this plant are still used by the "gifted" to find water, lost farming tools, and, by one enthusiast,

Indian graves. The faithful still claim it as efficacious, and he who doubts is sneered at if he expresses his opinion. All that the rambler can ask is that the plant be not exterminated, and that the fools may be.

While lingering by the witch-hazel, or standing under a cedar, through whose dense foliage no snow ever drifted, the botanist has an humble plant to attract him, all through the winter, in the pretty star-chickweed. Give it but a few rays of genial sunshine daily, and let the south wind sweep the dead oak-leaves away, and this little plant will blossom as freely as in early June. The flower, of itself, can scarcely be called pretty, yet in midwinter, when so little is to be found, small favors, such as this, are most thankfully received. Again, beneath some near-by sheltering cluster of trees, where the midday sun meets with no obstruction, and the north wind cannot reach us, a goodly space may be whitened with blooming whitlow-grass, and lead us, when a little distance from it, to think that snow has been slyly scattered there by some passing cloud.

While it is yet winter and bitterly cold, the hillside sassafrasses are often in bloom, when taller trees afford them shelter. Their yellow flowers are quite pretty, and a winter nosegay can be gathered that is worth the carrying by blending them with twigs of holly, brilliant with red berries. It is only the smaller bushes that bloom so early. Not far from the creek towers a tree, sixty feet high, and with a sturdy trunk two feet in diameter. This giant sassafras patiently waits until April, or March, if the spring happens to be an early one.

Another midwinter bloom, and also yellow, is the

graceful, hanging catkin of the smooth alder. These are too pretty to be passed by unheeded, and yet but few are familiar with them. I have had them scattered among roses from the hothouse, and they were stared at and toyed with as some rare exotic.

Because of its mephitic odor we are apt to shun it, and it is not to be carelessly handled, nor will any become enthusiastic over it; yet the despised skunk-cabbage must be considered in the list of the winter-blooming plants of Poaetquissings. Its purple-tinted, shell-shaped spathe will bear examination, and the ball of flowers it contains will be found in full bloom always in February, and sometimes earlier.

However disparagingly this vigorous plant is spoken of by most of those who know it at all, it is kindly thought of by many naturalists, for it harbors at its roots the earliest salamanders, the pretty Maryland yellowthroat nests in the hollows of its broad leaves, and rare beetles find a congenial home in the shelter it affords.

Back to the hillside, from the swampy ground where we found the cabbage, let us look among the drifted leaves for more yellow bloom. It will not require long to make the search. In every nook that the frost has spared the dandelion has flourished, and is even now, in midwinter, in bloom.

We can justly claim at least two thirds of March as strictly winter, and so the bloom of the first three weeks of the month may be considered here as the botanical attractions of Poaetquissings at that season.

Already seven blooming plants have been named that

add to the interest of a winter's walk. If the weather stays open, even in February, and usually in March, blue violets peep from beneath sheltering leaves. There is one interesting point with reference to early violets. They are always more advanced where there is a comparative absence of oak-leaves. I have so often found this to be the case that it would seem as though there were in the leaves something inimical to the flowers. Throughout the summer, however, violets flourish in oak woods. The explanation may be that the thick covering of broad leaves prevents the frost from "coming out," and the growth of the plant is checked in consequence. Whatever the reason, under any other leaves than those of the oak are winter violets more likely to be found in bloom.

On Washington's birthday, in a distant upland woods, a friend claims he can always find, at least, one blossom of trailing arbutus; and so, too, on the bluff that guards Poaetquissings and shields it from the north winds, he can always find the liver-leaf, with its beautiful white, pink, and purple flowers. It grows at the bases of tall trees, where the shelter is effectual in protecting it from all the assaults of Jack Frost. My own experience is not equal to my friend's. I find it only in March, and then, when there has been a week of sunshine and an absence of frosty nights.

Lastly, even as early as the middle of March, one may gather eardrops. These are the most striking of all the flowers of winter, and, as they hang from a smooth, naked scape, six or eight inches high, are quite sure to attract the botanist's attention.

Whether one must wade through the deep snows of the uplands, or labor through the deeper mud during a January thaw, there is sure to be ample recompense for the exertion required to reach Poaetquissings in winter. The animal life will be so far abundant that the naturalist will find the time to pass all too quickly, and the botanist will, perhaps, not think his labor has been in vain. If, indeed, he can find no flowers, there are still trees in abundance, and their winter aspects merit more attention than they have yet received.

Shillings and pence—shillings and pence. This was the ever uppermost thought of the thrifty Quakers who succeeded the Indians, and no bit of nature was allowed to remain undisturbed, if, by any possibility, a little more grass, or any grain, could be coaxed from it. The tide was too much of an encroachment upon available pasture, and, by an ungainly floodgate, was shut out from its ancient domain. Poaetquissings once gloried in a tide that swept its channel clean, and brought a wealth of lusty fishes to its depths. This must needs be changed. Nature, as provided at first hand, is never good enough for the white man. Even when on top of a mountain man longs for stilts, or frets for higher heels to his boots. The floodgates were built. Great oak logs were hewn, squared, jointed, and placed in proper position, and planks set upon them, to let the creek water flow over, but keep on the other side every drop of tide water that might come up so far. The disgraced creek fretted at the insult, but could do nothing more than fret; not even when reinforced by many a winter freshet could it move those ponderous gates. At times, indeed, it bore great trees against them, and held them open for a while. Then its courage rose. The river rushed in and made a raid upon its former territory; but this was but for a few days at most. The greedy landlord reset the gates, and the baffled river could only fret and submit. But a worse fate was in store for Poaetquissings. Little creeks, it seems, like poor men, have few rights that rich men are bound to respect. It so happened that the canal must replace the river as a highway. Nature blundered, as usual, and made the river too broad and shallow. Man, therefore, must needs make a canal, deep and narrow; and this passes directly over the outlet of Poactquissings. Then and Now—think of it! Then, meandering leisurely through a forest of hickories, maples, and elms, and joining the river with unruffled flow—now, forced to crawl through a wooden trough, with a battered barndoor at one end, and under the canal at that! The tide is still shut out, it is true; but in all these changes the creek has had some little satisfaction for past indignities, for the old floodgates are in ruins.

Although not a natural feature of the stream, these ruined floodgates are not unsightly. Where they are the creek is very wide, pondlike, and even boasts of a little island. Here, in midwinter, there is a beautiful skating-ground, but one that cannot be coursed over carelessly. Devote one eye, at least, to air-holes, or come to grief. When the thermometer suggests that the arctic circle is out of place, that it has slipped southward a thousand miles, look upon yourself as an Esquimau, and visit Poactquissings by moonlight. "It will pay," as my practical neighbors remark continually, when offering advice. The more striking features of the creek are congregated about the floodgates. The largest trees along the banks are at or near them, and the little island, with its one great oak, is a feature of wondrous beauty, when the snowclad limbs of the tree stand out against the blue-black sky. I have found, when skating, it is something to have a little wildness about me, and if a neighbor's dog barks it recalls the hungry wolves that chased the benighted Quakers—if they ever did. I once was startled by a stray cow that had wandered from the barnyard, and straightway took aim at it, with my cane, with all the eagerness that the hunter knows when levelling his rifle at the unexpected game he has suddenly discovered. This is childish, I am told. True, but is it not worth something to be able to be a child again—to forget for the moment the vexations of manhood, and recall the experience of "having fun"? For me, at least, such childishness is far preferable to the ceaseless round in a skating-rink, where even the ice is unnaturally rough, and the skater can only boast of tired legs when he walks home. Give me an hour of Poaetquissings by moonlight, with its shadows of the elms that fringe its banks, with its starry sky above, and dim distance mournful with the hooting of owls that fitfully fret when their domain is invaded; give me these, and the world is welcome to the modern rinks, with their gas-jets, stuffy atmosphere, and crowds. Zoology, too, can be studied to advantage when we are on skates. If a venturesome weasel bounds over the ice or a startled rabbit courses along the frozen surface, we can have an exhilarating race with the frightened creature. All of our non-hibernating mammals venture abroad at night, and know full well the new highway that firm ice offers them. The 'coon, opossum, otter, mink, and weasel all make short-cuts over the frozen creek, and no better chance to see them is ever afforded than now. Exception should be made of the skunk. He is uncertain, and my rule is to skate backward when he puts in an appearance.

There is a deep hole above the floodgates, where, in winter, hosts of fishes congregate, instead of hibernating; where to fish through the ice is no child's play. It is, in part, a question between fighting frost or mosquitoes; and the former is, I think, the less formidable foe. It is always practicable to have a fire either on the ice or on shore, and numb fingers can there be quickly restored; much more quickly, indeed, than the blotched and bitten digits that vex the gentle angler in June. It is wonderful how full of spirit is the winter pike, perch, or sucker. They seem to have acquired additional strength with the increase of cold—to draw a two-pound pike through a hole in the ice is a different matter from switching him to land in midsummer. The fact is, we have only the short line to hold, and have but little advantage over the fish. At times I have had them whirl round with astonishing rapidity and wear away the cord as it pressed the sharp edge of the ice, before I could draw them from the water.

This little creek is at its best in winter, when the ice is blue and without air-bubbles. At the old floodgates, where the stream is of considerable width, I have often lain down upon the frozen creek, and, covering myself with a blanket to exclude the light, peered down into the depths, when the sun was brightly shining, to watch the movements of such life as was active at the time.

After many repetitions of these observations on successive days the terrestrial life on the creek banks became quite accustomed to my presence, and soon inquisitiveness replaced fear. This was amusingly illustrated in one instance by a weasel, in crossing the creek on the ice, stopping to investigate the peculiar something lying in its path. Peering under the blanket, it either heard my blood circulating or smelled it. At all events, it gave my ankle a nip which brought me quickly to my feet, and sent the bloodthirsty wretch scudding over the ice with marvellous rapidity. How the crows laughed! I had noticed a flock of these birds when I went to the creek, and had been wondering if their incessant cawing was not a discussion of my curious movements. They were, possibly, disposed to think me a trap laid for them, but were astonished or amused at my sudden regaining of the perpendicular when the weasel offered to investigate the matter.

To return to the infra-crystic life. This proves to be nearly as abundant as in summer, and the changes of habits necessitated by the difference in the season is exceedingly instructive. Even the restless gyrinus, or scuttle-bug, that keeps the summer surface of the creek in constant commotion, is now active as ever, deep down in the water, each glistening with its bubble of air which it carries along with it. Where it gets a fresh supply when this becomes exhausted is easily determined; for, however severe the winter, there are always some airholes. These they seek, undoubtedly. They must know of them, and, remembering their whereabouts, are able to go to them; a little fact showing, I think, that even these whirligigs have a modicum of intelligence. But what do gyrini find to eat at such a time? I leave the subject, without reply or suggestion, for others to determine. But, while we are straining our eyes to follow the mazy threadings of the gyrinus, a fish or turtle passes leisurely by, and the insect is at once forgotten. Why are these greater animals not tucked away in the mud? Have we not been taught this in the books? It is a somewhat painful sensation to have preconceived notions and statements in print so emphatically contradicted; but, if you wish to know nature through books only, don't wander to Poaetquissings. I cannot find that any of our animals live strictly up to the rules laid down for them in the library; and, surely, it cannot be that this small creek's tenantry are exceptions, for the creek "is by nature provided with everything that man can desire," and man does not desire to continually find himself mistaken. Be this as it may, Poaetquissings' fishes are full of life in winter, and so, too, are many of her turtles, and even a small proportion of her many frogs. On the 12th of February, 1875, I visited Poaetquissings, and experimented in fishing with a net placed under the ice. There were no means of disturbing the fishes, if at rest in or on the mud, and any that might be caught would be such as were voluntarily moving about. After a lapse of half an hour the net was removed, and I found seventeen fish had been "gilled"—sunfish, catfish, lazy suckers, and little minnows. The creek here is shallow, and with a weed-choked bottom; at this time of the year, however, it is comparatively clear, as the frost has long since wilted the nuphar, pontederia, sagittaria, and nymphæa, until only blackened masses of their rank summer-growth remained. Just where the net was placed there was a different condition from that obtaining in the immediate vicinity. It was a little basin, from four to five feet in depth, and fully three feet deeper than the surrounding bed of the stream. This deeper water was warmer than that in the shallower places, and there was the added advantage of a constant supply of fresh water from two lively springs which bubbled up with great energy, keeping the sand in a constant whirl. About these springs the vegetation was green, and appeared vigorous, if not really growing. Here was a winter haunt of the fishes; the one that first led me to study their winter life more closely than heretofore; and ever since I have found in just such places a fair representation, during winter, of Poaetquissings' ichthyic fauna.

Indeed, I doubt if hibernation is so fixed a habit with any creature as is supposed. That many animals can strictly hibernate is unquestionable; that they always do is quite another matter. I am free to say that I believe the element of regularity in this matter is wholly wanting.

How quickly crows learn to know when the ice will bear them! Their keen eyes detect the first lacelike tissue of frost over the creek, and the steady growth of needle-like crystals from the shores outward. I have even seen them play at "tickle-y benders," but with the advantage over boys in that they can stay up always, even if the ice goes down; and later, when the creek is frostbound from shore to shore, these birds enjoy wandering over it fully as much as I do. They are ever on the hunt for food, and during deep snows their ingenuity fails them, and many starve to death. They appear to have grown so over-cautious of late that, rather than incur the merest ghost of possible danger, they will suffer for food in the midst of plenty. Poor crows! Really useful, and to the lover of nature an unfailing source of interest, they have suffered so much and so long that it would not be strange if they often wondered why, indeed, they were created. I have said they are useful, and I stand by the unqualified assertion. I admit their fondness for corn; I know that they love watermelons, and are excellent judges of them, always pecking a destructive hole in the choicest of the patch. What of it? The same crows have eaten grubs and young mice for ten months, and have paid thereby better prices for the corn and melons than ever farmer got from any purchaser. Frighten the crows, if you will, from the cornfields and melon-patches, but do not kill them. This is not the whim of a crank, but the advice of a farmer.

Poaetquissings is worthy of consideration in yet another aspect, during and after a snow-storm. When the creek is frozen, prior to a fall of snow, the outlook is even better; for the surface of the stream, particularly near the river, is then a trackless expanse of glittering white that is tempting to the lover of a winter walk. The crooked elms and bending birches, drooping beneath burdens of snow-lined branches, hem in on either side the hidden stream, and nothing that ventures abroad can well escape our notice. But what does venture abroad? A few winter birds, of course, and it well repays one to watch such when the ground is covered with a foot of snow. The nuthatches are probably the most prominent bird-feature of the tall trees. These, with the brown tree-creeper, scatter the snow from the rough bark, and, peeping beneath the upturned edges of semi-detached pieces, find food, and chatter about it almost incessantly. During such snowy days great flocks of cedar-birds settle on the tall trees near Poaetquissings, and add an attractive feature to the scene. They are called chatterers by some, but they make little noise, and only when they take flight do they call attention to themselves by the lisping twitter that they utter as they start. But if the woods appear comparatively deserted after a deep snow, it does not follow that they are really so. During a recent ramble, I purposely left the monotonous surface of the creek, and clambered about the bushes that clustered between the trees upon the creek bank. Looking up into the branches of every tree as I passed it, I soon spied something worth miles of walking to catch a sight of. On a thrifty maple, sitting close to the main stem of the tree, sat a great gray owl, the largest of all our birds of this family. I stood and stared; he sat and blinked; and then, roused by my demonstrations of attack, the great bird spread his wings, and, without a trace of sound, sailed majestically across the creek and over the meadows. Before, the meadows were comparatively deserted, but not now. From every bush there came a sparrow, winter-wren, nuthatch, or kinglet, and, giving chase, screamed as they followed in the wake of the great gray owl. Would they pursue it closely? I think not; but each must enter a protest that this supposed enemy should so boldly appear among them. I could not follow this owl, he flew so far; but, later in the day, I found him again. A family of jays, blue as the sky above them, and restless as the feathery clouds that scudded by, had stumbled upon him as he sat in a dense cedar, and forthwith they sought to dislodge him by ceaseless jabbering. In this they failed, but their clamor drew hither the crows of the neighborhood, and all the small fry whose curiosity was greater than their fear. Such a din from associated birds I have seldom heard, and yet, probably, not one in a dozen knew why it was there, or why it was making such a noise. I climbed part way up the cedar, to scare the owl. It flew as I approached, and the noisy jays, I noticed, were straightway mum, and soon sneaked away. The little birds, as before, followed a short distance, scolding this unwelcome visitor, but never venturing very near. This is the third specimen of these great owls I have seen in New Jersey.

While it is clear, therefore, that Poaetquissings has bird-life enough to render it attractive even in midwinter, such is not its only charm. Southward from the old floodgates the creek has but a short reach of meadow to pass through before it joins the river. This short course, however, has many merits, prominent among which is the fringe of maples that, in single file, stand guard upon the banks of the stream. How beautifully, between these opposite rows of great maples, Poaetquissings at one time glided into the river! how prosaically now! A little more than half a century ago the creek had an ample flow of clear, evenly moving water, and passed its boundaries with becoming grace. Now, confined to an unsightly wooden trough, and that, too, beneath the bank of a canal, it sobs as it seeks its proper home through this dark passage.

The necessities of man are innumerable and inexorable, but who cannot regret that they ever necessitate the blotting out forever of the choicest bits of scenery. Think of the transition from the maple-guarded banks of a clear stream, a hundred yards in breadth, to a cramped wooden trough sunk in the mud. This eyesore passed, the canal crossed, and it, with all its unwelcome accessories, behind our backs, and we sight the Delaware, here more than half a mile wide, within the limits of tide-water, and deep enough for craft of considerable tonnage.

Unless cursed or blessed, as one chances to view it, with an open winter, the Delaware, in mid-winter, is an arctic-looking, desolate place, indeed. Often have I seen it, choked with great masses of ice piled up on edge, and so inextricably jammed that the boundaries of no one mass were clearly distinguishable. Here and there, in the wide expanse of ice-masses, shows a blue line that marks a brief space where the water reaches the surface, and in it, it may be, that a seal, with head well up, may be seen swimming. A volume might be written on the fauna of a frozen river. Every winter it happens that the river, sooner or later, becomes, first, dotted with cakes of floating ice. These, in part, become stranded along the shore and over the sand-bars. Once fast, they check the progress of other masses, until, finally, the open water is reduced to a narrow stream that threads its chilly way through a glittering expanse of tilted, jagged, towering, toppling ice-cakes.

To wander over such a surface is necessarily too dangerous to warrant venturing over deep water; but it sometimes happens that nooks and crannies near shore may be reached, wherefrom, in safety, a broad expanse of the river may be viewed; and there is little probability that such a ramble will prove profitless.

I once stood behind a tilted cake of ice to avoid a cutting east wind, and into the little pool in front a long line of beautiful "squaw" ducks came with a rush, and rested upon the water so lightly as scarcely to cause a ripple. A slight movement on my part startled them, and, with a grace and rapidity of movement unequalled by any grebe, they dived. To this day I am puzzled to know what became of them. I waited long for them to reappear, but in vain. An under-ice passage to the nearest open water could scarcely have been found, and yet I am loath to believe they were drowned.

It is when the river is thus choked with ice that the sharp eyes of some hunter, every winter, finds one or more seals in the river. I have never been so fortunate as to discover the first seal of the season; but have had to take my chances of a subsequent view, when the creature was being hunted by an army of idlers, armed with every conceivable weapon, from a Queen Anne musket to a hickory club.

Within historic times, seals do not appear to have ever been abundant, and yet every one who has occasion to be much about the water in winter has either seen or heard of them. In going over my note-books I find I have recorded in them the occurrence of seals at Trenton, which is at the head of tide-water, in December, 1861; January, 1864; December, 1866; February, 1870; and December, 1877. If the newspapers did not report the same seal more than once, there were five taken in the river in the winter of 1878-79; and they were more than usually abundant in the other rivers of the state and along the coast.

My impression is that during very cold winters they are really much more abundant in the Delaware than is supposed. Considering how small a chance there is of their being seen when the river is choked with ice, I am disposed to believe that an occasional pair or more come up the river, even as high as Trenton, nearly one hundred and fifty miles from the capes, every winter.

On examination of old local histories I find reference to the seals as not uncommon along our coasts, and as frequently wandering far up the rivers.

As the capture of a seal is usually noised abroad, I have examined with some care the files of local newspapers, for a period of fifty years, and not without some rather interesting results. I have found no notice earlier than November 20 or later than March 25, so it is fairly safe to conclude that in the five months from October to April seals are to be found in the Delaware, when found at all. The additional fact gathered is, that during the past fifty years seals have been seen or captured every year, in the state, and in thirty-two years of the half century one to ten have been taken in the Delaware River.

In the memorable winter of 1836, when the snow was fully four feet in depth, on a level, there were seven harpooned in the river, between Trenton and Bordentown, a reach of but five miles; and two were found to have wandered up Crosswicks Creek to where that stream makes a sudden bend at the base of the bluff, and there, in a deep hole, they thrived admirably on the bountiful supply of chubs and suckers that the deep water contained. These two seals were seen by many people, and various attempts to capture them alive were made; but I cannot discover that they were ever taken. Local gossip does not mention this fact, and there are several old hunters still living who would probably have heard of it, had some one been lucky enough to catch or kill them.

Although this occurrence of seals was beyond the boundary by a mile or more, and the circumstances were very unusual in every respect, still I think it but fair to claim that the animal is to be included in the fauna of my farm. Indeed, were it not that they are shut off by a high canal bank, it is probable that whenever a winter freshet occurred these animals would appear on the meadows; but I am pained to admit I have never seen one there.

It must be confessed that the stray seal, as it appears

in the river, is not an interesting object. Possibly, aware that to be seen is to be persecuted, it keeps out of sight as much as possible, and it has puzzled me to know how the animal was recognized. I have never seen them clamber up on the firm ice, or show an inch more of their bodies than their round heads, that bobbed about like cocoanuts, and then were gone for a long time. Possibly the old fishermen that linger about the river, long after any chance for fishing has gone by, constantly bear in mind the possibility of their finding a seal, and so report every seal-like object to be one. In such a case, if there does happen to be one about, it is pretty sure to be recognized, reported, persecuted, and killed.

Other mammals also wander into and over the frozen river, and it is no unlikely occurrence to meet with otters, musk-rats, minks, and even meadow-mice, that have wandered far from the river shore and seem bent on some important errand. Of course, the presence of the otter is readily explained, for there is often a vast number of fishes in the patches of open water, upon which the animals feed. The same may be said of the mink; but why mice should undertake to cross the river on the ice is by no means clear; unless it be the peculiar disposition of these creatures to migrate in bodies, from one spot to another.

It is when the river is frozen that, in all probability, grebes will be seen swimming on and diving into the pools that dot the frozen surface of the stream. Would these birds be content to act with some deliberation, it would be a pleasure to observe them; but, as it is, they aggravate rather than entertain. You say to yourself, there is a grebe; but before the assertion is finished, the bird is not there, and you stand with a vague impression that you did see something, but cannot be sure. Between winks, it reappears, and your doubt is redoubled, for now you cannot be sure that it ever disappeared. This feathered uncertainty I was accustomed to call a crested grebe, but it now proves that I was mistaken. On the contrary, there are two, not one, and neither is crested. One is the red-necked grebe, the other the eared diver. This is a pleasant mistake, whereby I have added a bird to the previously large list found in this valley. Along the sea-coast, and probably in the bay, these divers are numerous from early autumn till spring; but this does not appear to be true of them as frequenting the river at this point. I have seen none except when there was an abundance of ice and snow; yet, after all, why should I be so positive? A near neighbor, last summer, had a pair of mocking-birds nesting in his garden, and I. never knew of it until long after they had gone south again. I must often have heard them sing, and I must have given to cat-birds and brown thrushes all the credit.

Such, in brief, are the suggestions of a walk in winter, when the Delaware and Poaetquissings are alike ice-bound; when, as yet, no trace of spring is to be found; when, for all that greets the eye, we might as well be miles within the arctic circle, rather than hundreds of leagues below it.

CHAPTER III.
'TWIXT COLD AND HEAT.

TYPICAL spring is one of the lost arts: actual spring is the mother of disappointments. Since the February sun began rising more and more to the east, and edged westward along the horizon in the afternoons, I have been looking for some evidence of spring, with her reputed ethereal mildness; and I have not found it. The difference between March and December has not been one of importance, even as regards temperature. Indeed, December proved far the more springlike of the two, and during its closing hours the frogs piped merrily.

And all through March, that month of broken promises, I was lulled to sleep, time and again, by a gentle south wind murmuring in the pines, and dreamed of frogs croaking their satisfaction that there shall be no more winter—for a season. I awoke, and only to find the north wind roaring in those same pines, and the fields snowclad.

Days of impatient waiting pass; the thawing of the snow is tardy; but finally the fields are bare. Surely, now, spring will come. It is near the twentieth day, and the well-thumbed almanac says that upon that day spring commences. The sun crosses the line, but who, except astronomers, would imagine anything unusual in that? The mercury in the thermometer runs up and down, with all the precision of a pendulum's side-wise course. It is winter at night and, faintly, something else at noon. The month comes and goes, at least this last one came and went, with ice, snow, north winds, and all the plagues of winter, yet it is said not to be that season, but something else. Just what, it would be hard to say.

As some lifelong wanderer, returning to the scenes of his childhood, expects to find green the grave of his grandsire, but, instead, meets the gentleman, still hale and hearty, although a centenarian, so now, after a night-long ramble in the land of dreams, I awake, not to find flowers covering the grave of winter, but his frosty grimness still overshadowing the land.

If we have spring at all, it is limited to a brief part of April, and is as little prominent as a season of the year as is mortar between bricks or the thin layer of cement between the dressed stones of the building.

Even limiting the mythical season to half a month, what are the distinctive evidences of its arrival? It is not, as we have seen, a matter of temperature. To be doubly sure of this, I asked a practical farmer when he thought the season had fairly set in. "When it's too warm to smoke on the south side of the barn," he replied, and here, I found, he sat, half the winter, to enjoy his post-prandial pipe. I asked him again, about blooming flowers; and he told me of dandelions and green grass that had amused him "by their pluck, seein' sometimes they were covered with snow."

Is spring the date of the reviving of hibernating

animals? If so, how is it that the January thaw rouses even the most methodical of them all, the jumping mouse? The fishes have been in the deep waters since last November, and active too, as when you saw them last, during an October ramble. A few have been lying dormant, in the mud, but their rousing from such slumber may occur at any time, and so the significance is wanting.

Is it the batrachians that, by their united chorus, proclaim the advent of spring? Then how explain their full-voiced chorus on December 31 and on New Year's Day?

As to the birds: it is not the fish-hawk, which did not come on the 21st of March, this year; nor yet the kill-deer plovers, for sometimes they appear on the meadows in February; nor can we say that pee-wees bring spring with them. They are sometimes at their haunts of the past year as early as February 22, and have been called "Washington birds;" "cherry-tree fly-catchers" would be better, for the cherry is a favorite tree with them, particularly when its fruit attracts the flies.

As long ago as 1799, Dr. Benjamin S. Barton, of Philadelphia, wrote of our spring birds as follows: "Although, in Pennsylvania, and many other parts of the United States, the arrival of our birds does not appear to be as uniform as it is in many of the countries of the Old World; the arrival of several species is, nevertheless, so regular, that it may be considered as the signal for commencing certain agricultural operations. Thus, the Muscicapa fusca, which we call Pewe, is one of the earliest spring birds of passage, visiting the neighborhood of Philadelphia about the middle of March. We have seldom hard frosts after the arrival of this bird, which seems to give a pretty confident assurance to the farmer that he may very soon begin to open the ground and plant."

Not so accommodating are the pee-wees of to-day. They have a trick of coming even in February, and, if there be sunshine, sing suggestively of early spring; but I have never known their cheery *pēē wēē* to escape the sad change to dreary *Ah, me!* before the ethereal mildness of the poet's spring proved a matter of fact. There lives no farmer now that holds the pee-wee either a weather-prophet or a barometer.

I do not know how often the learned doctor was about, in winter, to see, but I suspect that then, as now, there were pee-wees beyond the city's limits at earlier dates than he mentions; if not, there has been wrought a curious change in their habits.

For years it has been a source of amusement to see how promptly the early pee-wees accommodate themselves to that change to wintry conditions which is sure, sooner or later, to follow their arrival. March frosts or a snowstorm drives them from their perches on the leafless branches to the roomy shelter of empty out-buildings, and here they find a sufficiency of food by hunting the ever-present spiders and various forms of dormant insect life.

Of course such a change brings them into conflict with the quick-tempered Carolina wrens, and the battles are both long and loud. The wrens scream their displeasure, the fly-catchers screech their indignation, and neither appears to gain a decisive victory.

Nevertheless, to hear these birds for the first time does suggest that winter draws to a close. The late T. A. Conrad, the geologist, always dated spring in New Jersey from the pee-wee's arrival, ignoring the fact that often the bird's appearance was followed by a foot of snow. Once, when fossil-hunting, away from home, the notes of this bird fell unexpectedly upon his ear, and he recorded his impressions as follows, on the spur of the moment:

"Sweet promise of the sunny days,
    Thy restless form is dear to me;
Though homely are thy plaintive lays,
    Thy simple carol, brown pee-wee.

"I see thee build thy rustic fort
    Beneath the bridge's mouldering arch;
And joy to hear thy love's report
    Above the boisterous breath of March.

"Thou comest from distant wood or bower
    To scenes which smiled upon thy birth,
While trees are bare, and scarce a flower
    Is scattered o'er the cold, moist earth.

"While Spring is in her changeful moods,
    And now unlocks the icy rill;
When in the hollows of the woods
    The unsunned snow is lingering still.

"Thou living memory of the days
    When I was young and gay like thee,
Thou lead'st me thro' the gathering haze
    Back to the light of infancy.

> "To morning hours when oft I trod
>   The spongy fields in search of thee,
> When Draba starred the chilly sod
>   In a pale, tiny galaxy.
>
> "Once, in a kindly winter day,
>   By Alabama's waters rude,
> I saw thee on the mossy spray
>   That stretched in leafless solitude,
>
> "Upon the steep bank's crumbling side,
>   Enriched with many a fossil shell;
> And truly, 'twas with joy and pride
>   I saw thee in my precinct dwell:
>
> "For then it lost its alien face,
>   And Fancy dwelt in home once more;
> I seemed in early Spring's embrace,
>   Beside my far ancestral door.
>
> "And when shall come the fatal night,
>   Amid my weakness, grief, and pain,
> I would behold thy circling flight,
>   And die while listening to thy strain."

Of our migratory birds collectively, it may be said that they come so near the first of May, when the foliage is at least one third grown, that they really mark the commencement of summer; for, after all, what is summer but green leaves and torrid sunshine, both of which are often as marked a feature of May as of any of the four succeeding months. Of course, this remark does not apply to the so-called "pioneer" birds, which, as stragglers, sometimes appear a week or even two weeks in advance of the main flight. Dr. Barton, in the essay already quoted, referring to summer in May, remarks: "It is an old observation in Pennsylvania, that when the whip-poor-will (Caprimulgus Virginianus) arrives, it is time to go bare-footed; that is, the spring season is pretty far advanced, and sufficiently warm to admit of laying aside the use of shoes, without much inconvenience. This adage originated in the days of greater simplicity than the present (1791). Some of our Indians believe that this bird is a messenger sent to call their attention to the planting of the ground. Accordingly, upon the arrival of the whip-poor-will, they say to one another, 'The *wee-co-lis* is come: it is planting-time;' and, while the bird is uttering the sound of whip-poor-will, or wee-co-lis, they will repeat the word 'hackibeck,' which is, 'plant the ground.'"

This holds good to-day. The whip-poor-will cannot, or will not, accommodate itself to circumstances, and either the weather must be warm or the bird tarries southward; and if, as is so apt to be the case, a cold rain-storm occurs in May, these birds leave their haunts and return to warmer quarters. At least, they disappear, and I cannot believe, even temporarily, hibernate, as the writer quoted considers as possible, but not actually demonstrated.

Unfortunately the whip-poor-wills are comparatively scarce, and the opportunity of closely observing them does not offer. They, like their cousins the night-hawks, have greatly decreased in numbers during the past half-century.

Let us return and consider the scattered April flowers that bloom on the beautiful north bank of Poaetquissings. Under favorable circumstances, the delicate flowers of the yellow corydalis, a cousin of the cardrop, that bloomed last month, will be apt to catch the eye of the plant-hunter. If we do not mind a few scratches from the gordian knots of smilax, a little hunting will discover another yellow blossom, the erythronium; a gracefully nodding, lily-like flower, perched upon a stem six inches high, which, in turn, springs from between two mottled brown leaves, that are themselves quite pretty. Yellow buttercups, too, are now ready to be gathered; and who does not love them for the recollections they bring up of those irrecoverable days as full of sunshine as are these flowers' golden chalices.

Again, a little closer search discloses the beautiful tricolored violet, often starring grassy spaces between the larger trees, and crowding out even the grass that struggles to maintain itself in the same places. It almost causes the recollection of the past winter to vanish, to be able to gather violets; and resting at the foot of a tall tree, basking in noontide sunshine, and holding a nosegay of these pretty flowers, one can almost say, "Spring has come;" but when we reach the top of the bluff, and a breath of searching north wind whistles in our ears, we laugh at such a thought as a childish fancy, and resign ourselves to further waiting for the departure of winter.

But the botanist cannot rest here. There is early saxifrage, with its large cluster of white flowers on a scape high above the dead leaves of the overarching trees, and its hairy spatulate leaves at the base of the stem. Blood-root, too, with its single white flower, will not escape notice; and better than all, as we venture out upon the meadow, are the beautiful "Quaker girls."

Conrad, whose verses on the pee-wee have been quoted, calls them "beloved Houstonias" in his "Wissahickon in April," and, referring to this very bank and meadow of Poaetquissings, writes:

> "In other scenes,
> O'er starry meads they court the sun and gather
> In loving groups, robed by the breath of Spring
> In azure-tinted mantles—they so pure,
> So exquisitely simple in attire,
> Merit the endearing name of 'Quaker Girls'—
> On tearful April's bosom none more lovely;
> None whose fair multitudinous crowds recall
> More vividly the idols of our youth,
> When our free hearts exultantly went forth,
> Beating beneath the touch of April joys,
> Born of the illimitable blue and fanned
> By zephyrs dallying with Viola's breath,
> And rioting in the freedom of the hours,
> When the song sparrow's airy notes are blending
> With the Eolian music of the pines."

And the end is not yet. In the same ramble that has disclosed all that have been named there may also be gathered bright yellow blossoms of the marsh marigold; purple-red bloom of the spotted geranium; jack-in-the-pulpit, grape hyacinth, with flowers as blue as the cloudless sky above them; Jacob's ladder, and daffodils. Are you not satisfied with these, oh! lover of plants? Then wander still farther, and if the month be well advanced, you may chance upon rue anemone and wind-flowers; and although

> "climbing columbines
> In niches of the tall, precipitous rocks,
> Reserve their banners for victorious May,"

it may chance to be your fortune to find them blowing

now, and the same may be said of the bellworts and Solomon's seal. In one nook, sheltered by cedars and a noble beech, there is also to be found, more beautiful than all, a roseate bush of blooming azalea. Before its leaves are grown, and a week or more in advance of its kind elsewhere, this "wild honeysuckle" anticipates May, and gives us a pleasant foretaste of the coming month.

Nevertheless, April along Poaetquissings is not like the April on the Wissahickon, only thirty miles away, of which it has been written:

> "Oh, Spring! how lovely is thy garlanded
> And fresh young brow! how sweet thy varying voice!
> What a glad music rings in every note
> Of love aërial! Brilliant is thy green
> New robe! and far along the rippling waters,
> How breaks the blue into a myriad stars—
> The glittering river, which is sprinkled o'er
> With diamonds of the sun. Swift Progne bathes
> In that blue radiance of reflected heaven
> Her ardent breast a moment ere she speeds
> In twittering joy on her aërial course.
> Here is an Eden for the young and gay,
> For hearts unshadowed by the raven wing,
> For the fresh, roseate cheeks Hygeia loves;
> For the defiant laugh, the careless carol,
> And the free tread of angel feet o'er flowers
> As pure and bright as only childhood knows—
> O'er moss-embowered trailing epigæa,
> Clear as Diana's alabaster brow,
> The gem of April's robe—sweet epigæa!
> Thy purity is stamped upon my heart
> In "angel whiteness," and thy odorate breath
> Redeems the grossness of the earth and links
> Our senses to the spirit world beyond!"

Animal life, in April, must not be ignored. Many creatures that have been comparatively inactive during the winter are now gradually assuming their summer restlessness. Among the countless hundreds of objects worthy of the rambler's attention, perhaps none are so beautiful and full of interest as the fairy shrimps that throng the dark waters of an upland sink-hole. This hollow in the field has a foot or more of water in it from November to June, and during the past winter it was frozen to the bottom until the 1st of April. A hard time, therefore, thought I, have these fairy shrimps had, with not a drop of water to move in; but they are not to be judged by the delicacy of their anatomy. There was a soft spot in the mud, somewhere, and when, later in the month, I waded between cakes of ice, and looked long into the depths of this upland pool, finally I found the fairies in abundance, a few well grown, but mostly mere babies. They were earlier in '84. On the 22d of the month I gathered a great many, and all fully grown.

To describe them is impracticable. They are liliputian lobsters, pearly white, picked with crimson; and with eleven pairs of feathery legs that move with the perfection of grace. They swim upon their backs, and the movement of these legs or paddles is the very poetry of motion. While the water remains cool, they will dart, float, and ramble among the dead twigs and leaves in the bottom of the pool, but disappear promptly, after a few hot days, or more gradually, as the waters soak away, if the weather is cool. Dr. Packard says of them: " At Seekonk, Mass., they occurred abundantly May 2, in a large pond which completely dried up in summer; ... when I visited the pond ... May 13, none were to be found. It seems from this quite evident that the animal probably dies off at the approach of warm weather and does not reappear until after cool weather sets in late in the autumn, being represented in the summer by the eggs alone; and thus the appearance and disappearance of this Phyllopod is apparently determined mainly by the temperature."

Bearing this in mind, I took several lumps of the dried mud, last summer, and placed them in ice-water, hoping to have the eggs, if there were any, hatch, and so puzzle the doctor with midsummer specimens, but the plan did not work. Either I got no eggs with the mud, or the water was too cold; at any rate, my plan was a failure, and, as it was intended to be a joke, deserved no better fate. Returning to pure science, I waded the waters of that upland pond faithfully until it froze. I could find no specimens. Even in March of '84 there were none to be seen; and this year, '85, they were apparently but a few days old, as late as April 1.

In an aquarium they are very beautiful, but must be kept by themselves. A dozen were placed in a small tank containing mud-minnows and sunfish. The latter ate the beautiful fairies as though they were an ordinary article of their diet; but the mud-minnows would not touch them. Later, I placed innumerable minute leeches in the same tank, and these the minnows greedily devoured, but the sunfish ignored them completely.

The fact that during the month of May nest-building

is at its height, makes it a busy and instructive time for the practical naturalist.

Birds when nesting, more than at any other time, show what they really are, intellectually. If one is lazy, stupid, or disabled in any manner, the fact will then become patent, and leads, at times, to divorce among mated birds. Among catbirds, wrens, and orioles I have known quarrels to occur, arising from such causes as I have mentioned, and which led to permanent separation, abandonment of half-constructed nests, and even a full complement of eggs.

Having met, in the summer of '84, with many instances wherein birds have shown considerable ingenuity in overcoming the ill-results of accidents to their nests, such as often arise during violent storms, I determined to test their intellectual powers generally, by a series of simple experiments, hoping thereby to be able to determine to what extent birds exercise their reasoning faculties.

My experiments, and the inferences I drew, are as follows: Noting the material being gathered for the partly constructed nest of a chipping-sparrow, I placed a small quantity of the same in a conspicuous position near by. It was seen by the sparrows, and examined, but none was removed. I placed a portion of it upon the margin of the unfinished nest: it was promptly removed by the male bird, who used only such materials as were brought to him by his mate. The following day the task of lining the nest with hair was commenced. I placed a quantity of this material on a branch near by, but it was passed unnoticed. I next placed a few hairs on the margin of the nest: these were promptly removed. On replacing many of these in the nest, the entire lining was thrown out. I replaced it, and the nest was abandoned.

A week later, finding another nest with three eggs, I added a few white cat-hairs to the lining: these were removed. Others of dark colors were added: they, also, were removed. I replaced both dark and white hairs: the eggs were broken, and the nest abandoned.

Did the sense of smell, in this case, lead them to suspect that a cat was prowling about? Birds are not always, perhaps not usually, disturbed by the chance occurrence of a foreign object in their nest. Stray feathers, bits of thread, a piece of paper, any such objects carried by the wind may settle upon a nest, and will simply be pushed aside. In this case, it would seem that the hair was recognized as something not so likely to be carried by a passing breeze, and only the near proximity of the cat could explain its presence, therefore danger threatened them. Have we not here a complicated process of reasoning and a logical conclusion drawn by these birds?

Four eggs found in a third nest were removed without touching the nest, a wooden spoon whittled for the purpose being used. In three days the female commenced laying again: four days later three eggs had been laid. I replaced the four I had removed: they were promptly thrown out. I then removed the nest, and, substituting another, carefully replaced the eggs without handling them. After what appeared to be a serious consultation, the new nest was accepted. These birds suffered no further annoyance, and reared their brood without mishap.

Why should not these sparrows, in the first two instances, have utilized the material for their nest which I offered, rather than gather similar stuff from distant points? They could not have been frightened by any odor attached to the material through my handling, as I was careful not to touch a particle of it, using a pair of wooden tweezers in every case. Neither did they see me carrying anything to or from their nests. As these, in all cases, were nearly or quite completed, the birds had necessarily become thoroughly familiar with the surroundings, and doubtless recognized the fact that these offered twigs and the hair were brought by unusual agencies to the spot, thus arousing suspicion, as I have pointed out. When a nest not of their building was substituted for their own, the sparrows were sorely perplexed and exhibited fear, and only after a strong mental effort—of itself a telling evidence of intelligence—the maternal instinct overcame the timidity of the female, and she resolved to brave the danger or solve the mystery, and cared for her eggs as usual. The male bird kept aloof for several days, I think; but of this I am not positive. These several incidents, collectively considered, clearly demonstrate that this social sparrow, which under other circumstances is so tame and unsuspicious, when nesting is wisely cautious, never acting without due consideration of the probable results.

But it is not every bird that is so particular as to the origin or location of suitable nesting materials. Only a few days ago I found a pair of English sparrows and mated Carolina wrens building within ten paces of each other. Both nests were but just begun, and anticipating a row before many days, I was consequently constantly on hand. To precipitate it, I placed a tempting roll of threads and carpet ravellings in a conspicuous position, and lingered near until they were discovered by the birds. As luck would have it, the sparrow and the wren spied the mass at the same moment, and both, with hawk-like rapidity, darted at it. They met. "The deuce!" chirped the sparrow. "Who's afraid?" twittered the wren; and there they sat, facing each other. But sitting still is not an accomplishment of the wren family, and this one thrust his beak into the mass to carry it off. "No you don't," ejaculated the sparrow, and he put his foot in it, in both senses of the phrase. The interference was too much for the wren, and he "went for" that sparrow. Head over heels through the air and over the ground went these angry birds, and their noise called out the other birds, who had been waiting for more nest-building materials. These newcomers took matters very philosophically. The sparrow followed her mate, to see which would whip; the wren, with full faith in her husband's prowess, glanced about for nesting-stuffs, and, spying the "bone of contention," lifted it up, although as large as herself, and bore it off to her home.

Tired of fighting, or having agreed to compromise, the combatants separated, and shortly returned to the wood-pile, where the coveted materials had been lying. Were they going to divide it? They hopped to the very spot, and lo! it was gone. I imagined those birds looked foolish. The sparrow twittered to its mate that it was only fun between them; the wren whistled "mighty queer," and departed.

Another series of experiments were as follows: finding a nest of the summer warbler in a low alder, the foliage of which was about one third grown, I girdled the supporting growths a few inches below the nest. The leaf-buds withered, and the nest, which under ordinary circumstances would have been quite concealed from view by the full-grown leaves, was now exposed. The nest was abandoned.

The next girdling experiment was made on the nest of a white-eyed vireo found attached to a low limb of a small beech. The leaves quickly shrivelled, and the nest, although just finished, was abandoned.

A second experiment of the same sort was tried, with identical result.

A nest of the summer warbler was found in a low shrub, containing young birds, and the supporting branches were girdled. The leaves withered and fell, exposing the nest to full view. The parent birds remained and successfully reared their brood.

In these cases we have evidence of mental operations of a more complicated character than any exhibited by the sparrows. It is evident that, in every case, these birds, in selecting the position for their nests, knew that the growth of the foliage would afford a desirable, if not necessary, protection. Finding that the growth of the foliage had been checked, that the little shelter at first afforded was daily growing less, they foresaw that the nests, under these circumstances, would be too much exposed to be safe from molestation, and they were abandoned, even after a full complement of eggs had been laid. Can we explain this by any other means than by using that very suggestive term "foresight"? But mark: when the same circumstance occurred after the young had appeared, the claims of the brood upon the parents were too strong to be overcome, and the danger of occupying an exposed nest was deliberately braved.

Other pairs of nesting birds were experimented upon that I might determine their intellectual status; first, by placing a nearly life-size chromo of a cat near the nest, when unoccupied, and watching the result. This depended much upon the character of the bird, whether naturally timid or brave. When a song-sparrow found itself stared at by the cat, it rushed precipitately from the nest and did not return until the picture had been removed. When the chromo was left for several hours near a nest, it was permanently abandoned. In no case did these birds offer to attack the animal, or express alarm, and so call other birds to their aid. It was otherwise with thrushes. I placed the same picture near nests of catbirds, song-thrushes, and the brown thrush. Immediately a cry of alarm was uttered that brought birds of the same and allied species to the rescue, and the excitement steadily increased, as it was found that no amount of scolding caused the intruding cat to retire. It was particularly amusing to see their puzzled expressions when they chanced behind the picture. Then, of course, there was nothing to frighten, and they were proportionately bold. In one instance a catbird, coming from behind, alighted upon the top of the picture, notwithstanding the warnings of the other birds. Chancing to look down, it saw the cat, and with a scream gave a double backward somersault and left. This, however, seemed to open the eyes of the other birds, and they gradually became accustomed to its presence, as though they believed the animal to be dead. In no cases were the nests abandoned.

When the same chromo, although now rather dilapidated, was placed near a wren box, the occupants took matters very coolly, and after finding the cat showed no disposition to leave, determined to drive it off. With impetuous fury they assaulted it, and struck it about the ears and eyes several times. Of course, this experience soon told the quick-witted wrens that the cat was harmless, if a cat at all, and they paid no further attention to it. I found this to be true of both Carolina and common house wrens, in every case. Taking the battered picture to the muddy meadows, the marsh-wrens merely glanced at it, as they would at any unusual object, and passed by. They, at least, are not troubled by cats in the marshes.

A small mirror placed near a nest produced conflicting emotions. The bird was usually indisposed to leave her nest, and yet was much annoyed by the apparent intruder. I do not think in any case the bird learned to recognize it as but a very vivid shadow of itself. Sparrows and warblers were rendered timid, and expressed their alarm so frequently as to keep their mates near by, but in no instance was the supposed intruder assaulted. As I expected, the case was very different when wrens were tested. These immediately became very angry, and finally, an over-excited house-wren pitched headlong at the supposed interloper, with the doubly fatal result of killing itself and breaking the glass. Subsequently, taking a larger glass, that was thick enough to withstand ordinary attacks by wrens or larger birds, I placed it on the ground, and soon found that it was supposed to be water. Chickens tried in vain to drink, as did small wild birds; and none seemed to be surprised at seeing their own reflections. It would seem, from this, that such reflection in water is a common occurrence, and they gave it no thought, but recognized a difference when they found the glass in a perpendicular position, near their nests. Did they realize that in this latter instance it could not be water? If so, birds have gotten so far as to have some knowledge of physics; which, after all, is not much to be wondered at, when they are, all of them, excellent mechanics.

Experiments of another character were as follows: I placed a series of short pieces of woollen yarn, fastened together at one end, near the tree containing a partly constructed nest of a Baltimore oriole. These yarns were red, yellow, purple, green, and gray. An equal number of strands of each color were thus offered to the orioles as building-materials. I purposely placed the red and yellow strands on the outside of the tassel-shaped mass, so that these would be first taken, if the color was not objectionable. To my complete surprise, the gray strands only were taken, until the nest was nearly finished, when a few of the purple and blue yarns were used. Not a red, yellow, or green strand was disturbed.

Here we have an instance of the exercise of choice, on the part of a bird, which is full of interest. The woollen threads being otherwise identical, it was the color only that influenced the choice of the birds: they realized that the red or yellow yarns would render the nest conspicuous, although well protected by the foliage of the branch to which it was attached. Why the green threads were not taken I cannot imagine. As a result of this experiment, I anticipated that the orioles would reserve the brightly colored yarns for the lining of the nest, and the gray and green for the exterior. This was a result obtained two years ago, when I tried a similar experiment; but the use of red yarn as a lining may have been merely accidental.

Out of mere curiosity, for I could not anticipate what might be the result, I made a few transfers of the eggs of one species into the nest of another bird. The results were not, however, particularly suggestive. I placed the eggs of a catbird in the nest of a song thrush, and *vice versa*. The eggs of the former are dark green; of the latter, light blue. No act indicative of recognition of the change was observed. I placed eggs of the song sparrow in the nest of a pee-wee, and *vice versa*. The fly-catchers rejected the eggs of the sparrow; but the latter accepted the situation, although disturbed by it. Many other changes were made, with similar results; and I concluded that, unless the eggs were greatly different in size and color, about one half would be accepted; but when a single egg was placed in the nest of another bird, it was destroyed in nearly every case. This I found to be true, even when I tested such birds as are subjected to the annoyance of the cowpen bird's egg being deposited in their nests. I was surprised at this result, and am led to believe that large numbers of the eggs of this bird are destroyed. It is well-known that our summer warbler frequently outwits the cowpen bird by building a new nest directly above the old—a two-story nest, in fact—leaving the egg that has been left to her care to rot in the basement, while she rears her young on the floor above. It will be seen that from these experiments no very positive results were obtained. I did note, however, that, where the change was accepted, it was not because it passed unnoticed, but was submitted to, notwithstanding the evidences of much misgiving on the part of the birds. In one case, the nest was practically deserted for twenty-four hours, and the eggs were chilled in consequence. The birds sat upon them for five days, when, as they did not hatch, the nest was abandoned. In previous years I have made these changes occasionally with success, but was not able to determine that the young were recognized as not the offspring of the attendant birds. In such cases the young were tended with the usual care up to the time for leaving the nest. This may possibly be indicative of stupidity. It appeared so to me at the time; but I am now disposed to see in it an indication that the maternal instincts here, as in other cases I have mentioned, overcame all other feelings, and that the fact was accepted by the birds with as good grace as they could command.

The co-operation of birds, when constructing their nests, is a subject that demands a good deal of close attention, and is one surely worthy of more systematic observation than has as yet been given it. The many ways in which birds assist each other in nest-building offer, perhaps, the clearest evidence that they have a very intelligent notion of what they are doing, or propose to do. I feel warranted at the outset in making the somewhat startling assertion that the choice of location for a nest is made only after protracted joint examination of suitable sites, and is the choice of both birds. I doubt if it ever happens that one of a pair of birds "gives in" to its mate. Certainly, such a thing as madam giving in to her lord is unknown in the bird-world. My impression is, that the female birds of every species are exacting, obstinate, and tyrannical. I have seen marked instances of this among house-wrens, pee-wees, and even known a cooing turtle-dove to exhibit unmistakable evidences of a quick temper. These may seem to be trivial matters, and not within the range of the scientific study of animal intelligence; but it is an error to look upon such proofs of individuality in this light; they are among the most convincing evidences of a high degree of intelligence.

So much for quiet studies during May; but it is not a month that suggests a minimum of physical exertion, and often the days are too beautiful to make a roof desirable. One longs not only to be out, but active, and then to go a-birds'-nesting is the very acme of a naturalist's enjoyment. Not to gather eggs or even frighten the birds do we go, but simply to see how many can be found nesting, and, better, to find some that had not been found in previous years. This, at least in my tree-climbing days, was the height of my ambition; it was a red-letter day when I could add a new bird to the list. And how often, when on such excursions, would inaccessible nests be found. How often have I vainly attempted to climb some neighboring tree, that I might look down upon the contents of a nest far out of reach. It was a satisfaction to verify the statements made in the books, although there was no reason to doubt them. At such a time one longs for the surely coming days of aërial locomotion, although it will be a sorry time for many a timid fly-catcher, now living in remote tree-tops, when, with a balloon in one hand, we can sail above the topmost branches and inspect the contents of what now are usually inaccessible nests. The sight of such nests and a glimpse of the builders is really all that one needs; to shoot the birds that they may be identified is an abomination; but it takes years often to overcome the mania for tree-top scrambles. Every naturalist must at least risk life and limb once in his time, although others have done so sufficiently often to settle every important point in North American oölogy. Happily one desperate adventure sometimes cures—as it did me.

A few years ago, in one of the big elms at the "bend" in Poaetquissings, far out over the water, was the nest of a yellow-throated vireo. I contemplated that nest for half a day. I dreamed of it that night. Have it I must, and, telling no one—another proof of insanity—I went alone to the quiet corner of the creek. To reach the nest I must not only climb the tree to a considerable height, but must then creep along an overarching limb, with no supporting branches near. Once there, the creek only would be beneath me, except a single outreaching branch of a large maple that stood opposite the elm. If I fell, this might catch me; if not, a plunge into the creek, twenty or more feet below, was the only alternative. Foolhardy as it was, I resolved to try, and up that elm I clambered, with, I must admit, mixed feelings of determination and doubt. The upward climb alone was easily accomplished, but that outward creep—ah! it makes me shudder to recall it. Needing all the grasping power I possessed, I took off my shoes, and found that bared feet were far more available as claspers than one might suppose. So effectively did they cling to the rough bark that I was forcibly and favorably impressed with the derivative theory of man's descent from an arboreal, simian ancestry. The outward creep was commenced, and a yard brought me fairly over the black, deep water. I dared not look at it, but keeping my eye steadily fixed upon the nest, slowly crept forward. I was my length from the base of the limb, and over the middle of the creek. A half length was yet to be accomplished and I was within reach of the nest. Carefully I moved forward yet a little farther, and tremblingly put out my right hand and took up an egg. I placed it in my mouth; then another was secured, and now I was content to withdraw—but how? I tried creeping backward, but it was not practicable. My clothes caught in the bark and held me fast. I must go forward or drop; but the former was, of course, impossible. Must I drop, then, into the water? At this moment the birds returned, or, if hitherto silent spectators, were now emboldened to attack me. That they recognized my utter helplessness I do not doubt. The little feathered furies dashed at my face with wonderful vehemence, snapping their beaks viciously in my very ears. I feared for the safety of my eyes. I was forced to continually move my head from side to side to avoid them, and finally, in so doing, relaxed my grasp so far as to slip from the upper to the under side. Here was a dilemma I had not foreseen. Hitherto my weight was equally distributed along the limb of the tree, and the necessity for exertion at a minimum; now I was forced to cling by my arms and legs crossed over the branch, and to remain in such a position long was impossible. There seemed no alternative but to let go and drop into the creek. I was in utter despair, and then, it seems, the brain puts forth its best efforts. I suddenly thought of the maple branch beneath. Could I reach it with my feet? A downward glance showed me that I might, but how the deep waters sparkled with glee at the probability of receiving me! Could I not baffle them? Grasping, with all the energy of despair, the elm bough with my hands alone, I let my feet drop, and they both pressed the branch. What a relief! But, alas! the maple bough could not sustain the pressure without some yielding, and I was swung between the two, with a firm hold upon neither. There was but one way to proceed. I could not regain the elm—I must trust wholly to the maple. Even when one has but a single chance he often hesitates, hoping, like a fool, for impossible aid. In spite of the strain, I faltered, as though I had full faith in Campanius' statement that the creek below me was really "provided with everything that man can desire," and so would provide me a comfortable means of getting to the ground. But very soon my arms rebelled and I was forced to relinquish my hold. It was, to be sure, a matter of one chance in a hundred, but, as it happened, proved a success. I fell forward flatly upon the bough, and secured a firm hold, without a scratch or bruise. Slowly I dragged myself forward towards the trunk of the tree, and, once grasping it, was so eager to feel the firm earth under me that I could not take time to clamber down. I gave a jump, and touched Mother Earth with a cry of joy. But the eggs —alas! I had swallowed them.

May, then, becomes a full month to the rambler. What with animal life, then exhibiting its most striking features, the vegetable world in the climax of its activity, and archæological researches then prosecuted to the best advantage, time will not hang heavily on the hands of him who loves a quiet stroll along the bluff that guards, the woods that conceal, and the meadows that bound Poaetquissings.

CHAPTER IV.

MARSH-WRENS.

In localities beyond the range of the average pedestrian, and unheeded by the boatmen, as they hurry by, intent upon mere progress, and all unmindful of the half-hidden beauties of reed-grown shores, there lives, in perfect content, a countless colony of little birds, the very existence of which is known only to a few. The little birds to which I refer are the marsh-wrens, the long-billed and the short-billed species. They are strictly aquatic birds, yet never get their feet wet, if they can help it.

One of the charms of studying the habits of our birds is the well-grounded hope that we may discover some feature of their lives that has been overlooked; but the marsh-wrens do not vary from what has been written of them. There is no variation from their ordinary habits —no wandering from the spots they are accustomed to frequent. They live in reeds and rushes growing in and about the water, and, except when migrating, do not wander so far from their home as to have dry land beneath them. They hold in horror any approach to an anhydrous condition of their habitat; and along Crosswicks Creek and in the muddy meadow are as sure to be over water as fishes are to be in it. Here, the reeds grow with such rankness that no foe can follow them; therefore they are happy as they fitfully flit above the tall weeds or clamber through them. To be appreciated, these birds must be seen in just such spots as I have named: neglected nooks, rankly overgrown, and daily washed by the creeping tides—at times a widespread lake, then a stretch of seething, slimy, bubbling mud. I know not if it holds good elsewhere, but as these wrens have been observed along Crosswicks flats, I have never seen one leave the reeds in which it was nesting and fly half a dozen yards in any direction. They come to the tops of the waving vegetation, twitter, and, closing their wings, sink back into the cover. I have tried to drive them from such clusters of weeds, but never succeeded. They could be flushed easily, but never forced to leave their chosen haunt. Wilson remarks of the long-billed wren, it "arrives in Pennsylvania about the middle of May, or as soon as the reeds and a species of nymphæa, usually called splatter-docks, which grow in great luxuriance along the tide-water of our rivers, are sufficiently high to shelter it."

This brings up a very interesting feature of bird migration. These wrens arrive very irregularly, but in accordance with the season. They require a given condition of aquatic vegetation, and when that obtains these birds appear in and about it. It is, indeed, scarcely to be wondered that the crude idea of the hibernation of birds should have arisen. It is apparently true of the marsh-wrens, yet I believe they have escaped the charge. In the past eleven years, the reeds and other water-plants have been moderately grown as early as April 15, and often not earlier than May 10, and these birds have been found in abundance as early as the middle of April, but sometimes not until nearly a month later. And they come at once. Yesterday, not a wren was to be seen or heard; none were to be flushed, however carefully the search was made—to-day, their united voices make the reedy growths of the riverside fairly to ring. By what means could they know just when to come? Do they send out an advance guard to explore, return, and make a report? This has been seriously suggested, but is too much to believe of a bird's wit and wisdom. It is more reasonable to ask, do they judge of the advance of vegetation in one river valley by the condition of that in the next? The reeds in the Chesapeake are earlier than those of the Delaware; the Potomac is earlier than the Susquehanna; very little, to be sure, but still there is ordinarily an appreciable difference; and if the migratory birds do go upon such guess-work, they appear never to make a blunder. The wrens come when the reeds are ready, and as soon as they are ready. Never a week too early or too late. The weather afterwards, whether cold or hot, matters nothing. The birds have but two needs, food and shelter; and given these, they will laugh at ice and snow, both of which have caught them in the Jersey marshes. The reeds must be killed outright by severe weather, under such circumstances, to drive the birds away, and I have known this to happen but once. As a general thing, April ice and May snow-storms do no serious damage, except to cultivated plants.

The careful collating of facts with reference to the presence of the birds and condition of the weather after their arrival, shows conclusively that temperature alone has almost or quite nothing to do with a bird's movements. I know of no one of our birds that cannot withstand a low temperature; and were the food supply kept up, whether it was hot or cold, the migratory birds in New Jersey would become resident with scarcely an exception; and when we come to compare the accounts of our birds as recorded by Wilson, seventy years ago, and the habits of these birds as they now are, it is remarkable how variable are certain features which Wilson sets down as governed by fixed rules.

Evidence of this is, of course, readily obtained by daily observations made throughout the year, and continued for years, in given localities. The results of a single year will have but little bearing upon the regularity or want of it in a bird's movements. The observations of the same person in the same locality must extend over at least a decade before it is safe to arrive at any general conclusions. My own conviction, that summer birds can withstand a winter climate, is based on the fact that I have now a record of nearly thirty instances where sensitive summer birds have been slightly injured, and, unable to undertake a migratory flight, have wisely not attempted it, but seeking a sheltered nook for protection against severe storms, have wandered about in search of food in a thoroughly cheerful and contented manner; even singing at times, with much of their springtime earnestness. Such single birds wintering on my hillside were several cat-birds, a brown thrush, two indigo birds, several orchard and Baltimore orioles, a summer warbler, and a golden-crowned wagtail.

It is necessary to presume, of course, that Wilson was correct in his statements to make my own conclusions worthy of consideration; but the later authors, Audubon and Nuttall, follow so closely in their remarks upon the same birds, it is not probable that any serious blunders were committed. At present, the irregularities in migration are most noticeable in autumn; and one potent fact that the return southward is then under protest, is that the action of frost is very variable, and sheltered nooks, of perhaps an acre or two, may escape for several weeks, while the marshes elsewhere have only wilted weeds to cover them; and these sheltered nooks are often so densely overcrowded with the birds, and birds, too, of other species, that it is difficult to conceive how they keep alive. This occurs, at times, among the strictly upland birds, but much less frequently. They, on the other hand, I suppose, often find food becoming less and less abundant, and leave before there is any apparent reason. I have known some of our birds, notably thrushes, to quit a neighborhood directly after nesting, or early in July, and not one again to be seen until the following spring, when they returned, as usual, and remained in abundance until there was not only hoar-frost, but thin ice. Temperature and migration are largely coincident, but cannot be considered as cause and effect. Whether the bird is an insect eater or granivorous, it matters not. The food, in either case, has its allotted time of growth, and while this continues the birds are sure of a supply, for premature frosts do not affect either animal or vegetable life so far as to cut off the food supply suddenly, and thus the bird has simply the inconvenience of a lower temperature to contend against, if it really is an inconvenience. We are too apt to measure the effects of frost by what is seen in our gardens among cultivated vegetables and flowers, which is no criterion whatever. The occurrence of a drought—an irregularity in nature, from which it has not yet evolved self-protection—is far more disastrous to the comfort of birds, and influences their movements more than cool evenings, shortened days, and the early frosts of autumn. The contemplative rambler, as much as the farmer, has cause to dread a midsummer drought.

Be it April or May, sooner or later, the marsh-wrens will be with us, and their many curious habits are well worthy of even closer study than they have as yet received. Speaking now exclusively of the more abundant species, the long-billed wren, it may be stated at the outset that they are not shy, but have not that fearlessness characteristic of the upland species. Still they will resent interference, sometimes, and express their displeasure with all that impetuosity so very generally displayed by the house-wrens of our dooryards. Let us consider, now, two prominent features of this abundant species, its song and its nest.

Wilson remarks of the notes of the long-billed marsh-wren, "it would be mere burlesque to call them by the name of song. Standing on the reedy borders of . . . the Delaware, in the month of June, you hear a low, crackling sound, something similar to that produced by air bubbles forcing their way through mud or boggy ground when trod upon; this is the song of the marsh-wren." I rejoice in not being so critical, and I cannot see why the joyous utterances of these wrens should not be spoken of as songs. Under what circumstances do these birds sing? Up from the tall reeds, "with many a flirt and flutter," a moment in mid-air on trembling wings, out from its panting breast rolls a short, sweet series of mellow notes, without one trace of harshness. "Air bubbles through mud," indeed! They are rather flute-notes through the sparkling waters, which the bird tarries to catch as they float away, and then sinks back into the reeds. Another and another wren comes into view in like manner until often half a hundred of them have, in quick succession, taken their turn; then for a few minutes silence intervenes. It would seem as though Wilson had but seldom heard these birds, or, preoccupied at the time, not lent an attentive ear; or could he have heard a whole colony suffering at the time with sore throat? I can think of no other reason. The most recent accounts of this bird follow Wilson closely, but may it not be that such copy merely his statements? All the world to the contrary, the Crosswicks wrens sing sweetly. Wilson, however, does the nest-building of this bird full credit. He remarks: "As, among the human race, it is not given to one man to excel in everything, and yet each, perhaps, has something peculiarly his own; so among birds we find a like distribution of talents and peculiarities. The little bird now before us —marsh-wren—if deficient and contemptible in singing, excels in the art of *design*, and constructs a nest which, in durability, warmth, and convenience, is scarcely inferior to one, and far superior to many, of its more musical brethren. This is formed outwardly of wet rushes, mixed with mud, well intertwisted, and fashioned into the form of a cocoanut. A small hole is left two thirds up, for entrance, the upper edge of which projects like a penthouse over the lower, to prevent the admission of rain. The inside is lined with fine, soft grass, and sometimes with feathers; and the outside, when hardened by the sun, resists every kind of weather. This nest is generally suspended among the reeds, above the reach of the highest tides, and is tied so fast in every part to the surrounding reeds as to bid defiance to the winds and the waves."

This elaborate description is but partly correct of the thousands of nests annually built in the Crosswicks marshes. Wilson, it will be noticed, refers to excellence "in the art of design;" let me add, that, during the construction of the nest, there is also abundant evidence of the possession of conversational powers. Indeed, it would be impossible for these birds to build such nests unless they possessed the power of communicating their thoughts. In this case, it is by spoken and not gesture language. As I have had occasion, in another connection, to remark, I have seen one of these birds adjusting one end of a long blade of rush-grass, while its mate held the other, until the former had completed the task to his satisfaction. It was evident that the weight of the ribbon-like growth, quite a metre in length, was too heavy to be moved to and fro, and at the same time prevented from slipping from the unfinished nest. Only by assistance could such materials be utilized, and only by intelligent joint labor could these little birds build such large and complete globular nests. Now these birds were not silent, nor yet did they sing, while at work; but uttered frequently short, sharp, sibilant chirps and twitterings, such as I have never heard at any other time. It was plainly their *conversation.*

Wilson's description does not agree with my experience in the study of these nests, in two particulars; and this suggests either a change of custom, as has taken place with other birds, in nest-building; or that the nest may vary in different localities, and has always done so. First, in regard to the cover over the entrance. I have found but one such projection, and that was by no means sufficiently prominent to effectually shield the interior from rain. During the past summer I examined a very large series of nests, but found nothing that could be likened to Wilson's description; not even a single strand of rush projecting more at the top than the bottom. As so much stress is laid upon this feature, by Wilson, I visited the marshes during a "driving" rain, to see if, in lieu of such projection, temporary provision for protection against rain was now adopted, but could discover nothing. A very few of the nests were so placed as to face the rain, and were apparently fated to be thoroughly wetted, but I could not find that any were penetrated by the rain to any important extent. One of the old birds was, in every case, in each nest examined, and in eleven of twenty-three nests visited, the mate was sitting *in the entrance.* In every instance, therefore, the eggs were wholly out of harm's way; for what little rain might enter the open entrances the sitting bird would receive on its back, and either retain or cause to trickle beyond the eggs; and in those nests where the mate sat in the entrance, of course no rain could enter. I do not know that this has become a common habit, taking the place of a nest built as Wilson describes, but such is probably the case. A general survey of the nests then found and all such seen since then bear me out in saying that, as a rule, the nests are not built so as to be exposed to wind or rain. They are placed sufficiently low in the reeds to be sheltered quite effectually by the overtopping growths, which, of course, bend over them and become sheltering roofs during high winds and driving rain-storms.

The mud cementing the outer materials of which the nest is composed is the second feature, mentioned by Wilson and subsequent writers, which I have usually found wanting. I have never, indeed, found much mud in the walls of any nest, and in others so little that it might readily be only the still adherent particles that were on the leaves when they were gathered for the structure. In by far the great majority of the nests there was not a particle of foreign material clinging to the rushes and grass that formed them.

A curious feature of the lives of these wrens is, that they seem to be always nest-building. After the second brood is on the wing I have found new nests in course of construction; nests which were finished in August, and probably never occupied, even as roosting-places. Furthermore, I have been inclined, at times, to believe that polygamy was practised by these wrens. I have watched a colony of the birds, by the hour, and I am sure I have seen the same bird, presumably a male, enter first one nest and then another, carrying food to the young that they contained. The liability to err in such observations is obviously great, but it would be no surprise were it to be determined beyond question that some super-gallant wren had the responsibilities of two mates and two nests resting upon him. Considering the energy, restlessness, and wealth of animal spirits, nothing that a wren does need excite surprise.

A few words in conclusion about the far less common, short-billed species. Occasionally, I have had the good-fortune to find an isolated cluster of rank, aquatic growth tenanted by a colony of these birds. They are true wrens, every inch of them; quick, restless, high-tempered, and brimming over with both song and chatter. Of the song, perhaps more can be said than of that of the preceding. It is fairly soft, varied, and to a certain extent wren-like; but is certainly not fully expressive of that wealth of energy characterizing the bird, or its kindred, the house and Carolina wrens. So far as I have had opportunity to observe, these wrens are more retiring than their long-billed cousins, and stay closer to their nests and the surrounding reeds; often singing while clambering through them, something the other species never appears to do. This, possibly, may have arisen from the proximity of a much larger colony of the allied species; and there certainly is no surplus of good-feeling existing between them. I have seen them quarrel, and never found the nests of the two species in the same cluster of rushes.

The nests of these short-billed wrens do not differ

essentially from those of the long-bills. Those I have found were all in similar localities, and if the birds were not seen, could only be recognized by the fact that the eggs are white.

What I take to be a curious error in Barton's "Fragments of Natural History" reads as follows: "Motacilla Troglodytes? (marsh-wren) commonly continues with us the whole year; in the winter-time taking shelter in our houses, stables, etc." Certainly both species of marsh-wrens are strictly aquatic, and we have seen that they are migratory. Here we have no evidence of a change of habits, but a confounding of the marsh-wren with the Carolina wren. This is the more interesting, inasmuch as, in Wilson's time, and later, when Audubon wrote, the latter was held to be a rare bird in this vicinity, and my own inference that a recent colony had become established as far north as Philadelphia, falls. Certainly, Carolina wrens are resident species in the strictest sense; and how they could have been confounded with the aquatic marsh-wrens is not readily comprehended.

A word with reference to a feature common to both marsh-wrens. Given clear skies, as the moon fulls in May, June, July, and August, these birds forego sleep, unless they take short diurnal naps, and with that same restlessness that marks their movements "from the rising of the sun even unto the going down of the same," these wrens are ready to greet the rising moon and sing to her a sweet sibilant serenade until the day dawns. With singing-birds generally, such performances at night are occasional or uttered while dreaming, for I have seen a caged canary sing for several seconds while certainly sound asleep; but it is otherwise with the marsh-wrens. They are fully conscious of their singing, and, indeed, fly up from the reeds, as in broad daylight; and to him who has not heard this concert by moonlight, with its pleasing accompaniment of rippling waters, booming of bitterns, far-off cry of the whip-poor-will, and the sudden quok! of the night heron, a pleasing experience of out-of-doors yet remains.

CHAPTER V.

A COLONY OF GRAKLES.

FIFTEEN pine-trees, in negligent array, shade three sides of the house. They are at various distances apart, yet in nearly every case the branches interlock with those of the next tree, and thus give to the dwellers of their needle-y tops a chance to hop from the front yard to the back without flying more than a yard or two at any one time. Of course, the birds generally like such a cluster of tall trees, none of them less than fifty feet high, but of these various small birds I have nothing now to say. It is to a colony of grakles, or crow-blackbirds, that yearly make of these trees a home, from March to August, that I wish to call attention.

Grakles are both migratory and resident, for never a winter passes that a few are not seen along the river shore. Indeed, when the usual January thaw arrives, quite a host of them are to be found feeding on the mud-flats, when these are not covered with ice. The sudden coming and going of the grakles, abrupt as the changes from frosty to mild weather, has given rise to the supposition that, like swallows and rail-birds, they hibernate, and respond even more promptly to any decided change from cold to comparative warmth. The truth is, of course, that no birds hibernate, but, in the case of the grakles, a limited number of hardy individnals, finding sufficient food, prefer the discomforts of remaining throughout winter to the exertion of migration, and so tarry with us the year through. In March, however, those that did migrate come slowly trooping up this way, and, congregated in considerable flocks, chatter of good times coming, as they crowd the bare branches of the meadow hickories. No severity of weather, in March, disheartens them. Even such a March as that of 1885 was not sufficient to send them southward.

Pleasant as it is to have the grakles among our winter birds, it is in April that interest particularly centres in them, and when one is seen bearing a twig in its beak you may rest assured that it has had a hint of the coming summer the discouraged farmer has failed to recognize.

While noisy at all times, it is in April that they most frequently essay to sing. Perched where he knows his mate will see him, with partly uplifted wings and spreading tail, he gurgles a few notes that have, at least, the merit of good intention. It is a pleasant sound, because suggestive of longed-for seasonal changes. Particularly was this the case during the past winter, for winter lasted until late in April. The forest was gray until after May 1, when it should have been green, and the frost-nipped anemones, bluets, and arbutus were all hidden in the heaped-up leaves of a year ago. Except that the spicewood sparkled with scattered gold, and the Draba was starring last year's mould, there was no hint of coming summer; yet the grakles were full of faith, and chattered the day long never so merrily.

How do these grakles recognize their mates? If we could have placed those that nested in 1884 in one long row, the most that could have been determined was that there were eleven males and as many female birds. Certainly, to human eyes, there was no difference of expression. This is no proof that the birds themselves could not recognize distinguishing marks, and it is assumed by ornithologists that they do so; but is there no other way, and one equally probable? I refer to their power of communicating their thoughts by vocal sounds. It may be said that if these birds presented no individual characteristics, the possession of such a power would be of little value. A continual mistaking of one individual for another would undoubtedly lead to no end of direful results; but, on the other hand, the peculiarities might as readily be in the voice as in the features, and just as we can recognize our friends by their voices, when we cannot see them, so grakles may possibly know their mates from others by vocal peculiarities, their features presenting no recognizable differences.

As a further test of this, I transferred the broods from one nest to another, the young in each case being of exactly the same age. The parent birds, I am sure, recognized the difference immediately, and each pair sought for, found, and fed their own young, and the change of broods was accepted in good part by both parties concerned. It is possible that I confounded the parent birds, but I think not; but, if so, then these birds could see no difference between their own young and those of their neighbors, which renders it the more probable that their power of distinguishing adults is not from individual peculiarities of expression, but of voice. When I changed a single bird, a few days younger, for one of another brood, there was a commotion at once, but in no instance was the changeling injured or forced from the nest; and I did not detect any searching for the missing one by the old birds, or any discussion between the persecuted parents as to what should be done. They simply discovered the change, and made the best of what they doubtless considered an inexplicable circumstance.

In the spring of 1884 there were eleven pairs of grakles nesting in the pines, seven pairs of which raised two broods. In April, 1885, there were seven pairs busy building their nests, and the backwardness of the season made them ludicrously in haste, when, on the 20th, it became suddenly very warm. Prior to that date the cold winds and daily prevalence of ice and frost kept the poor birds in a constant state of bewilderment; they located their nests, marking their claims by a few sticks, and waited. Shivering and chattering, they waited for three weeks, and then, literally in hot haste, with the thermometer over 80° in the shade, ran up their rude structures in so short a time that their strength to withstand high winds is a matter of doubt.

Let me particularize the grakles of '84, for these were more closely observed than any previous colony. They came early in February, and held many consultations as to the best localities for the nests. The three beeches, sole survivors of the forest primeval, are large enough to hold a thousand nests, and have often held all that a colony has built. The elm and lindens could hold a hundred without crowding. These trees were considered, I thought, for they apparently underwent a very searching inspection, but during February there was nothing to indicate that a choice of locality had been made. Making no sign, they left on the approach of a "cold snap," and were gone for weeks; and when, in March, they came again, the whole proceeding was repeated, and the pines were elected the nesting-trees of '84. They lingered about them much of every day. They tore away the rubbish that marked last year's nests, a proceeding I never witnessed before; and then, although no active operations were commenced, these grakles stayed about the trees until the time for building had arrived. Any one to whose attention the matter was called would prophesy without hesitation that the grakles, even early in March, had decided upon nesting in the pines—and so they did.

The nest is usually a bulky and strongly-built structure, every twig and blade of grass being well intertwined with the others; but there is one very prevalent defect in the architecture of these nests: they are insecurely anchored to the supporting branches of the tree. It is no uncommon occurrence, during a high wind, for the nests to become loosened from their places and fall to the ground. They always come down bodily and remain intact, and it is seldom that enough twigs remain in the tree to point out the former sites of the nests that have met with such irreparable disaster.

One such nest that fell late in the summer I took pains to unravel twig by twig. It was a tedious task. There were four hundred and eighty-two twigs, and two hundred and four blades of grass, used as a lining. With these were bits of inner bark of certain plants, a number of chicken feathers, and a long, black shoelace.

Another nest was lined with many feathers, some hair, ravellings of rope, and bits of lead-colored muslin; and over all these, as though they had not been found as comfortable as it was thought they would be, was quite a thick layer of long grass, beautifully wound about the sides of the nest, and here and there placed among the twigs so that each should retain its proper place. It was the most ingeniously finished grakle's nest I have ever examined. Indeed, were it not that they trust too much to luck, as to the force of winds, grakles would be very fair nest-builders. But this is not asserted with the intention of conveying the idea that a parallelism obtains between intelligence and nest-building. The latter is a much less intricate proceeding than has been supposed, and the labor of collecting the materials is greater than the skill required to make a comfortable nest with them.

Every colony, I think, commences nest-building at the same time, and there is little difference in the number of days required to finish the structures. Certainly some pairs are quicker motioned than others, and so get ahead with their work. This is true of all birds, just as it is true of mankind; but the difference in the case of the colony of grakles, in 1884, was but five days, and this was kept up in all that subsequently transpired.

The last brood departed from the nest just five days later than the first.

The nests are built at last, and straightway the eggs are laid, five or six in each nest; but five is the usual number, and the odd one generally does not hatch. They are as ugly as eggs well can be: dirty green, streaked with dirtier brown; dull, rough emeralds rolled in the mud.

And all this while, although there is nothing much to do until after incubation, an incessant chattering keeps up. I have tried to fathom the secret of such ceaseless jabberings, but without result. It can scarcely be the scolding of ill-tempered wives, and the efforts of impatient husbands to check the clamor; for, if so, there is not a patient, easy-going grakle in existence. At any rate, as is always the case with birds, and so on up, madam has the most to say, and also, that sweetest solace of female existence, the last word. Still, there is no quarrelling, either among mated birds, or between near neighbors. So far as the colony in the pines truly pictures grakle life, they are exceedingly well-behaved, a fact which does not shield them from much unmerited persecution at the hands of prejudiced agriculturists, of all people those that should be practical ornithologists, and who, as a class, are most ignorant of the subject.

The eggs once hatched, something like work commences. From early morning until late in the evening —so long, indeed, as there is sufficient light to enable them to see a worm—the male bird for the first week, and then both parents, hunt for and carry to the five hungry infants their food. To get an approximate idea of the amount of food required to keep these young birds in growing condition, I timed the movements of a pair. I chose the hours from 10 to 11 A. M., and 2 to 3 P. M. In these hours each bird made thirteen trips to and fro, carrying in every case a worm, larva, or large insect — living animal food in every case. The five young birds were supplied, therefore, with food at a rate nearly equal to every other minute; but, as there were five of them, each bird got a "square meal" at least once in every ten minutes. This feeding was kept up for fully ten hours of each day, there being less activity in the matter towards evening, when the parent birds were probably taking their own meals; but, at this rate, it is a matter of two hundred and sixty worms a day, or fifty-two for each young bird every twenty-four hours. What digestion! Of course, this must be active, and the fact is evident, as, in every departure from the nest, ejecta are carried away in the beaks of the parent birds, and dropped often at a distance of a hundred yards from the nesting-tree.

The young birds are twenty-five days old when they leave the nest, and are supposed to shift for themselves. In the meantime each has been supplied with fifty-two worms a day, or thirteen hundred during its life in the nest; and the five, collectively, have consumed sixty-five hundred worms, larvæ, or insects. But there were eleven of these nests, which, therefore, means the destruction of seventy-one thousand five hundred worms or insects. Again, seven pairs of the colony of twenty-two birds raised a second brood, which means a further check upon insect life of some forty-five thousand five hundred more worms and grubs, or a total of one hundred and seventeen thousands of insect life, in larval or mature state. The food of the parent birds has not been considered in the above calculation; this added, and we have a grand total of about one hundred and fifty thousands of forms of insect life destroyed, all of which would have proved more or less destructive to the growing crops.

Grakles early attracted the attention of the settlers in this country, not only because of their great numbers, but from an unfortunate habit which they then had of eating too much corn. The Swedes called them *maize-thieves*, and considered that, of all birds, they did "the greatest mischief in this country." Peter Kalm, writing from Swedesboro, N. J., in February, 1749, says: "They have given them that name because they eat maize, both publicly and secretly, just after it is sown and covered with the ground, and when it is ripe. . . . As soon as the leaf comes out they take hold of it with their bills and pluck it up, together with the corn or grain, and thus give a great deal of trouble to country people, even so early in spring. . . . When the maize grows ripe . . . they are continually feasting. They assemble by thousands in the maize-fields, and live at discretion. . . . As they are so destructive to maize, the odium of the inhabitants against them is carried so far that the laws of *Pennsylvania* and *New Jersey* have settled a premium of threepence a dozen for dead maize-thieves. In *New England* the people are still greater enemies to them; for Dr. *Franklin* told me, in the spring of the year 1750, that, by means of the premiums which have been settled for killing them in *New England*, they have been so extirpated that they are very rarely seen, and in a few places only. But as, in the summer of the year 1749, an immense quantity of worms appeared on the meadows, which devoured the grass and did great damage, the people have abated their enmity against the maize-thieves; for they thought they had observed that those birds lived chiefly on these worms before the maize is ripe."

And the people did right in allowing their enmity to abate. The grakles did far more good than evil, even then; and now, and for years, they no longer molest the cornfields when the grain is ripe. The habit of opening the husks at the ends of the ears, and so blasting them for half their length, is no longer characteristic of these birds. They have cured themselves of their greatest fault, and now what little corn they take is that which has been recently planted. But even in this case the birds do not so much seek for the corn as for worms, and finding the former, as it were by accident, devour it. An examination of the stomach contents of grakles killed while foraging in a newly-planted cornfield tells the whole story. Place them in the worst light, and still their good qualities far exceed the evil, so-called, of their natures.

The fact, already alluded to, of a change in their habits is of much interest, as showing how altered environment affects the modes of living. Grakles, in the western states, I am informed, still damage the ripened and ripening ears, as has been described. Audubon figures this bird as tearing away the husks that the ear might be exposed and the juicy kernels pecked off. This was true of the grakles about here, but is true no longer. We have as many acres of corn as formerly. It matures at the same time as in early colonial days, but the grakles still prefer animal food, and through August and September are still hunting for and feasting upon animal life in the meadows. I have seen a flock of fully a thousand, early in October, chasing the untold millions of grasshoppers over the meadows, and feeding upon them until they were actually surfeited.

The old Swedish settlers told Kalm, "this part of *America*, formerly called *New Sweden*, still contained as many maize-thieves as it did formerly. The cause of this they derive from the maize, which is now sown in much greater quantity than formerly; and they think that the birds can get their food with more ease at present."

Here, I think, is an error, for it is not certain that the Swedes had more acres in corn than did the Indians, when in the height of their prosperity. I quote here Lucien Carr's elaborate memoir on "The Indian as an Agriculturist," from volume ii. of the "Memoirs of the Kentucky Geological Survey." Speaking of the Delaware Indians, the writer says: "They occupied both banks of the Delaware, or 'South,' River, lived in forts, and raised corn and beans, which they sold to the Swedish and German settlers. Later, about the year 1682, William Penn found the Delawares and Shawnees still occupying this region. . . . Speaking of their manner of life, he (Penn) says that 'their diet is maize or Indian corn, divers ways prepared; sometimes roasted in the ashes, sometimes beaten and boiled with water, which they call hominy.' Loskiel, A. D. 1788, takes up the story, and tells us that corn was the chief product of their plantations."

Local traditions, old documents, and fragments of journals dating back nearly two centuries, clearly show that the ground upon the bluff that forms the eastern bank of the Delaware, from the head of tide-water to where Burlington now stands, was, for a considerable part, a cornfield, and the grakles had as much maize then as ever since to raid upon. That the Indians were forced to devise all manner of scarecrows is certain, and these birds have, probably, not been affected by any changes that have taken place, so far as their numbers are concerned. Why they are no longer as destructive to corn as formerly is not to be explained.

To return to the grakles in the fifteen pines. The even tenor of their way comes to an abrupt conclusion when the young are ready to leave the nest. Their last day at home is their noisiest. The excited parents evidently talk far faster than they think, and neither old nor young pay any attention to the uproar, but, instead, add their quota thereto, without knowing why. It would appear that every bird was asking questions of its fellows, and never waiting for or receiving a reply; but, as the day wears on, the exodus takes place. With scarcely any preliminary trials by the young of wing-strength, the birds, both old and young, mount to the topmost branches of the pines, and, as though at a given signal, wing their way, in a compact flock of six or seven individuals, to the meadows. So superlatively noisy are these birds when they are about to leave their nest that the fact is published as unmistakably as the undue excitement among bees shows they are about to leave the hive. And once the last grakle's nest is vacant, and for weeks after, each gloomy pine seems silent as the tomb.

CHAPTER VI.
FOUR RED BIRDS.

Red, of any shade, is not a common color among our birds. Some, like the woodpeckers, have a little patch on the back of their head, the kingbird a little at the base of his crest, and the smaller blackbird red-and-gold shoulders; but, as we walk through the woods, over the fields, or about the meadows, we certainly see very little red plumage on any of the many birds hovering about us; and yet, the year through, we are never without a wholly red bird, or one with that color greatly predominating. While purposing to speak particularly of but four, there are really seven such birds, if we include the two crossbills and the purple finch.

In summer the red-bird, par excellence, is now rare, but the scarlet tanager is abundant; in winter we have the crested cardinal and the pine grosbeak. The former is quite common all winter long, whether the season is mild or severe; and, I believe, only when we have an arctic winter can we confidently expect the pine grosbeaks to haunt our cedars. Let us consider these four birds, as they appear in the same locality—two as summer visitants, one as resident, and the fourth as a stray comer, when the thermometer ranges low.

So recently as thirty years ago the summer red-bird was as regular and almost as abundant as any of our thrushes. The farmer looked for them when the apple-trees were in bloom, and welcomed them, too, for to him they were trustworthy barometers. Did they not say, "Wet, wet, wet!" and did it not shower sooner or later? Surely no better weather-prophet could exist.

What has happened in the past thirty years to have influenced these birds is undeterminable; but now summer after summer passes, and not more than one or two are seen, and sometimes not one. Even when Wilson wrote, seventy-five years ago, summer red-birds were rare about Philadelphia, and that author says he had to cross the river to Jersey to find them. This statement may seem almost an absurd one at first, but it is really not so. Jersey could boast of a beautiful bird, in abundance, which was really rare across the river. Why was this? If the physical geography of the east and west sides of the river are compared, it will be found that they are as radically different as they well can be, from Trenton, or the head of tide-water, southward; and this was the northern limit of the bird's usual migration. Now, throughout South Jersey, there is a sandy soil and a flora largely similar to that of the southern seaboard states, while in Pennsylvania the soil is a heavy clay-loam, and the flora so far different that many trees which occur singly in New Jersey there are congregated as forests, and in the smaller growths this also obtains. Such variation in conditions the bird would be very sure to recognize, and, in its gradual northward travel, in May, come as far as it found those conditions obtaining which characterize its favorite haunts in Virginia and southward. We all know the peculiar flora of southern

New Jersey, and how hard and fast the lines are drawn that mark the habitat of certain plants. Why, then, should it not be true of animals? Let us see if other equally marked instances cannot be readily pointed out as occurring in the same locality. Late in February, 1885, I spent a few days on the Pennsylvania shore of the Delaware, at Bristol, ten miles away, as the crow flies, and there, in the thrifty evergreens along that beautiful river-bank, were purple finches. Not one finch, but many. Now, here there are pine-trees as tall, cedars as dense, cosey nooks as sunny, food, I suppose, as abundant, yet not once this long winter has the song of the purple finch enlivened my rambles about home. If they come at all, it is but to look about in disgust, and soon, with a loud twittering of discontent, away they go. I am told that about Bristol these birds are common winter residents. I know that about the same river, some ten miles up the stream, they are never abundant.

Again, the black-throated buntings, on the higher grounds and colder clay-soils, above the limits of tide-water, are abundant year after year. The sandy soils of the region south of the rocky ridge upon which the clay-soils rest offer these buntings no attraction, and it is a rare experience to see one of them there.

In a lesser degree the same is true of the arctic snow-bird and the horned larks. These birds are often common on clay-soil areas, and very rare in the lower-lying sandy fields. They prefer as low a temperature as we can offer, and their preference for the localities mentioned is explained, at least in part, by the fact that it often snows on the clay when it is raining on the sand. Indeed, this may be the sole reason for all such marked peculiarities in the distribution of our birds.

To return to the red-bird. I have heard it stated that their disappearance was largely due to the destruction of the old apple-orchards. To prove this, it would have to be shown that the introduction of the apple and general planting of orchards caused a decided increase in their numbers. This cannot be done; and yet it is not improbable that extensive orchards have, in a measure, modified the habits of some birds. Ornithologists well know that, in these extensive collections of fruit-trees, certain species of birds are more surely found than in the ordinary tracts of woodland; and many birds show a marked preference for apple-trees as nest-sites.

The summer red-bird, although so conspicuous a species, was not seen by Kalm, who mentions at length the cardinal grosbeak. Might it have been a rare visitor then, and subsequently become abundant? If so, it may again come back to us as the years roll by. So may it be! The same has happened with reference to the mocking-bird. In 1734, and for many years after, these outnumbered the brown-thrushes here in New Jersey. We all know how rare they now are.

The few glimpses that we now get of the summer red-bird make him the more interesting, because they afford us all the pleasure of a genuine discovery. So unreasonable are we, generally, that we demand the flavor of novelty in all that kindly nature vouchsafes to offer us, and often affect weariness because there may be only the attractions offered by our most common birds for the time being. The summer of '84 proved delightfully novel, however; for a pair of red-birds spent half the summer within walking distance. They came in May, nested in June, and, scared by the senseless snapping of fireworks on the 4th of July, quitted in disgust on the 5th.

While watching the many birds that were in the woods and thickets, on May 11, I saw a large gray-green bird start up before me, uttering a loud cluck as it flew. I took it to be a female tanager, but was not sure. I followed a few paces through the briers, and then saw the mate of the stranger. It was a splendid specimen of a summer red-bird. I stood perfectly still, with my arms behind me—birds fear men's arms more than their faces—waiting for him to sing. Presently his head was thrown back, the neck swelled, the beak slowly opened, and that "strong and sonorous whistle," of which Wilson speaks, sounded through the woods. It recalled familiar scenes of thirty years ago. The old orchard reoccupied the now open, sunny field, and the merry days spent there came trooping back, but wrapped in mist, not sunshine. I could not, unhappily, forget, even for the moment, that it was but a day-dream; and while I stood there the bird, as if in pity, ceased to sing.

Day after day I watched this pair of birds. A week later I found them building a nest on the extreme end of a long horizontal branch of an oak growing on the hillside. This nest was an ordinary twig structure, lined with grass, and as much like the nests described by Wilson as those referred to by Brewer, with so much uncalled-for criticism. The eggs, four in number, were laid by the 22d, and hatched on June 3. When the female was sitting the male bird did not remain very near, and at all times moved in such a manner through the trees as never to be conspicuous. I never once saw him out in the open fields, and when occupied in insect-hunting he remained closely to the tops of the taller oaks, and seemed to move with reference to the foliage, so as to be shielded by it. The bird recalled a remark of Wilson's about a red-headed woodpecker that nested within the limits of the city of Philadelphia. This woodpecker "took in the situation" carefully before leaving the nest-tree, and made directly for the country, once upon the wing.

When just four weeks old the young were able to shift for themselves, although their flight-power was not fully developed; and at this time, as I have mentioned, both old and young left the neighborhood.

During the stay of this pair of birds the male sang a great deal, and, as it appeared to me, with much cunning. It joined in with the general chorus far more frequently than it sang alone, and never sought a conspicuous position when whistling its fife-like notes. This marked shyness could scarcely have arisen from the mere fact that it was conspicuously colored, for in the same woods were numbers of tanagers and rose-breasted grosbeaks, which certainly did not try to conceal their colors as they passed from tree to tree. They were as readily seen as catbirds, and did not hesitate to occupy the most exposed positions. I am forced to be content with the aggravating fact that the red-bird was inexplicably shy.

My inquiries among old people about this bird have not been satisfactory. All seemed to have a confused idea of it, and the scarlet tanager and the cardinal grosbeak were so clearly referred to in many of their remarks that I practically learned nothing. In local history, however, I find an unmistakable reference to this species. There is an entry in a "common-place book," under date of May, 1797: "The smooth-headed redbirds have not appeared this year, as is their wont, and I much miss their shrill whistling from the walnuts on the hilltop. Those that have wings and tail of black are, as usual, in the orchard; but these whistle not, nor sing, like any of our smaller birds." Very true, they do not.

Wilson calls attention to a curious statement made by Du Pratz, to the effect that this bird stores up food for winter use. If this is a mere "make-up" by that author, or if he was deceived by some native, then there the matter ends; but it is best to examine a little closely into all such apparently absurd statements, for sometimes they have arisen from facts that were unknown, and the tracing of the origin of an erroneous impression has led to an increase in our common stock of knowledge. Here in New Jersey, certainly, no storing of food by this bird takes place, and, of course, such a habit would be least likely among migratory species; but, on the other hand, certain small mammals do have extensive magazines of nuts and seeds, and it might happen that a bird should learn this fact, and profit by the knowledge to the extent of making an occasional raid upon the animal's stores, particularly if a scarcity of food arose. These raids do not occur here except in the case of crows, which often scratch out the less-carefully concealed stores of food laid up by the white-footed mouse. The summer red-bird, when here at all, does not remain late enough in the season to profit by the accumulations of food laid up for winter use by squirrels and mice; and, indeed, very rarely would such stores be accessible to them; but I have known a cardinal grosbeak to nest near a hollow hickory, and feast, the summer through, on the insect larvæ that were so abundant among the shells of the nuts stored by the squirrels during the previous autumn. In the hollow of this hickory-tree—a great cavern freely exposed to the weather—there was always an accumulation of nut-shells, left by the squirrels, and an abundance of fat white grubs was a feature of the heap at all times. This rendered life free of care, so far as food-getting was concerned, and a careless observer, never seeing the squirrels, might suppose the bird had gathered the nuts for the sake of the insect-food always found with them. Perhaps, after all, Du Pratz was simply mistaken. A little learning *is* a dangerous thing.

Surely there is little to be said of the scarlet tanager. Every one knows the bird, and believes he knows all about it. Although we admit this, mention must at least be made of it as one of the four red birds; for such it is, although its black wings and tail make it less so than are the others; but, nevertheless, it is quite as conspicuous. The brilliancy of the plumage exceeds that of the others, and it rather delights than otherwise to sport in the bright sunshine.

I have asked a half-dozen observing persons living near by what were their impressions as to the times of arrival and departure of tanagers, and, curiously enough, they all agreed that not until the apple-blossoms were fully blown did these birds come, and before the hot week of September was spent they were gone. This would imply considerable irregularity in the coming and uniformity in the date of departure, for the first week of September, for nine years in every decade, is the hottest week of the summer. As has been often remarked concerning migratory birds, they are frequently supposed to be absent because not looked for. The truth is, not a year passes but that I see tanagers earlier than apple-bloom. For instance, in '84 I saw a tanager as early as April 27. It was on the top of a tall sassafras, and sat there for half an hour, singing, in its own fashion, "Chip'-pă-ra'-ree!" This bird was fully sixty feet from the ground, and, seen from below, the deep-red color of its body was not to be recognized. The bird appeared to be of a uniform black or brown. Although I knew it by its song, I waited until it flew away, when its color was at once apparent, and the identification no longer a doubt.

It was not until the following Sunday, a week later, that I saw others, and then the summer birds generally were here. It is not to be supposed that we have no summer birds until they have all appeared. There are always a fair number of early arrivals antedating the main flight by one or two weeks; and I am convinced that, since the days of Wilson, these advance birds have been coming earlier and earlier, and that, decade after decade, the main body has tarried later and later.

Just as our seasons are becoming more and more evenly divided into six months of heat and six of cold, so the birds, as a whole, are likewise prolonging their stay beyond the four months that seems formerly to have been the limit of their sojourn north.

Tanagers and apple-orchards are as much associated as bees and flowers. That they are found in scores of other places is, of course, true; but, when elsewhere, they seem quite out of place. Where they tarried in Indian times we can only conjecture, but probably in the wild fruit and nut trees that were often planted extensively near village sites. Indeed, the walnut seems to be a favorite tree with this bird, and I have knowledge of one being occupied for several summers by a pair of tanagers, the nest being always on the same branch. They regularly built a new nest, and removed every trace of the one they had occupied during the previous summer. To see how far their attachment to a particular limb of the tree extended, I removed it after the birds had left us, and in the following spring discovered that, by so doing, I had lost the company of one pair of birds. They left the neighborhood in disgust.

Curiously enough, these birds do not appear to have given rise to any weather-proverbs. At least, I have not been able to find any reference to them in the scores of "sayings" I have gathered. This is the more strange, as these birds do appear to have a fancy for cloudy weather, and sing more frequently then than when it is clear. Dull, doubtful days in summer, when the question of a picnic is to be decided, are those when the crude song is likely to be heard, and I am puzzled to know how it comes that the country-folk have overlooked them.

It is a source of regret that tanagers, beautiful as they are, should offer no peculiarity of voice or habit. Except in color, they are the very opposite of brilliant. Their existence seems really whittled down to the one matter of passing through life with the least possible exertion, except that they do not, cuckoo-like, use another bird's nest. Had tanagers the quick wits of a wren, or the general intelligence of a crow, they would be the most charming feature of our woodlands and orchards; as it is, they would not be known to exist to others than the professional ornithologist, were it not that Nature has bedecked them with such gaudy color, that to escape notice is impossible. Not accepting the idea that Nature is beyond improvement, and leaving this gayly colored blunder, as the tanager seems to be, what a wonderful change for the better do we find in the cardinal grosbeak, yclept, hereabouts, the winter redbird. In him we have a fixture of the farm; as much a part of it as the hickories in the meadow, and the beeches on the hill-side. On the bush that concealed his nest, in June, he perches and whistles throughout January. Wilson speaks of them as preferring, in winter, "sheltered hollows covered with holly, laurel, and other evergreens." This is misleading, to a certain extent. They do not seek such situations for shelter from a low temperature so much as from winds. The latter distress them, as they do most birds; but if the day is still, whatever the temperature, they are found as frequently in the most exposed situations as in sheltered nooks. It too often happens that when any bird is seen a few times in some one locality, it is thought that such places are universally its favorite haunts. In the case of the cardinal, it is only true that they avoid exposure to the wind. I have often heard them singing, while perched upon a hyssop or mullein stalk, when the ground was covered deep with snow, and the thermometer at zero. Let the wind spring up, and they are gone in an instant, and a week may pass without seeing or hearing them again. But to see them, in winter, to advantage, find a clump of bittersweet bushes on the hill-side, where the sun shines with some vigor, and not a breath of north wind can reach you. There the cardinal loves to linger from dawn to gloaming, and whistle he never so carefully, no notes excel those of his midwinter days. Wilson says further, they are in song from March to September. True, but they are far more so from September to March. They are in the height of their glory in the height of the season, and sing louder and sweeter songs during the Christmas holidays than in May or June, when the nest and young occupy their time and attention. Unless the matter is an omission on the part of Wilson, there has evidently a considerable change taken place in the habits of the cardinal.

On the home hill-side cardinals nest every summer, choosing generally a tangled clump of blackberry-briers. They seldom go elsewhere, and always pick out as tangled and thorny a locality as can be found. It has sometimes seemed as if they had arranged the briers with a view to extra prickiness. This serves, no doubt, to keep meddlesome creatures away, and probably neither squirrels, snakes, or blue-jays molest them. Certainly, all such broods as I have found came to maturity.

In the latter part of summer these birds are skulkers. They flit about in tangled bushes, and seldom show themselves or sing during August and the first weeks of September. They may be moulting at this time, and, at all events, keep so much out of the way that the unpractised observer would probably overlook them. The cool days of the coming winter changes all this. When titmice and nuthatches aim to monopolize the woods, and troops of twittering tree-sparrows crowd the fields, then the cardinal again asserts his supremacy and out-warbles all the host of winter songsters.

Of course, in leafless woods, the bright red plumage is a detriment to this bird, or would be, if increased intelligence did not enable it to obviate the inconvenience of being too conspicuous. The smaller hawks are the principal source of danger, and yet I have never discovered that red-birds suffer more than the dull-colored sparrows. The truth is—and herein lies the evidence of the bird's cunning—that it always scans its surroundings closely, the moment it alights on the top of a bunch of briers, and then, satisfied of its safety, sings; furthermore, it stays mostly in dense thickets, and comes up from below, instead of making a considerable open-air circuit, before alighting. At the first faint intimation of danger, it will cut short its song and dive into the tangled depths.

I never saw the attempt made, but I believe it can baffle a sparrow-hawk, unless the latter has some very unusual advantage. The red-bird, itself, is not strong upon the wing, yet, as a dodger, it is nearly equal to a humming-bird, and this compensates for the danger incident to very bright coloring.

The cardinal did not escape the notice of Peter Kalm, who, however, tells us very little of the bird as he saw it, in 1749. He refers to its fine vocal powers and the fact that many were shipped to London; also that it was an enemy of honey-bees, preying largely upon them. It would be an interesting fact to determine if there has been any change in habit, in this respect. I certainly never should have supposed it had any predilection for bees, and never knew it to capture one, although I have known a pair to have a nest within fifty yards of a bench of beehives. I have no data bearing on this point, but must express my doubt as to the habit being common to them. It is not an uncommon circumstance for individual birds to develop very peculiar tastes, just as this happens in mankind, but that all cardinals are bee-eaters is questionable, to say the least.

Stranger than all, I find in a back volume of "Science Gossip" (1881), the utterly absurd statement that these birds are "pests," and should not be introduced into other countries, and again, that they are "adepts at eating cherries and shelling peas." These statements are said to be based upon personal observation. If so, then the cardinal of New Jersey is greatly different from the cardinal of Virginia, a fact that has not been recorded by our own ornithologists. The truth is, there is no more perfectly harmless bird in America than a cardinal grosbeak.

While in a critical mood, let me call attention to other statements, made at home. In the elaborate tomes of Baird, Brewer, and Ridgway, it is stated that the cardinal is by no means common in Pennsylvania, and that a prominent ornithologist has but seldom seen it in New Jersey. This is all utterly, inexplicably absurd. It is true, if not looked for in their favorite haunts, they would be seldom, perhaps never, seen; but systematic search would never fail to discover them.

As the cardinal is known, at least locally, as the winter red-bird, it is fitting, at such a time, to bid him farewell. In the first snow of the season he delights to disport himself, and when the air is full of feathery flakes he fears no prowling falcon, but, mounting the topmost twig of his brier-patch, whistles so cheerily that the dreariness of on-coming winter is forgotten.

Leaving the brave cardinal singing in a snow-storm, let us now turn to the last of the series of four red birds, and this the rarest of them all, the pine grosbeak. The first snow-storm, often in November, fails to bring him. A steady cold of several weeks must elapse; the indications must all point to a severe season, and then, in January, if on the lookout — for these birds do not flock to our dooryards — the pine grosbeaks may be found. A winter that is even more than ordinarily cold will sometimes come and go without these birds appearing. Fortunately, the winter of '83–'84 was suited to their fancy, and they appeared in considerable numbers. Wherever there were clusters of pines or cedars, these birds were a marked feature of our avifauna, from December 29 to March 2; about which time they left us. At least, I saw none after the later date mentioned.

I am forced to admit that, although comparative strangers, these grosbeaks were not particularly interesting. They never sang and seldom chirped. They were always in companies of three to six, and wandered but little. Even in bright, clear days, they stuck as closely to the evergreens as do butterflies to flowers. A very depressing regret that they had wandered so far from Canada seemed to possess them.

During a roundabout ramble, after a deep snow, I chanced, last winter, on a clump of cedars, on my neighbor's hill-side, and

> "I tarried a bit,
> As a crested tit,
> Whistled his call so cheery,
> It seemed a tune
> In leafy June
> Sung by a nesting veery."

I never saw so many birds congregated in a few trees, except when flocks of red-wings gather in the meadows. Sparrows and titmice; linnets, nuthatches and kinglets; all, without discord, twittered, chirped, flitted and hopped through the maze of interlocking branches. I was puzzled to identify one harsh *tship!* which I occasionally heard, and to unravel the mystery I snowballed the trees. A perfect shower of little fellows flitted into space, and each scolded vehemently at such thoughtless disturbance, but their protests were of no avail. I continued throwing soft balls, until finally a large bird appeared and flew to the fence near by. This it was that had uttered the loud, harsh chirp: it was a pine grosbeak. Its tameness was remarkable. I stood within six paces of it and fully exposed to view; yet it sat on the fence, looking towards me, wholly unconcerned. I threw a handful of loose snow at it and sent it reeling to the ground, and before it could recover from its astonishment, I had my hat over it. With a little care I got a safe hold upon it, and brought it to light. It became quiet in a moment, and seemed perfectly contented. There was no external evidence that the bird was injured, and in a few minutes I tossed it into the air, supposing, of course, it would fly to some near tree. What was my surprise to hear it utter a shrill chirp, several times repeated, when out from the cedar came four others, which, joining it, all rose to a considerable elevation, and taking a northern course, flew off. I trust they were not disgusted with my rude treatment, and did not report ill of me in their Northern home. If they will come back, I promise to snowball them no more.

In December, '76, all Northern birds were unusually abundant, and several flocks of pine grosbeaks were seen in the streets of a certain town. Their presence was explained by the statement that a ship had been wrecked upon the coast, the cargo of which was made up, in part, of a large number of Brazilian birds and mammals; the birds had escaped, and were now shivering in the streets: and in all that town there was no one that knew these birds, and could contradict the absurd statement of that newspaper's imaginative reporter.

CHAPTER VII.

THE SPADE-FOOT TOAD.

In a sink-hole in a dry upland field, not far from the house, on April 10, 1884, there suddenly appeared a large colony of hermit spade-foot toads, which, by their remarkable cries, attracted the attention of every one passing by. So unlike the cries of any other of our batrachians were their utterances, that all who heard them were attracted to the spot, and wondered, when they saw the creatures, that so great a volume of sound could issue from so small an animal. One need not wonder, however, on this point if they will but examine the development of the animal's vocal cords. The machinery for producing sounds equal to an ordinary steam-whistle are apparently contained in the throat of this rare and curious batrachian. Holbrook, in his diagnosis of the genus Scaphiopus, refers to the "sub-gular vocal sac" of the males; but it must not be inferred that the females are voiceless. That they are not so noisy is probable, but, occasion requiring, they can readily make themselves heard.

These spade-foots remained in the shallow waters of this sink-hole until April 15, when, the weather becoming considerably cooler, they as suddenly disappeared as they had come. In May, 1874, these toads appeared in like manner in the same locality, remained but a few days and were gone. In the intervening ten years not a specimen was seen or heard, although careful search, annually, was made. I supposed, when they appeared in April of the past year, that they spawned previous to their sudden disappearance, but neglected to investigate the matter, in consequence of a press of work in other lines of investigation. The spade-foot toads were soon forgotten. The wealth of bird life that came trooping in from the South during May, and their subsequent nesting, occupied my thoughts, and were the prominent objects sought during my daily rambles.

It was not long, however, before the spade-foots again became the prominent feature of the fauna of the neighborhood. During the night of June 25–26 a violent northeast storm arose, and rain fell in torrents. The sink-hole, which for weeks had been nearly dry, was again flooded, and on the afternoon of the 26th was literally alive with these rare toads. Sitting upon every projecting stick or tuft of grass, or swimming with their heads above the surface of the water, were spade-foots by the hundred, and every one apparently uttering those shrill, ear-piercing groans that only these batrachians can utter. Not only during the day but all night their cries were kept up. The following day there was no abatement, but during the night the sound decreased. On the morning of the 28th not a specimen was to be seen or heard.

During this brief interval these animals spawned, the eggs being attached to blades of grass and slender twigs. These eggs hatched on the 2d of July and a large series was gathered a week later.

To return to the eggs. During the time that intervened from the laying of the eggs until I gathered specimens of the tadpoles, there occurred four moderately heavy showers, so that the water in the sink-hole at no time disappeared, but was much below the level that it reached during the protracted rain-fall of June 26. Very much, therefore, of the spawn that was laid was high and dry for from two to four days before hatching, and I suppose was destroyed.

On the evening of July 9, I found the water in the sink-hole confined to a few very shallow pools of limited area, and in these pools were a few hundreds of spade-foot tadpoles. In comparison with the abundance of eggs seen June 26, and of young seen a week later, it is evident that a large portion of the eggs were destroyed and a vast number of very young tadpoles were killed by the soaking away of the water.

I have never known any like disparity between the eggs of frogs or common toads and the young in the tadpole state; and it is at once very evident that if the spade-foot toads habitually or usually deposit their eggs in temporary pools, then we have an obvious reason for the positive rarity of the animal, as apparently it is the rule, rather than the exception, for the egg to be destroyed or the young perish.

The tadpoles gathered July 9, which were then seven days old, were curious creatures. At this time the hind-legs were well developed, although small, and did not interfere with the anmial's natatorial locomotion. The bodies of these young Scaphiopi were short, stout, and oval, and, when viewed in the water, deep velvety black; but when closely examined it was found that the two irregularly parallel, yellow dorsal stripes, that are so prominent a feature in the coloration of the adult male, were plainly discernible.

The movements of these tadpoles were not different from that of the young frogs and toads in this stage of their existence. Those that I had in an aquarium moved in companies as though following a leader, and occasionally one would drop out of the ranks, come promptly to the surface, eject a bubble of air, and dive again quickly to the bottom of the tank. Like all tadpoles, they had enormous appetites, and when fed with bits of raw meat quickly attached their sucking mouths to the food offered, and did not remove it, I think, while a particle of blood remained in the mass.

A week later, July 16, the majority of these tadpoles had acquired their front legs, and the tail had perceptibly diminished in size, but still was used by them when moving through the water. At this time, however, the movements of the animal are far less active than before or soon after, and for a few days, if exposed to the attacks of any enemies, they would suffer far more than at any other period of their lives.

A very curious feature in the growth of these animals is now to be noticed. Of the specimens I had under examination, in an aquarium, about five per cent. did not progress beyond the condition in which all were on July 9. These "retarded" tadpoles proved to be voracious cannibals. They seized their more matured companions by their tails and legs, swallowing the member, and thus sustaining their own lives at the expense of their fellows. They generally killed their victim in the course of twenty-four hours, and often in less time, and then promptly seized another. So bloodthirsty were these few "retarded" tadpoles that I was compelled to protect the lives of the little hoppers, their brethren, which now, in spite of stumps of tails, sat in frog-like fashion on their haunches, and were in all respects miniatures of the adult spade-foots that in April and June made night hideous with their unearthly cries.

Having tested several specimens, a few days previously, as to their ability to assume the land-life of adult Scaphiopi, by placing them upon damp sand, and finding that they throve fairly well, on the 25th of July I removed the water in the aquarium and put in earth to about an inch in depth, and very carefully smoothed the surface. Upon this the young spade-foots were placed, and in less than one minute many had commenced digging little burrows, into which they disappeared as the excavations deepened. In all respects these burrows were like those made by adult spade-foots, oval in outline, oblique in direction, and generally with a slight angle in the course. In twenty minutes all but two, of forty-four specimens, were below the surface of the earth stratum I had placed in the aquarium.

It now became monotonous in the extreme to watch them. Not a movement occurred that was other than might be expected of adult toads or frogs of any species.

I did not see them eat, but as only living food would now be accepted by them, it was simply because minute insect life did not come within reach; but while yet in the water these young spade-foots found some food, as shown by the examination of the stomachs and intestines of several specimens. Dr. A. C. Stokes kindly made this examination, at my request, and reported as follows: In the stomach of one was found fragments of a fly and of a small moth, and in the intestine a mass of sand grains cemented together by dark brown amorphous matter, with numerous rhizopods (Arcella) and several diatoms. In the stomach of another a species of Thrips, and a few diatoms in the intestine.

These two specimens had been thirty-six hours out of the water when the examination was made. But if my friend did not find much food in the stomachs of the little spade-foots, he did find an abundance of microscopical life. Let him tell us about it in his own words:

"While making a microscopical examination of the intestinal and stomach contents of young spade-foot hermit toads, I observed two forms of apparently undescribed endoparasitic Infusoria so crowding the rectum that it seemed only a thin-walled tube surrounding a semi-solid, writhing mass which, viewed with a low power objective, brought to mind the idea of a shimmering cloud of heated air, or a wavering flame of colorless fire, through which here and there glistened a yellow spark.

"The rectum of toads and frogs has long been a kind of happy-hunting-ground for endoparasites, especially for the Opalinæ; but so far as I am aware only colorless species of the genus have been observed. In this instance, however, the yellow points within that living mass proved to be Opalinæ of a lemon-yellow tint. The periphery and, to a much less extent, the deeper portion of the endoplasm are tinged, the color, which appears to be a stain and not an aggregation of particles, being collected in a layer near the cuticular surface, with a quite sharply defined line of demarcation between the lower margin and the internal body-sarcode.

"Their numbers are not great; perhaps a dozen were noted in the contents of the rectum. Neither are they always to be found. Compared with its more numerous associates, however, this yellow creature is a giant among pygmies, and it rotates through the mass with a carelessness as to results quite in keeping with its bulk. It measures from $\frac{1}{330}$ to $\frac{1}{350}$ inch in length.

"The intestinal fluid seemed thickened by the throng of bacteria, bacilli, vibriones, and spirilla accompanying the Opalinæ; and associated with them was not only an undescribed flagellate zoöid, but a large species of Opalina, which I have, after some hesitation, identified with *O. ranarum* Purk. Their appearance and structure are those of the latter, but the size is much less. They are quite active. As they pressed each other beneath the surface or forced each other upward, the aspect of the field of view was comically like a pool of furiously boiling soup with big dumplings bobbing about."

During this simple series of observations of young spade-foots in confinement, I watched also the development of those left in the sink-hole. The water there soon was confined to mere puddles concealed in the dead leaves, and before the young had their limbs fully developed the depth was nowhere sufficient to permit of swimming. Three days in advance of the maturing of my confined specimens, I saw, in the sink-hole, a few individuals which had fairly assumed the land-living, air-breathing stage of existence. Supposing that, like those I had at home, they would burrow in the earth *where they were*, I did not visit the locality from the 21st to the 31st of July, on which date I made an exhaustive but unsuccessful search for them. Not a trace of either young or adult could I discover. It cannot be said that they were overlooked. My search was too careful and comprehensive for this, and I believe that these spade-foots, both old and young, wander farther from their breeding-grounds than is supposed, or else dig far deeper into the earth than a depth of six or eight inches, as stated by Holbrook and DeKay.

Since the above was written I have received a most interesting letter from Mr. Nicolas Pike, the well-known naturalist of Brooklyn, L. I., and I take the liberty of quoting a few lines of his concerning the spade-foot toad. He remarks, it is a "most interesting and curious animal, well worth study. It changes its color much during hibernation. As you must have many around you, by looking on sandy, gravelly elevations I think you would find their holes. They make a turnip-shaped hole, a few inches deep, leaving an opening at the surface, and in this they live. They are nocturnal, seldom venturing forth in the day. There is always a secretion around their house to attract insects."

I sincerely wish that I could add that I have found their subterranean retreats, such as Mr. Pike describes, but, so far, luck has been against me. If all the spade-foots that I saw in the sink-hole had burrows in the adjoining fields, I am puzzled to know why I overlooked them all. It was not for want of painstaking search for them.

I have already referred to the wonderful noises made by these animals when they congregate in pools for the purpose of spawning. At no other time do they appear to be vocal, and the question naturally arises, why, when the animal leads a life that requires no such power except for two or three days in a year, should its utterances be far louder than any or all the frogs and toads of the same locality combined? Although the animal is strictly crepuscular, and not diurnal, it could readily find a mate guided by sight, and the purpose of the deafening epithalamium is somewhat hard to determine. If it could be shown that they call to each other from far-distant points, the difficulty would disappear; but this they are not known to do. Apparently it is not until they are congregated in some available pool that they sing, if singing it can be called. No words yet in use in our language can fairly describe their utterances, which, it may be presumed, are expressions of delight at meeting.

A word in conclusion with reference to the peculiar spur-like process which gives the common name to this batrachian. Holbrook describes it accurately as follows: "On the internal margin of the metatarsus is a horny, spade-like process, containing a bone, which moves by an imperfect joint; the breadth of this process is about a line and a half, its length one line; the cutting edge is jet black." By viewing the foot from beneath, this little spade can be readily seen. It will also be noticed that the little toe terminates also in a horny knob, a fact which has hitherto, I believe, been overlooked.

I have already mentioned how quickly the young hoppers dug little tunnels for themselves when placed upon the earth. At that early age the growth of the "spade" had commenced. This is now a white, soft, cartilaginous process, differing greatly from the same feature on an adult foot. It can scarcely be of use in digging, at this time, and so leads us to infer that the young choose more yielding earth and remain nearer the surface than do the adult spade-foots. In such a case the older the creature and better developed the spade the deeper are the subterranean homes wherein they seem to remain so closely, and from which, moved by some common impulse, they mysteriously come forth, in multitudes, to startle the passer-by with their weird cries, and then as suddenly disappear.

CHAPTER VIII.
TRUMPET-CREEPERS AND THE RUBY-THROATS.

I KNOW of a little garden planted one hundred and forty years ago, and wholly neglected for the past half-century. Were it not that the squat wooden fence surrounding it had the stoutest of locust posts for its support, this would long since have wholly disappeared. As it is, but a small portion remains, and the few fragments of lichen-coated and worm-eaten palings that still cling to the posts will scarcely bear handling. In their place, however, is a wayward, untrimmed growth of gooseberry-bushes that conceals what little remains of the old-time fence. This, even as it now is, forms a pretty hedge, and is the delight of sundry song-sparrows that haunt its tangled recesses the year through. I have often thought that nowhere else have I heard as sweet music from sparrows as when listening to the occupants of these bushes.

In one corner of this gooseberry-hedge stands a quince-tree that is a veritable relic of the past. Tradition has it that it was brought from England as far back as 1684, which is probably true. However this may be, it is now a gnarly, bent, and rheumatic-looking growth, quite dead at the top, and when at its best so sparsely covered with leaves that one may well question whether it is not more dead than alive. So far as can be ascertained, there is no tradition even as to when it last produced any fruit. I am sure, for twenty years it has never had a blossom. The tree has one great merit, however. It is held in good repute by the sparrows, and is the stage whereon are performed their choicest concerts. At sunset, and often later, these birds perch upon the outermost limbs of the tree, where they project upward for some distance from the bushes, and sing as only an old, experienced sparrow can.

Following this gooseberry hedge a distance of some fifty paces, we come to another corner of the weed-grown garden, which is even more attractive. What is here wanting in bird music is made up in wealth of color, and, with no lack of proper appreciation of the old quince and the sparrows, I often pass them by, in midsummer, and seek this gaudy corner, where, reclining on an oval mat of ribbon-grass, I gaze by the hour at the rank growth of an aged trumpet-creeper that monopolizes every vestige of the ancient fence and all other available supports. The rank growth of tangled vine, however bloom-laden, is not of itself the attraction. It is the humming-birds' paradise. Given a warm day in August, with a clear sky, and the vine in full bloom, and the fourth feature that completes the picture will not be wanting.

By the time these old-fashioned flowering vines are in full bloom the nests of the ruby-throats are deserted, their young are strong upon the wing, and during the few remaining weeks of summer no one spot is so much frequented by these birds as where the trumpet-creepers grow. I have often seen a dozen, at one time, hovering over the wealth of crimson bloom, and witnessed, I am sorry to admit, not only remarkable exhibitions of flight-power, but some of the fiercest battles ever fought by birds.

Perhaps no one of our birds, not even the wren, is more ready to enter into a fight, has uniformly more courage, and, when worsted in combat, yields more reluctantly. Quite recently, I was forcibly impressed with the fact of their fiery tempers, by chancing to witness a free fight between three of these birds, that happened to meet near the old trumpet-creepers. The day was absolutely perfect; warm, without being oppressive; sunny, yet without too great a glare; with bees and butterflies all astir, and tireless locusts " z—ing " in all the tall trees near by. The swallows were abroad in unusual numbers; the wood-thrushes sang in the shady covers; the noisy crows were cawing ceaselessly. In truth, nothing was wanting to induce one to take a good long walk. Realizing this, I wandered as far as the old garden, and, fashioning a soft cushion of the rank ribbon-grass, sat down to watch the restless ruby-throats that were busy among the blossoms.

There were but three of them when I reached the spot, and for a few minutes all went well; but very soon it became evident that each considered the others as intruders, and when by chance two visited adjoining flowers or crossed each other's paths in their short flights, an ominous buzzing, and at times a sharp squeal, suggested "bad blood." I left my place and drew nearer, that I might see the proceedings more distinctly, and it proved a lucky thought to do so. No sooner was I re-seated in a more favorable position than the battle began. Minute description is, of course, impracticable. It was

> "Too like the lightning, that doth cease to be
> Ere one can say—it lightens!"

Withdrawing from the flowers, the three birds circled over the spot where I had been sitting, and rushed at each other with impetuous fury. Turning as quickly as they passed each other, again each assaulted the other, and all the while they drew nearer together. A loud bee-like humming was clearly audible, and in less than a minute they were so near each other as to be scarcely distinguishable. I could only determine that their method of attack was an effort to stab with their sharp beaks. This, finally, one succeeded in doing. His beak was thrust its full length, I thought, into the breast of another, and the two birds fell together to the ground. The third, thinking, perhaps, he had vanquished both, returned to the flowers.

I stepped quickly to the spot where the two birds were lying on the grass, and as I reached forward to cover them with my hat, one darted off; the other I caught, as it was sorely wounded, and for the time disabled. It proved, however, to have simply a flesh-wound, and in the course of half an hour was able to fly, very weakly, however, and the blood upon its breast showed that the hurt was no trivial scratch.

Such occurrences as this are not unusual. So long as the trumpet-creepers are in bloom the ruby-throats continue to frequent them; each desirous of the choicest blossoms, and angered by every interruption. Bees, wasps, and hornets they always attack, but not always successfully. They are not mere honey-suckers, as is often thought, but tireless fly-catchers, a fact generally unknown and probably overlooked by the Philadelphia poet-naturalist, with whose lines I close:

> "Thou tiny spirit of the air,
> With sylph-like motion, glad and free;
> Who can thy meteor presence spare,
> Whose childhood passéd near thee?
> For near our door thou lov'st to dip
> Thy bill in the Bignonia's bloom
> And of its nectar juices sip
> 'Mid summer's choice perfume."

CHAPTER IX.

THE DRAWING OF THE SEINE.

There are moments of extreme felicity in the life of a naturalist, and one of them is at the drawing of the seine. For how long had I looked at the broad, blue expanse of Poaetquissings, near the mouth of Back Creek! While sitting on the little beach at the Sand Point, how much I have wondered what strange creatures might be beneath that glassy surface. To be sure, I had peered into these depths so often that I knew every pebble and water-logged tree on the bottom. Still, I imagined it the home of creatures unknown to me, and possibly of patriarchs of those that were known. I had dreamed of ten-pound pike and monster catfish—now the reality was at hand. A net, such as had never before been used in the creek, was in place. Encircling a large and deep portion of the stream, it was being slowly drawn to shore, and steadily narrowing the range of the life within its contracting boundaries. How my heart leaped as angry pike struck wildly at the cork line, and a myriad of shiners rippled the muddied waters. Now and then some black, smooth, shining object loomed up, as though a small whale was about to breach. A bit of wood, merely, but so lifelike in its movement that to ignore it was impossible. Nearer and nearer the lines approach the shore, and carefully the lower, weighted cord is kept upon the bottom. The net becomes a great bag in the water, and this now slowly emerges. The water, that, as tangled drops, had been held by the weeds now rudely dragged ashore, is again free, and hurries to the pond, wearing threadlike channels in the sand. With one mighty lift the net, fairly quivering with the splashing, struggling, sobbing mass of terror-stricken creatures within its folds, is borne to the dry land and laid upon the trampled grass and muddy beach.

The prosaic matter of assorting and gathering the valued portion of the catch commences. Pike, perch, bass, catfish, and a few great land-locked gizzard-shad are picked from the weeds and thrown into a basket; the net is gathered, freed from sticks, and placed in a wagon. The fishermen's work is done, and mine begins.

As I bend over the refuse, what a wealth of small fry is visible, from which to pick and choose! The ill-mannered fishermen laugh in derision as I wash a soiled minnow, rescued from the weeds. This is an experience a naturalist soon becomes accustomed to, and a judicious show of fight will sometimes prove desirable; but it is well to take such matters with reasonable good-nature, for these same men are often good observers in their way, and may prove the means of securing rare objects that otherwise would be lost. I do not profess to be very patient, but self-control has often worked well, and secured me friends where I least expected to find them. A bully that once was too troublesome for endurance, and was thrashed, a month later brought me the first living gar that I had ever seen. The fishermen having departed, I was left in peace to pursue my studies.

Of diminutive cyprinoids, now dead and faded, there were hundreds; and of the tougher toothed-minnows nearly as many more. I was at once struck with the great difference between these two families of fishes. The slender, silvery cyprinoids made scarcely an effort to escape, and, gasping a few times, were dying or dead. Not so the blunt-head toothed-minnows or cyprinodonts. Their gill-covers shut closely, and retained a supply of water on their branchiæ or breathing apparatus. They lost no muscular power by exposure to the atmosphere, and seemed to have so far a sense of direction that all were making intelligent efforts to reach the open water. I saw cyprinoids lying within a hand's breadth of water into which they could have jumped with but little effort, and yet they remained and died; while the cyprinodonts, often two and three yards distant, found their way to it, and escaped. Their movements recalled what I had read of the strange periophthalmus, a little fish found in the Philippine Islands, which, leaving the water, "skip along the strand with long leaps, evidently seeking their food, which, besides insects, consists principally of" onchidia, a genus of mollusca. I have never seen these blunt-headed, hardy minnows leave the creek and go insect-hunting, it is true, but the pluck and method of the fish when removed from the water show very clearly that but little experience and teaching need be added to make them as hardy and active out of water as their distant cousins of the Philippines.

Fingering the mass of wet weeds and its entangled prisoners, I supposed I had gathered a full series of these small fishes, but a careful inspection, as they circled about the glass jar, revealed the fact that I had done more, for one of the cyprinodonts was double-tailed. The vertebræ branched, a half-dozen joints from their termination, and each branch was well equipped with bony framework, muscles, nerves, skin, fins, and all the requirements of a first-class tail. These deformed minnows, like deformed trout, are quite common; but never, I believe, have I seen any aberrant form so perfectly symmetrical as this. It swam with all the ease of normal specimens, and quite as rapidly.

All deformed fish that I have met with were healthy. Their mishap resulted in no inconvenience, and every humpbacked and crooked fish seemed to have as good times as its associates; a happy condition of affairs that usually does not hold good with the higher vertebrates; for, with birds and mammals, unfortunates are often ostracized, and more frequently killed.

Speaking of the "good times" enjoyed by fishes, what of such an occurrence as the drawing of the seine? I have always insisted upon the fact that fishes were intelligent creatures; probably more so than batrachians, as a class; and if so, may it not be that they suffer considerable mental as well as physical discomfort when tangled in the meshes of the net? Logically, this should be so; and when we look an angry pike or bass straight in the eye, our faith in the logic is strengthened. When either of these fish makes a lunge for your hand, and bites you severely, theory vanishes, and you are practically convinced that some fishes are no fools, whatever others may be.

While still peering into the nooks and crannies of the mat of weeds, I caught a glimpse of one little fellow that I failed, at the moment, to recognize. It was too "deeply, darkly, beautifully blue" for any of our cyprinoids or other small fish found in Poaetquissings Creek. Carefully bringing it to light, it proved to be a little four-spined stickleback, such as is often found in creeks farther down the river, but does not often wander into this, the uppermost stream affected by the tide. Every spring, since the summer of 1870, I have been on the lookout for their curious nests, but without success. Every old fisherman to whom I applied for information made reply to the effect that he had never seen either such a fish or its nest. In the upper waters of the creek they were very abundant during the summer of 1865, and I found several nests; in succeeding years they were present, but in fewer numbers, and during the summer of 1869 they had disappeared. Sometimes it happens that a freshet in summer restocks our streams with fishes not otherwise occurring here, and so it may have been in this case.

The little stickleback that I found to-day exhibited a degree of irascibility that gave it claim to a high degree of intelligence as a fish. Indeed, they are much among fishes what the wrens are among birds. My captive resented all interference with promptness and pluck, and was particularly incensed when jostled by large fishes. In this, as in all its movements, it reminded me of one of its kind captured several years ago. This I placed in an aquarium with many other fishes, which, while it lived, it kept in a constant uproar. A more ill-tempered creature, even among snakes, I have never seen. It was only satisfied when chasing small fishes or snarling at large ones. Its method of attacking even large fishes, biting such exposed parts as were not covered with scales, and by tearing the fin membranes, showed that it comprehended its disadvantage in size, and made up for it by systematic attack, absolute fearlessness, and a degree of energy that was inexhaustible. In another and very marked manner this stickleback showed its intelligence. It once made bold to attack a half-grown pirate perch, a fish that will, less than any other species, tolerate any interference. The stickleback once darted at the pirate and tore the membrane of one pectoral fin. Instantly the attacked fish gave chase, and in such determined manner that the stickleback saw it was likely to be worsted, and took refuge in a little crevice between two stones, where it was safe, and ever afterwards only issued quickly from this vantage-ground, and nipped at the pirate as it passed by, never making an open attack. This betokened a certain amount of cowardice, I know, but it also showed so much discretion that this individual stickleback must be credited with rare good-sense, if such a blessing cannot be accorded to the family generally. But I think it can.

Having, as I thought, made a complete collection of the small fry the net had dragged in from the creek, I carefully turned the wet mat of vegetation and small sticks, thinking that possibly something had been overlooked, and such was the case. To my great delight, lying unhurt upon the sand were several young pike and a beautiful bill-fish; the latter still alive, but not active, as were the pike. I gathered it up with much care, and placed it by itself in a large jar. It soon revived, and the wonted brilliancy of its silvery and steel-blue back and sides returned. This is one of our most striking fishes, and I have always lingered by the water's edge when they chanced to show themselves at or near the surface. These fish do not like still water, and if they wander into quiet ponds, and do not find the exit as readily as they found the entrance, they become amusingly restless, if, indeed, they do not suffer. It would seem as though they required water that was thoroughly ærated, and could not live long in the warm and "dead" waters of a shallow pond.

Recently a bill-fish was found on the sandy shore of the river, at low tide. It was apparently unhurt, and twisted and squirmed vigorously, but did not move towards the receding waters, as doubtless it desired to do. Why did it not leave with the tide? was the question asked by each of those who saw the struggling creature, but no one offered a solution of the problem. Reaching the spot, the cause was evident enough. The inquisitive bill-fish had snapped at the extended soft parts of an open mussel, and the enraged mollusk had closed its shell with a snap, and caught the fish by the lower jaw. The mussel showed no inclination to relinquish its hold, and now that the water had gone, was evidently striving to bury itself in the sand until return of tide, as is their usual custom. It could not, however, drag the fish down with it, nor could the captured bill-fish lift the mussel from its bed in the sand. Both were prisoners, each being the other's jailer, so long as they chose to remain so. It was a most curious and instructive sight.

I find that locally this fish is, or has been, called snipe-pike, from the fancied resemblance of its attenuated jaws to the bill of a snipe. Now the name is corrupted to "snippick," and the remark occasionally heard among the fishermen, "sly as a snippick," shows that this fish is credited with considerable intelligence by these practical observers. Asking an experienced shad and herring fisherman recently about bill-fish, he told me that they had, to all appearances, a great deal of curiosity, a mental condition not common to fishes. That when a number of them were caught in a herring-net they seldom made any effort to escape, which they could easily do, by leaping over the cork-line, but followed the corks and played about them to the very last, and only when crowded by the herring, or approached by man, would they give a leap far over the cork-line and be off. It seemed, said he, "as though they wanted to see what sort of a muss the herring were in, but felt entirely sure of their own safety," and he added, "it isn't very often we catch them, unless we take extra pains to do it."

The few young pike that remained, for many escaped while I was engaged with the bill-fish, were still alive, but weakened by exposure to the atmosphere. I noticed particularly how changeable were their colors. A moment silvery, then dark blue; the bars and dots visible at times, and then fading out. Some had escaped.

These probably had received no injury, and their unclouded senses told them the direction of the water. They are intelligent fishes. How well I remember the cunning shown by a number of pike when in danger of capture. A gilling-net had been placed across the outlet of a small tributary of Poaetquissings Creek. In this little spring-brook several large pike had wandered in search of minnows. Being disturbed, they rushed with great impetuosity towards the net, and the foremost was at once securely entangled in its meshes. Straightway the others stopped as suddenly as they had started, and, recognizing that their fellow was in trouble, "took in the situation" at once. Each pike evidently realized the true condition of affairs, and reasoned thus: that pike tried to go through this obstacle in the water, and is in trouble; it is necessary for me to avoid it by some other means. There were five of these fish that paused close to the net; and each acted, I believe, as it *thought* best. One of them came to the surface, and, after a moment's pause, turned upon one side and leaped over the cork-line. Seeing the success of this effort on the part of one, a second did the same. A third came to the shore near where I stood, and, discovering a narrow space between the brail and the net, passed very slowly through, as though feeling its way, although the water was so shallow that its body was fully one third above the surface as it did so. The others were either more timid or less cunning. They turned to go up stream; but being met by my companion, who was making a great noise by whipping the water, they rushed again towards the net, but checked their course when their noses touched the fatal cords. Prompt action was necessary. They had not confidence in their leaping-powers; and both, as though struck with the same thought at the same moment, sank suddenly to the bottom of the stream, and burrowed into the sand and beneath the lead line, which was in full view. In a moment they reappeared on the other side of the net, and were gone. I could have prevented the escape of all of these fish, but was so much interested in the evidence of thought exhibited by them that the idea of molesting them did not occur to me. There was something in their manner not readily described, but something which gave an importance to their acts and added materially to the strength of the evidence that they were thinking in all that they did.

I have long insisted that fish can only be intelligibly described by using such terms as "cunning," "fear," "grief," "ingenuity," and "anger;" and if their actions indicate the possession of such emotions and faculties—and I claim that they do—then there is open to the practical naturalist a vast field for careful study and patient observation. Mr. Romanes, in his volume on "Animal Intelligence," has remarked, "neither in its instincts nor in general intelligence can any fish be compared with an ant or a bee." This I am forced to dispute, when I recall the habits of our fishes; the possession of the faculties mentioned surely narrows the gulf of which Mr. Romanes speaks. Fish collectively may not be the intellectual equals of ants and bees, but some species reach nearly, if not quite, to their standard; while probably none are so low in the scale of intelligence as Mr. Romanes believes. This view of the intellectual status of fishes is further strengthened by the consideration of their possession of a color-sense; and here I cannot do better than again quote from a recent work by the same author.

In his "Mental Evolution in Animals,"* Mr. Romanes remarks: "As further proof that a well-developed sense of color occurs in fish, I may remark that the elaborate care with which anglers dress their flies, and select this and that combination of tints for this and that locality, time of day, etc., shows that those who are practically acquainted with the habits of trout, salmon, and other fresh-water fish, regard the presence of a color-sense in them as axiomatic." As one "practically acquainted" with some sixty species of fresh-water fishes, representing a dozen or more distinct groups, I am reminded, by the above quotation, of many occurrences witnessed during my rambles about the Delaware River, or its tributary creeks, that have a bearing upon the subject. Besides recognizing the differences in insects by their colors, have fishes any knowledge of the fact that their own colors may or may not be protective? Are they aware that it depends upon themselves whether these colors shall be a safeguard, or a source of danger? That we are warranted in giving an affirmative reply is shown, I think, by their habits, and particularly by the fact that to a certain extent they have the color of their bodies under their control.

---

* "Mental Evolution in Animals," by George J. Romanes. New York, Appleton, 1884. 12mo, 411 pp.

Relatively speaking, the fishes of the Delaware River and its tributaries may be classified, in regard to their habits, as diurnal and nocturnal. It might almost be said that there are no "fixed" habits. I have found marked variations in every one of the most characteristic habits of our birds; and can see no reason why the same degrees of variability should not likewise obtain among mammals, reptiles, and fishes. In considering fishes as either nocturnal or diurnal, I mean that they are so to about the extent that owls are; *i. e.*, ranging from species as diurnal as hawks to those that are nocturnal, or, properly speaking, crepuscular. How often we hear the phrase, "as blind as a bat"! yet these mammals are not averse to daylight, and only shun the glare of noonday. In shady woods they are often found insect-hunting by day; and fly just as freely, and range abroad as generally, on cloudy days, as during the gloaming throughout midsummer.

Several years ago, when studying our fishes with reference to detecting supposed traces of voice possessed by them, I concluded that the nocturnal, dull-colored species had the power of uttering certain sounds, especially during the breeding-season; while the diurnal fishes were apparently voiceless, and were dependent upon their gaudy coloration as a sexual attraction. More recent observations have led me a step further, and I am convinced that the colors of many species continue to play an important part in the struggle for existence throughout the interim from one breeding-season to the next. It must be remembered that fishes, when undisturbed by man's presence, are very different from

THE DRAWING OF THE SEINE. 159

the frightened creatures that rush hither and thither in the most reckless manner when startled by his sudden appearance. We have only to take a favorable position, and, ourselves unseen, to gaze patiently into their accustomed haunts, to realize what animated, cunning, and mentally well-developed creatures fishes really are.

That curious group known as "darters," or etheostomoids, is always to be found, when not in motion, resting upon the bottoms of streams; and I have never found these fishes in localities where their color did not closely resemble the sand, mud, or pebbles upon which they rested. I have tested them in this matter in the following manner. Finding a spot in a small stream where many of these fishes congregated, I placed a large number of white-porcelain plates in the stream on a level with the surrounding sand. On disturbing the "darters," I found that they invariably settled between these plates, and never on them; and this after the dishes had been several days in position. Finally the currents covered the plates with a thin coating of sand, and then occasionally a "darter" would come to rest upon one of the plates. The motion of his fins in so doing usually displaced the sand, and exposed the white surface beneath: if so, the fish darted off, and settled between the plates or beyond them. It is evident, I think, that protection through their color must be quite essential to them; more so in the matter of procuring their food, perhaps, than as a safeguard against the attacks of enemies.

The mud-minnow depends very largely upon insects and smaller fishes for food, and the question of color is a prominent one in its life history. This fish frequently assumes what we may call an "inanimate" position, and, with a variety of colors streaking and spotting its sides, has much the appearance of a bit of dead grass, a twig, or a caddis-worm. Often such unnatural positions will be retained for many minutes, or until some object suitable for food comes within reach, when it darts at and seizes it with the rapidity and certainty of a pike. Now, in all such cases, there is great and constant changing of color. Often the tints deepen until the fish appears to be inky-black, then pale, until, from above, we can scarcely detect the fish. Such changes, of course, are very significant, and can only be explained as being serviceable to the fishes in rendering them inconspicuous, both to their enemies and to the wandering animal-life on which they prey. In precisely what way the extreme variations from very dark to pale are serviceable is not yet known, so far as I am aware; but the fact itself can scarcely be used to the disadvantage of the main proposition, that the color and its changeableness are of benefit to the fish, and are under the animal's control.

During the early spring, when the vigor of these fishes is at its maximum, the coloration is more pronounced in every particular; and the continual changing from dark to light, and *vice versa*, as seen in connection with its other habits, shows plainly that it is as much under control as are the folding and spreading of a peacock's tail.

The cyprinoids, or "shiners," known collectively as minnows, roach, and dace, so many species of which are conspicuously colored at least at one time of the year, are all essentially diurnal in habit. Their bright colors, as a sexual attraction, are essential to their welfare, but are, at the same time, detrimental to their safety. Have we any reason for believing that these fishes seek to avoid exposure to enemies when thus arrayed in extra-conspicuous dress? I think we have, in the fact that usually they deposit their ova and milt in rapid waters. Waters with a constantly rippling and troubled surface certainly protect them from such enemies as the kingfisher, fish-eating mammals, and probably from frogs and snakes. By drawing a seine through turbulent water at the foot of a mill-dam, I have frequently found scores of splendidly colored cyprinoids; and finally, very soon after spawning, all these extra tints fade out utterly, and the fishes return to their accustomed haunts. These facts certainly seem to indicate that they are aware of the disadvantage of unusually bright colors, which, notwithstanding, are essential to the perpetuation of their kind.

The common banded sunfish, a silvery white species, has a remarkable control over the color of the black vertical bands that ordinarily form so conspicuous a feature of the fish. At times when the water is rather clear, and the amount of vegetation not abundant, this sunfish will fade out, and show such ashen, faintly streaked sides, that it might almost pass for a dead leaf; but roused to action by the approach of other fishes, or the finding of food, the dull sides glisten like polished metal, and the faint bands become as black as ebony. Certainly these great and sudden changes are not involuntary. They cannot be likened to blushing, but are evidently under the fish's control, and are intelligently used to its advantage.

The bony gar is another fish having decided control over the coloration of its scales. When this fish is at rest the scales are pale blue, with a pink margin; and about the head and gill-covers there is a variety of brilliant hues. At times all these colors will suddenly disappear, and the fish has much more the appearance of a water-soaked stick than of a living animal. Unfortunately, I have had too few opportunities for observing this species to determine the reasons for these changes; but it is evident that they are under the control of the fish, and therefore advantageous.

The common pike also exhibits a variation of coloring, under different circumstances, and suggests the same facts that have already been stated with regard to other species.

When the chief aim of biological science seemed to be the naming and describing of "species," it was found that no description of the color of a fish, unless very unusual and marked, was at all satisfactory. Considering the subject of color, as I have here done, the cause is very evident.

A few fishes which had escaped both my first and second examination of the mass of aquatic plants yet remained in the refuse left by the fishermen, after the drawing of the seine. These were very young eels. These little specimens were enveloped in the slimy mass of leaves of the Nuphar pumilum; a splatter-dock which retains its foliage below the water's surface and which is but a mass of pulp when brought into the air.

They were strong, active, and apparently wholly unaffected by breathing the atmosphere, or by the slimy mass to which I have referred. None were six inches in length, and several scarcely measured four, yet these eels, evidently very young, were hatched in salt water, fully one hundred miles distant from the quiet nook in Poaetquissings from which they had been so rudely dragged. To reach this spot, what a journey they must have taken! As I looked at them, it seemed incredible that they should have been bred in the sea, and yet the journey hither need not, after all, have taxed them much. I tested the speed of several, and estimated it at one yard in two seconds. This is more than a mile in an hour, and if these eels kept a straight, up-river course until they reached the mouth of Poaetquissings Creek, four days would have brought them here; and these individuals were probably ten times four days old, and possibly a good deal older.

But why do they come? What impels these young eels, literally by the million, to go up stream as soon as born? Up, up, up, until the mere moist earth of some far-distant spring is reached. Even here, they do not always stop, but, leaving every trace of water, travel overland through the damp grass, and find a check to their progress only in stretches of dry sand; nor, by the way, is this so uncommon an occurrence as is usually thought. Eels are fish, and, of course, must be considered as aquatic, yet they are occasionally terrestrial creatures; but of this hereafter.

The life-history of the eel is very imperfectly understood. It is certain that such young eels as wander so very far inland never, in later years, show any disposition to return to the sea, and yet, beyond its boundaries they never breed. So far as is now known, a certain proportion of young eels annually ascend our rivers, and never return. These are barren, whatever age they may acquire; and why they come and lead a life so different from their brethren in the sea is an unsolved mystery. From my own rather limited observations, I judge that these young eels grow very slowly, even under the most favorable circumstances. Specimens which were fed with great regularity and kept under scrutiny for nearly two years were but one fourth heavier at the end of twenty-two months than when caught and placed in confinement. Some allowance, possibly, should be made for the fact that they were not under absolutely natural conditions; but granting this, it is doubtful if they double their weight every two years, under average conditions. At such a rate, some of the old five-pound eels of our millponds must be veritable patriarchs.

"If eels are very lively, it is a sign of rain;" so runs an old saying; but when, pray, are they not? Being nocturnal, of course, they are less active during midday than midnight, but I have never found them wanting in activity, and the relationship of their movements to the weather is not apparent in the neighborhood of Poaetquissings.

A word now as to eels as land-animals. It is not proper to speak of them as air-breathing fishes, and just how they get over the difficulty of respiration, when on land, constructed as they are, I shall not endeavor to explain; but the fact exists, that eels not only occasionally make overland journeys from one body of water to another, but they leave their proper element, at times, to feed upon animal matter lying on the shore, but quite out of the water. My attention was called to this fact during the past summer. A deep hole in the creek had had a net drawn through it, and nearly a bushel of catfish had been taken. These the fishermen dressed upon the shore, and left the heads, skins, and refuse portions lying on the sand, fully twenty feet from the water. Exposure to the hot sun soon caused decomposition to set in, and the stench was powerful. Two days later, having occasion to pass near by, I noticed a series of serpentine lines or channels in the sand, leading from the putrescent mass to the water. They were not the tracks of any mammal, batrachian, or insect, evidently. No mollusk could have worn so deep a path, and snakes glide too gently over sand to leave a trace of their passage. What, then, could it be? Certain that the visitors to the spot came at night, I hoped the visit might be repeated, and long after the sun went down I quietly approached the place, thinking to surprise the creatures, whatever they might be. In this I was successful, and no caution was necessary in making the discovery. I found a dozen small eels apparently feeding on the decaying fish-heads, and they made no effort to escape, when I reached the spot. These, it proved, were the animals that had channelled the sand between the, to them, savory food and the water. It is well-known that eels swim very near the surface of the water, at night, and often with the tips of their noses just above it, so that the surface is rippled as they move rapidly along.

Is it for the purpose of "locating" the presence of food upon land, not too far for them to reach? Doubtless, if an abundance of food is to be had in the waters, eels prefer to feed upon it then and there; but my observations indicate that the food is not necessarily out of reach simply because it is on dry land.

Abundant as were the number of fishes found that morning in the pond-weeds drawn from the creek, animal life was by no means confined to this family. Crustaceans were well represented in individuals, if not in species; and everywhere in the weeds were crawling, impatient crayfish, of two kinds, large, half-grown, and pygmies. The differences between these are not very apparent at first glance, but are persistent and readily recognized, after a little schooling. It consists mainly in the way the snout is pointed; in one, the slender crayfish, it is broad, of uniform width, and comes rapidly to a point; in the other, Blanding's crayfish, it gradually tapers from the base to the point. These two species proved about equally common in the mass of weeds to-day, but, considering the creek as one locality, probably the broad-snouted crayfish is somewhat the more abundant. In certain ditches, connected with Crosswicks Creek, on the other hand, the slender-snouted form is greatly in excess.

Some years ago I gave a summer to these crayfish, and learned a very little about them; but my observations during subsequent years have necessitated my unlearning a half of this too quickly acquired knowledge. Probably what little I now know of them will be held as scarcely worth recording. Crayfish are not easily studied. You may watch them for hours, and the fact that a crayfish has been before you may be the only one that you will have to carry away with you. They enjoy a game of stare, and will outgaze you, in every contest.

Twelve years ago, I felt justified in remarking that "on carefully approaching clear, running streams, Blanding's crayfish is to be seen resting on the plants, always with the head directed down stream. If disturbed, they would dart backwards down to the roots, apparently, of the plant upon which they were resting. After a lapse of about ten minutes they would return to their former resting-place, creeping up the plant down which they had so suddenly darted tail foremost." Here let me add, that if you approach streams that are neither very clear nor swift, you will probably see Blanding's crayfish that are less methodical in their movements; that head up stream or down, as they see fit, and if you draw a scoop-net through the weeds, these same crayfish will be quite as apt to dart into the mud as to dodge behind a lily stem. To suppose that they were confined to such beautiful streams as the head-waters of Poaetquissings was a grievous error.

Twelve years ago, too, I said the slender, broad-snouted crayfish was only found in the Delaware River, "usually frequenting the rocky bed, but also, in fewer numbers, on the mud-bottomed portions of the river." Here I was "at sea." Those in the river, "usually resting under flat stones," are Barton's crayfish; while the slender species is as common in the ditches as any species of true fish. Oh! a little learning, what a nuisance you are! A well-disposed critic once told me I was too fond of generalizations. Well, it is true, so far as these crustaceans are concerned; but I know now that I have gotten them straightened out. There are two species loving the ditch and haunting weedy creeks; there is one that prefers rapid water, and is found in the river above tide-water; and a fourth, which twelve years ago I knew nothing about, is more interesting than all the others. This is the burrowing crayfish, a semi-terrestrial species. I found none of them in the refuse from the seine, it is true; but having had so much to say of such as I did gather, it is well to complete the crayfish-survey of the region.

The burrowing crayfish differs from the others, in that it is not strictly an aquatic species, and is a prominent feature of the fauna of the meadows, from the fact that it has a subterranean retreat, and marks its site by an elaborate mud structure, popularly known as a "chimney." The creature itself, in general appearance, is much like the others, and is distinguished by a peculiarity in the wrinkles on its back, more easily pointed out than intelligibly described; but the reader can rest assured that if he digs down in the stiff loam of the meadows, to a depth of two feet, and finds there, often hundreds of yards from open water, a pretty little reddish-brown crayfish, that it is the chimney builder to which I have referred.

The burrowing crayfish commence as early as May 1 to erect their mud chimneys, or towers, as they are often called. Some of these are large, some insignificant, and a few, tall, slender, and symmetrically cylindrical. The character of the chimney does not depend upon the size of the builder, but does have something to do with the locality. Every variation occurs alike, whether along the bank of a ditch, or far out in the meadow, hundreds of yards away.

These so-called chimneys have attracted universal attention wherever this crayfish is found, and yet but very little notice has been taken of them by practical naturalists. Girard, some years ago, described the burrowing habits of the terrestrial crayfish, making one important statement, to the effect that the chimneys were usually closed with a ball of clay—this closing of the top of the structure being the customary completion of the crayfish's labors. After carefully examining a very large series of these chimneys, mostly when just completed, I have been led to the opposite conclusion—that they are intended to be left open, and become closed by accident, a ball of the clay from the rim of the structure being accidentally misplaced. Now this fact of some chimneys being closed and others open has given rise to a weather-proverb of this character: that when the chimneys are open the weather will be clear, but some hours before the approach of a storm the crayfish plugs up the chimney, to keep the rain out.

The truth is, the chimneys, as we shall see, are made up of pellets of carefully puddled clay, and the increasing moisture of the atmosphere sometimes loosens one or more pellets, on the rim, and they roll inward and get lodged. This simple fact has given rise to a weather-proverb, which in some neighborhoods, all the people swear by. Consider the absurdity of this from another point of view: of all the burrowings of this crayfish that I have examined, or that I have had examined by others, every one terminated in a little pool of water, scarcely big enough to let "Diogenes" turn around; and some of his burrows are on tide-water flats, which are alternately flooded and exposed. Why, then, should a passing shower induce the crayfish to close the opening of its chimney?

In *Nature*, No. 726 (June 5, 1884), Mr. Ralph S. Tarr gives an interesting account of his observations of the chimney-building crayfish (*Cambarus Diogenes*). His conclusions and my own with reference to this crustacean tally, except upon one point. Mr. Tarr remarks, "I do not think the chimney is a necessary part of the nest, but simply the result of digging." On the contrary, I am convinced that the crayfish *builds* his chimney or tower; that he often studies the locality with care and *builds* to suit the chosen site. My reasons for this conclusion are: That a large series observed during the present year were so placed on a steeply sloping bank of a ditch, that if the materials of which the towers were composed had been simply rejected matter derived from tunnelling, then it could have been rolled into the ditch without trouble; while in fact an artistic tower, only two inches in diameter and varying from eight to eleven inches in height, was erected; and in several instances the base of the tower was specially provided for by having the ground levelled and smoothed before the foundation masses of *puddled* clay were put in position. Of a series of forty towers built by the *Cambarus Diogenes* that I observed on the banks of a ditch, not one could have been the result of accident, as suggested by Mr. Tarr.

The towers that were found in the meadows, at a considerable distance from open water, were invariably broader at the base and never so high as those described as found on the edge of flowing water. These open-meadow towers or chimneys, however, were all found to be composed of pellets of clay so arranged as to render it highly improbable that their positions were fortuitous. Indeed, in the majority of instances it would have been practicable to have rolled the little balls of clay to a considerable distance from the opening of the tunnel.

Perhaps there is a bearing on the question of design in tower-building in the fact that often half-grown or even smaller crayfish of this species build the most elaborate structures. Some of the finest examples, *i. e.*, the most slender and tallest, were the work of diminutive little fellows which certainly could have avoided a deal of labor if the chimneys or towers were not designed.

But how does the burrowing crayfish build these chimneys? I am forced to admit they have, as yet, overtaxed my patience, and from personal knowledge I can only assert that the work is done only at night, and that often in a single night a tall and stately chimney will be reared.

Others have been more fortunate, and my nephew informs me that he has seen the crayfish at work. Finding, one evening, the base of a chimney about one and a half inches in height, he remained for some time to get a glimpse of the occupant. In this he was unsuccessful; so the following evening he determined to "make a night of it," if necessary, to see the crayfish at work. Placing a candle, with a mirror behind it, at a convenient point, he succeeded in getting a light upon the chimney about equal to that of the full moon, and he himself remained in shadow. After the lapse of some minutes, in perfect silence, my nephew saw the antennæ of the crayfish above the opening of the burrow. These were waved in the air, as if to scent or in some way recognize danger; for experiment showed that the slightest noise caused the crayfish to fall back into his burrow "like a lump of lead." An interim of fully five minutes elapsed, when the crayfish reappeared. Nothing disturbing it, the animal half-emerged into view, and brought on the back of its right claw a ball of clay-mud, which, by a dexterous tilt of the claw, was placed on the rim of the chimney. Then the crayfish remained perfectly quiet for a few seconds, when it suddenly "doubled up" and dropped to the bottom of its burrow. There elapsed some three or four minutes between each appearance; but every time it came it brought a ball of clay and deposited it in the manner I have described. About two fifths of the balls were not placed with sufficient care and rolled down the outside of the chimney. If all crayfish work as deliberately as did this one observed by my nephew, then the chimneys are not built in one night; but of this fact, however, I am so positive, that the crayfish that was seen at work was certainly an exception to the rule.

It being known that these chimneys are designed, and how they are made, let some one add an important item to the world's common stock of knowledge by telling it *why* they are built; and determine also whether or not this crayfish burrows from the nearest open water to the point inland where the chimney is erected, or does it travel overland to a convenient spot and burrow downwards? I believe I have knowledge of upward burrowing and the subsequent building of the chimney.

Bared fingers must not be thrust too carelessly into the mass of myriophyllum and lily stems. There are insignificant aquatic insects sure to be tangled there, that can bite as sharply as they can swim swiftly; and when, by chance, a half-dozen nip at your finger-ends at once, your ejaculations may startle your own self. It is remarkable how much emphasis rolls, ready-waiting, under the tongues of bug-bitten mortals.

The most numerous of the aquatic insects brought up by the net, and which have bitten me severely more than once, are everywhere known as water-boatmen, or Notonectæ, a much prettier name. Let us give them a moment's consideration. They are perfect insects, and not larval forms of some aërial creature; and are strictly aquatic forms. Still, they have wings, and if they find their home pond drying up, will take a prolonged flight in search of more comfortable quarters. A curious feature of their habits is, that they always swim on their backs, just as we saw that the little spring-time crustacean, Branchipus, does; and it is only when swimming that they may be said to be at home. They never know when to stop. They come to the surface with a series of most sprightly jerks, tarry a moment, and dive gracefully to the bottom, then up again; and so they continue until their appetite prompts them to seek for food, which it does pretty constantly. They grasp any available insect that comes within reach, and suck the fluids from its body. But they are not content with an insectivorous diet. Time and again, like some aquatic beetles, they seize a small fish, always at the gills, and soon draw from it most, if not all, the blood the body contains. Considering how readily they can pierce the thick skin of a person's finger, it is not strange that a minnow an inch or two long quickly succumbs when once a water-boatman has made good his hold.

There are other insects, of about the same size and general outline as the Notonectæ, for which I know of no common name. In the minds of many they are confounded with the preceding, from which they differ in habits as well as anatomy. So far as my personal experience extends, they do not bite, and I have never seen them attack small fishes.

While resting from my labors for a moment, after picking out a few water-boatmen for future study, I saw a single specimen of a long, attenuated, gray insect, with legs as exaggerated as are those of a "walking-stick" or Diapheromera. What to call them I do not know. My entomological friends say Ranatra, and we had better follow their example. They are apparently as lazy as water-boatmen are restless. When they do see fit to move, it is with great deliberation, as when they walk circumspectly along the edge of the still waters where sunfish eggs are likely to be. These they seize and suck, and so quietly that the guarding sunfish does not recognize the depredator from a chance twig that has floated thither; or is the fish afraid of the creature? They are bloodthirsty at times, and then attack small fishes. The specimen I gathered to-day may have been injured, but it did not resent handling, and seemed active enough when I placed him in an aquarium.

There is another of these aquatic bugs fully as interesting as the water-boatman. It is called a water-scorpion, but there is no sting in its tail or malice in its heart; it has the manner of a philosopher, or, at least, of a contemplative rambler. Unlike the peaceful (?) Corixa, which swims with its back up, or the Notonecta, which swims on its back, this so-called scorpion walks leisurely about the bottom of the pond or ditch, intent upon its own business, the character of which, by the way, I have not been able to determine.

Of course it can swim, and very well too, but this is not a favorite mode of locomotion, and when a summer pond nearly dries up, can fly to deeper and more certain waters. In this respect they have something to learn, for when they can recognize a temporary pool from permanent waters they will be saved the trouble of migration.

I have intimated that this water-scorpion is a bit of a philosopher, because I am really convinced that it is, yet to specify the indications of such a fact is impossible. I have never seen a single act that demonstrated its intellectual superiority over its associates, insects as quick-witted, possibly, as they; but something in the manner of the creature is certainly suggestive.

This may seem like trifling with the subject, but it is not. Those who are accustomed to study the lower forms of animal life will usually find it very difficult to detect pronounced evidences of cunning or skill, yet will always, I believe, feel convinced of a difference in the degree of intelligence among allied forms. Certainly, in mammals and birds this difference obtains and has been often commented upon, and, logically, the same should be true of invertebrates, although it is far more difficult to demonstrate the fact.

In bees, wasps, and trap-door spiders there is, of course, much to comment upon as proofs of these creatures' intelligence, but in the case of a water-scorpion all this is wanting, yet I believe no one can carefully watch them for an hour or more without being impressed that they are methodical, cautious, and—may I add?—contemplative.

And why may not a water-bug think, as well as a spider? A German naturalist says of the latter, "that they reflect is proved by the fact that they despise certain kinds of tough, chitinous insects which they have unsuccessfully attacked before. This reflection is to be distinguished from the instinctive dread which they have for bee-like flies."

While I doubt not but that the great majority of people will scout the idea that a mere impression, and an apparently very fanciful one, is of value in judging of an animal's intellectual status, I feel warranted in offering the suggestion that if such impressions, in the minds of unprejudiced observers, are uniform, whenever the animal is under inspection, even if no act can be specialized as thoughtful, then they are proper criteria upon which to base a conclusion.

Corixæ and water-boatmen are unequalled examples of tireless animal activity. Even when swimming with the distinct purpose of securing their prey, we look upon them in the light of machines rather than living animals: as self-winding engines wound up and set to capture diminutive insects and newly-hatched minnows —but the water-scorpion walks deliberately along the bottom of the pond, looking for food, seeking desirable shelter, and in all things taking the world so easily that we are led to admire it, while we simply wonder at, and are bewildered by, the others.

Unlike the other bugs that throughout summer are its daily companions, the water-scorpion does not appear to hibernate. However cold the weather, there will always be found numbers of these "scorpions" taking a quiet stroll, where the sun, here and there, lights up a corner in the ice-bound pond. When the ice is very clear I have often seen them stepping carefully along the mud, avoiding troublesome obstructions, peeping under bits of dead leaves, and giving now and then a sly kick at the caddis-worms that always thickly bestrew the level reaches of the sand. Perhaps it was accidental in every case, but the appearances were strongly in favor of the view that the bug deliberately gave the half-helpless worm a vigorous kick that sent it whirling end over end in a ludicrous manner.

One might think that, with these, little fish and all defenseless forms of aquatic life were quite sufficiently persecuted, if, indeed, they had not more than their share of life-destroying insect pests, but, on the fishes' account,

I am sorry to say there are two more, and one of them the largest and fiercest of them all. The smaller of the two is, in Poaetquissings, not at all common, but is a veritable crosspatch, and makes up in ferocity what may be lacking in numbers. Usually they are recognized as present by the collector being bitten, and they then may pass as water-boatmen, which possess the same inconvenient habit. It is to be presumed, however, that after years of experience a difference in the bite will be detected, and the more precise naturalist will proceed to investigate whether his fingers were nipped by a true water-boatman or a Pelocoris. For the benefit of the inexperienced it should be said that the same remedy, mud, is equally efficacious.

This water-boatman-like Pelocoris has the one good quality of being an insect-eater; and will dine off a corixa as readily as a new-born fish. The two insects are not very closely related, and so perhaps Pelocoris cannot be considered cannibal; just as we look upon it as a mere matter of taste whether or not man eats roast monkey, but—

The last but one, and largest, of the lot has not received a common name, and were not "water-tiger" preoccupied I would suggest it. Its scientific name, in English, is spearmouth.

This creature may be crudely described as a giant water-scorpion, for, instead of being a little more than half an inch long, it is nearly three inches, and wide in proportion. As the spearmouth is, in color, much like the muddy bottom of a pond, it realizes the protection afforded by this similarity of tints, as shown by its stealthy action when it creeps among the stems of water-plants, or suddenly squats on the bare mud, if the coveted prey approaches.

Here, at all events, we have an aquatic insect that not only possesses intelligence, but gives abundant evidence of the fact. There is exhibited by it all the cunning in hunting displayed by the most sagacious of mammals; and as it preys upon fishes of considerable size, seizing them at the gills, as mammals strike for the throat of their victims, one has but to place a spearmouth in an aquarium to see from how terrible a foe our fishes are called upon to escape, if happily they can.

But there is a much smaller species of these spearmouths or Belostomæ, which must not be overlooked. They are hardy, non-hibernating insects, and, with Nepæ, are found all through the winter in the mud of the ditches, or on it. Perhaps they have not as much vivacity then as in midsummer, or need no food, but, even as late as March, numbers of them, kept in an aquarium, were very peaceful, and lazy too, at times. Often they would lie flat upon their backs and, to all appearances, were dead; but any disturbance roused them, and away they would walk or swim, as they felt disposed. During the summer they doubtless cling to grass or twigs: but having no such support in the aquarium, they seemed to delight in riding about on the backs of the larger fishes, but not annoying them in any way; and one sat for half an hour on the snout of a small turtle, which seemed careful not to move so as to disturb the bug; and yet it had but to open its mouth to swallow the creature, had it chosen so to do.

The contrast between these small "spearmouths" and their larger cousins, as seen in midsummer, was very marked.

So much for water-bugs; and now a word about water-beetles. Of course, there were scuttle-bugs in abundance. Where was there ever a creek, in summer, that was not rippled by their erratic coursing? Unfortunately, they are so very common that they have aroused no curiosity in the minds of most people, yet they are curious creatures, and worthy of a passing notice. We all know they are not easy to catch, except with a dip-net; nor need we wonder, for they have eyes on the top of their head, wherewith to watch the upper regions, and a pair of equally good ones beneath, to guide them when they dive out of your reach.

These creatures have not escaped incorporation in local weather-lore, and their unusual abundance is said to be the sign of a shower. I have been for several years in quest of the difference between many and a great many of them; so, if they are noticeably numerous, do not turn back for an umbrella; the chances being there are not quite enough of them to bring up the shower.

Bearing some resemblance to the whirligigs or scuttle-bugs are those much larger, shiny black beetles, the young of which Packard aptly calls "water-tigers." They are voracious enough to be called by any bloodthirsty name, so water-tiger let it be; although I have caught the habit of my entomological acquaintances, and speak of it generally, to them at least, as the Dytiscus. There was one of these beetles in the mass of weeds. It did not bite me when I picked it up, but it had jaws that could have brought my blood if the creature had been disposed to try.

Happily, these large beetles are not very abundant, or small fish would have a hard time of it. They are quick as a flash, and seize a fish just as the little water-boatmen do, and, once seized, there is no hope of escape.

Dr. Packard considers the cylindrical larva of this beetle as voracious as an insect can be, remarking of them that their "large flattened heads, armed with scissor-like jaws with which they seize other insects," are also used to "snip off the tails of tadpoles," and they "are even known to attack young fishes, sucking their blood."

This is unquestionably true of these larval water-tigers. I took a half-dozen of them, some summers ago, from Poaetquissings, and placed them in an aquarium, where were several choice specimens of small fishes brought from a distance. During the day all went well, but next morning I found they had attacked the fishes and worried them to death. If, therefore, aquatic beetles are wanted in an aquarium, let them not be associated with small fishes, if you value the latter.

This, of course, does not close the list of water insects; but what else will be found will prove closely related to those that I gathered from the weeds after the drawing of the seine.

Some of these insects, as has been mentioned, prey

upon fishes, some upon mollusks, others upon insects not always widely different from themselves, but what enemies have these water-bugs? True, a Pelocoris will devour a Corixa, but this is a trivial matter, and there seems to be no decided check to their increase; and it is not improbable that the countless thousands of water-boatmen and allied forms may be the cause of the scarcity of fish in ponds apparently well suited to them. When we consider what defenceless creatures newly hatched fishes are, and that no sooner do they essay to lead independent lives than Notonectæ, Ranatræ, Belostomæ, or Dytisci, by scores, are lying in wait for them, it is not to be wondered at that, out of a thousand eggs, so small a percentage live to maturity.

Surely the fauna of that mass of water-weeds must end here! Does it, indeed? If the entomologist should take my place, he could give us a score of entertaining lectures upon the insect-life that, crawling from the mass, slowly made its way back to its home in Poaetquissings. If the microscopist should happen— but no, I will not let him come. Nothing short of eternity would enable him to get through. For fear of such a disaster I will kick the weeds back, before they become too dry to take root and grow again; only pausing for a moment over curious masses of amber-colored jelly, that I see adhering to bits of sticks. What are they? Jelly-fishes, my neighbors call them; and in the books they figure as *Pectinatella magnifica*. I am puzzled to describe them in an intelligible way. To the unaided eye they appear as a structureless gum or jelly; but, in fact, every mass is the home of countless thousands of beautiful animals. To describe them, except as a professional biologist might, is not practicable. Like so much of animate nature, it must be seen, not merely read about.

Prof. Hyatt says of these "jelly-fish:" "the tropical aspect and luxuriant growth of the clinging masses, frequently several feet in diameter, investing the summits of submerged stumps and the branches of water-logged timber, are unequalled among the fresh-water, or even among the marine, Saccata of our climate.

"The communities, assembled in countless profusion upon the gelatinous ectocyst, are crowded together, and, being compressed, become irregularly hexagonal in their outlines. The polypides upon the lobiform branches adorn the borders of these hexagonal patterns with a dense, glistening fringe, speckled with the scarlet coloring of their oral regions; and the bare cœnœcial trunks in the centre shine with a deep opaline lustre, completing the rich, coralline effect of the fringed outlines.

"In July and August specimens of Pectinatella magnifica are very abundant in shallows and in the depths of—Poaetquissings; but as fall advances, those in the shallows die, and in October they can live only upon the logs in deep, cool water, or in shaded situations. These autumnal specimens are old, and being unable to withstand the direct rays of the sun, disappear from all exposed positions, where they grow with impunity as strong and healthy adults earlier in the season. I have found them fifteen or twenty feet below the surface, showing a marked departure in this respect from *other* genera, whose species seldom occur below two or three feet, and are almost invariably near the shore line."

But to realize all that Prof. Hyatt has to say of these jelly-like masses, it must be remembered that a magnifying-glass is necessary; and further, the trouble necessary to see the beautiful animals included within the mass is nothing as compared with the delight that will reward the investigator. I have seldom seen anything so marvellously beautiful. A word more and I have done. How, it may be asked, do these animals reproduce their kind? Animals of this class, according to Prof. Hyatt, "have two modes of reproduction, one by buds, and the other by eggs. The former occurs in two ways; by statoblasts, either fixed or free, and by regular buds, which grow out from the side of each polypide. The first are the founders of new colonies. The last merely increase the number of individuals in each established community."

Let us follow up briefly the history of these wonderful statoblasts, or eggs, as most people would call them, although they are not such. On the contrary, they "bud from the funiculus, a cord-like prolongation of the outer membranes of the stomach. . . . They arise within beadlike swellings of the funiculus, and, enlarging slowly, push out to the surface of the cord, and upwards towards the stomach, until finally they hang upon the exterior, arranged alternately on either side, the youngest being at the lower end."

What do these statoblasts look like? Truly, they are not readily described. An oval, slightly double convexed disk, of a yellow-brown color, and about one thirty-second of an inch in diameter. By this description alone you might not recognize them, but, besides the features enumerated, these statoblasts have a series of hooks ranged about their outer rim which establishes their identity. Think of fifteen pairs of fish-hooks, placed back to back, and ranged at uniform distances from each other, in clusters of two, around a small coin, and you will have a fairly good idea of a Pectinatella's statoblast. These statoblasts are enveloped in gelatine until after death of the colony, it being needed in order to protect the parent from laceration by the pointed hooklets, and so is retained until lost by exposure of the bud to external influences. After the statoblasts are free from their parents, they still "lie loose in the cœnœcial cavity from this time until the death and decay of the polypides destroy the upper parts of the cells. Through the openings thus made, being lighter than water, they are readily floated off, and pass the winter unprotected by any other covering than their cellular casings, although remaining near the surface, and consequently, in higher latitudes, imbedded in the ice for several months. "Growth begins at the approach of spring, and the edges of the sheath are split apart by the increasing bulk of the polyzoön, which protrudes between them.

"The organs, when the little animal first makes itself visible, are well advanced in growth, and the polypide is already capable of retraction and expansion. For a time it floats freely in the water, wafted about by the cilia, which clothe the whole external surface, and increases in size until the sheaths of the statoblasts can no longer contain it; then, in some appropriate locality, the gelatinous ectocyst adheres to the surface, the cilia are absorbed, and the polypide enters upon a new phase of life as the founder of a community."

Of the weeds themselves, there is little to be said. What some of them are, other pages have made plain, except that, until now, no mention has been made of the carnivorous bladderworts. They are light, feathery plants, delicate as small ferns, and surely very innocent looking; and yet, insect larvae are often, and baby fishes, not being born botanists, are sometimes, fatally entrapped by them.

Some, who have studied these plants, hold that they are sensitive; others consider the movements of the valves of the "bladders," that entrap minute animal life, as merely mechanical. However this may be, they certainly act as if they meant to accomplish that which they perform. How do they do this?

Some of these plants have no roots, and float, unless there is no current, when they rest against the bottom of the pond or along the banks, if in a sluggish stream, such as in our meadow ditches. Scattered thickly among the little leaflets of the plant are numbers of very small green vesicles, which entrap various forms of minute animal life, said to then serve as nourishment for the plant. The form of these vesicles "is that of a flattened ovoid sac." Each "has an opening at its free extremity, somewhat quadrangular in outline.

"On either side of the quadrangular entrance several long bristles project outward, and these bristles, together with the branches of the 'antennæ,' form a sort of hollow cone surrounding the entrance, and there cannot be the slightest doubt that they act as a guide for the prey.

"The entrance is closed by a valve, which, being attached above, slopes into the cavity of the bladder, and is attached to it on all sides except at its posterior or lower margin, which is free, and forms one side of the slit-like opening leading into the bladder."

In other words, it is a mouse-trap arrangement that is easily entered but does not work both ways, and so, once in, there is an impassable barrier that bars all egress.

Of course, such a plant is of exceeding interest, and one is prompted to gather every specimen, and scan the bladders; but do not expect to find fish in them always. In the main ditch of a neighbor's meadow there is an abundance of the plant, and often I sweep the hand-net through them for such small fry as may be lurking in their midst; and it is very seldom, even in early spring, when the newly hatched fish are abundant, that I find any entrapped in the "bladders" of this plant. Minute larvae are found, and even diminutive mollusks, but seldom, indeed, any trace of the very youngest even of our cyprinoids, which, in fact, are the only species likely to be caught, as most of the others do not, when very young, frequent waters where this plant is likely to grow.

So much has been written upon the subject lately, particularly with reference to the danger of allowing it to grow in carp ponds, that it is fitting to call especial attention to the plant, the more so as it is so abundant in certain localities; but to find it feeding on fish will require much patience, and the collecting of a good deal of material.

The seine has been drawn. The fishermen and the student have secured their prey. The troubled waters have resumed their quiet beneath the overarching elms and stately birches; the day-dreaming herons are abroad; the last roostward-flying crow has passed by; afar in the maple thicket an owl ventures to hint of the coming night; and it remains, now, only to record that for me, at least, to linger so long on the shore of Poaetquissings has not been to waste my time. Surely I have had both a pleasant and a profitable ramble.

CHAPTER X.

A SUMMER AT HOME

"And what is so rare as a day in June?
Then, if ever, come perfect days;
Then Heaven tries the earth if it be in tune,
And over it softly her warm ear lays."

WHAT is, indeed? but such perfect days do come, when we have the rose-breasted grosbeak to sing to us. The month, in '84, came in clear and warm, and with grosbeaks in abundance. At sunrise they joined in the day's opening chorus; at noon they sang with unabated zeal, as if to cheer the weak ones that complain of noontide heat; at sunset, and through the gloaming, they are the leaders of the evening concert.

It is held by many that the wood-thrush is the finer songster, but have those that think this heard these birds as they sang to-day, when the hillside oaks and mighty beeches were aglow with the last rays of the setting sun, and happily no heartless robin interrupted? I trow not.

I love the thrush—no one can be more appreciative of it—but I worship the grosbeak.

The weather was all that could be wished, and, armed only with so peaceful a weapon as a spade, my companion and myself took a leisurely stroll over my neighbor's meadows, to search for such crayfish as burrow deeply, and then build high towers above their homes beneath the sod. We found that many had settled down quite near the open ditches, and were too cunning for us; and, long before we could reach them by way of their front doors, they had quietly slipped through a rear entrance into the open water and were gone. But this safe method was not employed by all. Others trusted to luck or the tall grass, and, believing no marauder would disturb them, had homes hundreds of yards from any ditch or other open water. Patient search finally rewarded us. Finding two mud towers, we dug beneath them, following the narrow, tortuous burrow leading to the terminal chamber, or home. This, in each case, was just at the water-line, and the animal, therefore, was either partly or wholly submerged, as it chose. This terminal compartment—it cannot be called a nest—was an oval expansion of the burrow leading to it, and measured, approximately, two inches in its long diameter, and half that transversely.

What, in such a place, did this crayfish find to eat? Whether carnivorous or, as my companion thinks, a vegetable feeder, it certainly finds no food in such a locality; and yet, once settled in these burrows, these crayfish do not appear ever to leave them. There are no marks of travel at the summits of the towers, no tell-tale refuse-heaps in their burrows or about them.

There is much yet to be learned of its habits, as of many another common animal.

Interested as we really were to-day, we could not continue the investigation; we were bent on other purposes, the main one to take a model ramble on this, the 1st of June.

Bagging our game, we botanized, after a fashion, as we neared the "great elm"—that one possession of my neighbor that I yearly covet.

To attempt a detailed description of the tree would be madness. A photograph would tell you its shape, a cunning artist give you an idea of its summer glory, but it can only be said that it, like other trees, is made up of a trunk and branches — but such branches! It is a tree that invites you. Whether there be a breeze or not, its long, outstretched boughs ever nod a welcome as you near them. Not only this; they lift you up tenderly, if you wish, and hold you as carefully and comfortably as a mother holds her child. It was there that we sat that long summer morning, discoursing of birds and flowers. Surely this was a fair beginning of the anticipated joys of a summer.

Later in the day we took yet another stroll, and made our goal a sturdy beech. Unlike the elm, it depended upon the surroundings for its attractions, being, of itself, quite like beeches everywhere; yet, had it a tongue, what pleasant stories of the past it could relate—stories of naturalists that have paused to drink of the clear waters rippling at its roots, and often carving an initial or a date while they tarried. We could decipher but one name positively, and this was carved sixty-five years ago —that of Conrad the paleontologist. Here, in the cool brook, he often placed watermelons, fresh from the dusty field near by, that they might be chilled to the very core; and here he truthfully wrote of them:

"I make thee, sweet melon, my favorite topic,
   Thou chief of the offspring of sun and of dew!
In spite of bananas, the pride of the tropic,
   Or famed chirimoyas, the boast of Peru.

"Give us cool 'Mountain Sweets' from New Jersey, nor ask us
   To sigh for the grapes of some Orient land;
The peaches of Persia, the figs of Damascus,
   Or the idolized fruits of remote Samarcand.

"I have shaken ripe oranges oft, where they fell on
   Floridian flowers; I have dreamed of the date;
But dearer to me is the dew-tempered melon,
   Fresh from the sand of my loved native state.

"The poet may sing of the Orient spices,
   Or Barbary dates in their palmy army;
But the huge, rosy melon in cold, juicy slices
   Is the Helicon fount of a hot summer day,

"Where I bathe the dry wings of the spirit; and sprinkling
   Sweet drops on the pathway of dusty old Care,
I hold Father Time from his villainous wrinkling
   Of features that never had graces to spare."

Is it not a common impression that no fruit is so prized as that which we first gather? The long waiting for the return of the season; the anxious watching of the budding plant, and then its bloom; the slowly growing fruit, hard, insignificant, and green. When will it be ripe? Day after day we watch, and, weary at last, give way to mild despair. It was so this year. A frost in May surely bodes no good, and we had three of them. Ah me! no strawberries; no strawberries!

How I regretted that my friend knew that there were any plants upon the farm. Not a syllable escaped me about fruit. I spoke only of "flowers," lest the word "bloom" might suggest berries; and only hope was left that the cunning of the cook might find some passable substitute.

Wearied with long tramping, some climbing, and a deal of flower-plucking, as the day closed we were again at home.

Surely, it was sad! The time-honored custom of strawberries on the first of June to be omitted, and a guest in the house at that. The hour arrived; the tinkle of the tea-bell was the laugh of imps that mocked me; but I took my place with a firm step and serene countenance. Was I, after all, responsible for the three frosts? What! Strawberries? Yes; there in all their blushing beauty they lie, heaped in a capacious dish. Ripe, ruddy berries, that will need carving, every one of them. O ye of little faith! What wonders, indeed, had three days of sunshine wrought; and it had been five since I had seen them, small, white, and unpromising.

I straightway grew enthusiastic, if not eloquent; and quiet satisfaction beamed from the countenance of my friend.

The first week of June is the climax of song-bird life. Earlier than this, we may always look for some new songster to join the company; later, one by one, the birds drop out from the ranks; so that what later music is heard is usually that of single birds. In the first week of June we have grand concerts—later, solos and duets.

In a cluster of oaks on the south hillside the birds

congregate, and one by one take their places in the trees. The thrushes on the lower branches open the concert, and all goes well, unless too many shrilly chirping robins interrupt by their incessant clatter. Think of an opera performed in a cotton-mill, and you have the songs at sunset, as they sometimes are, with this robin accompaniment. Such a time is a sufficient answer to the distorted notion that birds sing simply to please mankind. I have heard the statement made in perfect sincerity, even in these enlightened days. I have often thought how it must fret a tuneful thrush to be interrupted by a robin or blue-jay. Indeed, I am positive that they cease to sing from such a cause.

June 8 closed a week of perfect summer weather. An eager botanist rambled with me to Poaetquissings, and along its shady shores for half their length. His hands were only empty that he might gather fresh flowers, at every turn in our path. Purple and yellow oxalis, and star grass, slim, upright stems topped with yellow-centred bloom, made his first bouquet; and, as we left the creek-side, a handful of forget-me-nots were the fitting memento he carried home.

Stayed by a passing shower, we took shelter under the dense foliage of thick-set birches, and my friend grew eloquent as, from our leaf-house, he gazed wistfully at the dense clusters of arum on the shore, of pontederia in the shallows, of pond-lilies in bloom, and delicate Nuphar pumilum, whose leaves never reach beyond the water's surface, but whose golden, globular bloom peeps shyly above it.

I joined with him heartily, it was all so beautiful; yet my thoughts were with the many birds, now silenced by the rain. To this silence I referred when his eloquence was checked, and I prophesied that the robin would break forth into song the moment the sun struggled through the parting clouds. It was not so: a song-sparrow first and then the robin; but the reverse is true in almost every instance. Soon the greenlets, redstarts, and small finches were all in song.

"What are they saying?" I asked.

"Singing a hymn, and properly too, seeing it is Sunday," he replied.

"Would they not sing the same song, were it Monday?" I asked.

"Certainly; these birds do not assume to be, on Sunday, what they are not through the week," my friend remarked with much earnestness; and then added, "and now they are off for the meadows, all rosy with clover; let us follow;" and we did.

Botanists are not such slow fellows after all.

As we walked, we fell to talking about expressing bird-notes by syllables, and voted it could not be done; yet, strangely enough, persisted in trying whenever a bird chirped or sang near by. Finally, finding we appeared to be differently impressed by the notes of the same bird, we undertook to express these songs in writing and then compare.

One chirping sparrow, he remarked, said "phit." I had it written "tweet." To him there was no "e" sound, to me no short "i," in the bird's utterance. When it came to longer songs, which required several syllables to express, the differences were very marked, and sometimes ludicrous. Only a single example need be given. As we walked, a red-eyed greenlet commenced to sing in the top of a tall tree near by. "Let us take plenty of time," I suggested, and we stood for several minutes, listening to the tireless little musician. Then, satisfied we had it correctly written, after several modifications, our versions were compared. One was *weé-to klip-a-tcé-tcé;* the other *see-ro tut a tut.* One heard distinctly a syllable uttered by the bird that the other failed to catch, and the last notes were clear and ringing to one, while guttural and indistinct to the other. And each thought his own version much the more correct.

We did agree that the attempt to describe a bird's song, except in the most general way, would, in most cases, prove a failure. The "twittery-twits" and "chee-chees" that adorn our ornithological literature, we concluded, very inadequately describe the songs of our scores of singing-birds; and later, on reading the efforts of Nuttall to describe them, we were confirmed in our opinion, for, with his book in hand, and the birds singing near by, we could seldom hear the songsters he mentioned sing the songs as he described them.

The long-billed marsh-wrens that colonize the muddy meadow, and also the more melodious swamp-sparrow, were striking examples of how variously the same utterances impress different persons. My companion likened the notes of the wren to *phreé-ēē-ēē*, and the voice of the sparrow a little more prolonged, but similar. This description would certainly not have enabled me to identify the birds to which he referred. In the case of the wren, there seems to me a longer series of considerably varied notes, and the sparrow's song is as marked as an oriole's. I began to think, because plants were voiceless, botanists had no ears.

Illogical mortals we, verily! Having concluded it could not be done, we continued to try. Our last effort, whatever may be thought of the result, was the most elaborate. Taking our stands at a considerable distance from each other, but equally distant from the bird, we listened carefully to the same rose-breasted grosbeak, which sang without stopping for just three minutes—which is an unusually long time for any bird to continue in song.

Except that I used "ph" and "t," as the initial consonants, where he used "ch" and "d," we were in accord, using in every instance the same vowels. We concluded that possibly the following might be recognized as the song of this incomparable performer, *Kŭ-kŭ, ta-wēē-a, ta-wēē-a! Chēē-chĕ-wēē-a! Phēē-ta-tă-wēē-a!*

While discussing the matter in a general way, as we entered the yard, and admitting it was strange that in apparently so simple a matter people could not agree, a Carolina wren screamed at us, *cúri ous, cúri ous, cúrious!* We agreed that it was.

June 12.—My rambles brought me to the mucky meadow, and while gathering the beautiful broad leaves of the arum, I chanced upon the nest of a pair of least bitterns. Such finds make red-letter days. The nest itself was a loosely woven mat of twigs and grass, yet strong enough to be lifted from the tuft of bulrush upon which it rested. There were a single dirty blue-white egg, and four fuzzy baby bitterns, not a week old. They were clad in pale buff down, scantily dusted over them, and an abundance of straight white hairs, as long as their bodies. These young birds were far less awkward, even now, than herons of the same or even greater age. As I took one up, it thrust its opened beak at me, but, becoming quickly reconciled, seemed to take pleasure in the warmth of my hand. At times it uttered a peculiarly clear, fife-like cry, such as might readily be referred to a piping hylodes, or any one of several finches. Its clear voice, free from every trace of harshness, was noticed and remarked upon by all who heard it.

My efforts to rear this little bittern were not successful. Although I strove hard to imitate nature, the little fellow persistently refused to take food, and to reject all that was forcibly thrust into his stomach.

The spring-brook passing through several upland fields widens at one point to form a shallow pond, and there the steep banks are most intricately burrowed in many places, as though pygmy muskrats were in great abundance. I have watched the openings of these underground retreats for hours, as it seemed to me, and yet have never seen their occupants, or any creature, great or small, in the act of burrowing.

There are two ways of solving such a problem as this in reference to the identity of the burrowing creatures whose works have been mentioned: by persistent watching and digging along the course of a tunnel, until you find the occupant; and by reference to the proper books. Of the two methods, the former is much to be preferred; the latter, however, is much the more expeditious. In this case I combined the two, and the creature proving to be an insect, the mole-cricket, I then took a spade, and dug out a half-dozen, to be quite sure, and found the creature and the book's description to tally.

While, as yet, these burrowing crickets have wrought no damage, it is very evident that about mill-dams and permanent embankments they might prove quite destructive; as much so, indeed, as muskrats.

I carefully traced one burrow from the bank of the pond into the field. It was a trifle more than two feet in a direct line, at a uniform depth of one foot from the surface, then, obliquely turning, it sloped slightly upward, and at a distance of thirteen inches from the angle the burrow terminated in a capacious chamber. None of the others that I examined were as long, but all ended in chambers large enough to permit the cricket to turn around comfortably. Many were so near the surface that the roots of the grass had been destroyed by the cricket's progress. These could be traced along the sod, by the line of withered grass above them. Some were very crooked, as though a new course had been taken by the little burrower, whenever a pebble or root had been met with.

Of mole-crickets, themselves, little need be said. Their enormously developed fore-feet, by which they dig, at once enables them to be recognized. Excepting these, their appearance is much that of an ordinary black cricket. Of course they sing, insect fashion, but I have never seen them when so engaged. Prof. Riley says: "The males sing during the warm, still nights of spring and early summer. The song is a low, continued, rather pleasant trill, quite similar to that of the common toad, but more shrill;" so many a midnight serenade I have attributed to toads has doubtless been the stridulations of burrowing mole-crickets.

June 13 and 14 proved to be summer days of quite another type. A cold northeast rain prevailed. Such a storm comes, it is said, every summer—but it does not —and, if a week earlier, is the "strawberry storm," if later, that of some other berry. It is strange that every tree, flower, bird, and bug has not its particular storm; for so frequently have names been given to changes of the weather, no invidious distinctions should have been made. Raspberries, blackberries, and huckleberries are all very good, if not equal to strawberries—why, then, not give each of them a rain also?

But such a storm has one pleasant feature. It leaves us just before sunset, and there is a chance to see, before the day closes, what it has accomplished beyond soaking the surface soil.

During an evening stroll I passed along the main ditch of the meadow and overtook a stray muskrat. There was no water here sufficiently deep to enable it to swim or dive, nor any hole in the banks in which it could hide. I headed it off, as it ran, in a clumsy manner, through the shallow water and soft mud; upon which it abruptly left the ditch and in a moment hid in the tall grass. I was struck by the ease with which so large a mammal could find secure cover from pursuing foes, if the latter are guided only by sight. Although I was positive the muskrat was within a few steps, yet, search as I would, I could not see it from where I stood. In fact, when directly over the animal, a careful parting of the grass was needed to find it. The creature had drawn itself up to a mere ball of apparently dull brown earth, so that, if upon bare ground, it would not be recognized, except after the most careful scrutiny.

On attempting to pick the muskrat up it showed its teeth, but did not offer to bite. When touched with my cane, although not in the least hurt, it uttered a faint squeak, that would not be noticeable if attention were not directly called to it.

How much nonsense, of late, has been written of muskrats and fresh-water mussels! That this rodent is extravagantly fond of the mollusks named is known to every one, but lovers of the marvellous have long insisted that a muskrat never injures a mussel's shell, when extracting the animal it holds, so the question, of course, arose, How do they accomplish this? They don't, and never did. That is the common-sense reply to the whole matter. Muskrats adopt two methods of procuring mussels for food. They carry out of the water, in their mouths, quantities of the mollusks, and leave them to sicken on the shore, and when the dying mussels open their shells, no skill is needed to get at the soft parts of the animal within. They also, if in a hurry for a meal, nibble at the hinge or edges of the valves, and so effect an entrance. The assertion, so often made, that the shells are never scarified by the muskrats is absurd. Of course, when the mussels die on shore, the scarification of the shells is reduced to a minimum; but it needs no patient searching to gather hundreds of shells which as plainly show the marks of the muskrat's teeth as the nibbled nutshells prove the presence of squirrels.

Probably the most remarkable of the stories is to the effect that a muskrat was seen to carefully approach a mussel which at the time had its foot extended. When sufficiently near, the muskrat put forth one paw very quickly and transfixed the mussel's foot with one or more toe-nails; then taking the captured mollusk in its fore-paws, swam to the shore—of course, using its hind-limbs only—and then, in a necessarily erect position, walked up a steep bank, and, once on level ground, proceeded to eat the mussel. Now, even if this muskrat had accomplished three impossibilities, it never could have gotten through with the fourth, that of releasing the mussel from its shell without injury to the latter; yet this marvellous account was given to a scientific society as an explanation of the curious phenomenon that the shells of mussels eaten by muskrats were never broken.

Is there not a sufficiency of wonderful things in the most commonplace corners of nature, without investing the most simple of occurrences with a veil of mystery?

June 15.—I found a cosey seat in the midst of a dense growth of ferns, many of which were shoulder-high. This, the largest of these plants, is called Pteris aquilina by botanists, and certainly a noble plant it is. I could but think of the tropics, and recall the wonderful pictures of forests during the carboniferous era. The likeness to the tropics was largely strengthened when a scarlet tanager came, and, resting in a tree just above me, spread his wealth of color to the sun. Among our birds, usually so sombre-tinted, he seems out of place; yet none would willingly forego his presence. The no-less-strongly marked rose-breasted grosbeak also came near, tarried a moment and was gone; but no birds, great or small, seem partial to the ferns themselves. The warblers wander all about them, but seldom rest among their waving fronds. Do they offer no foothold, or are they actually offensive? In my limited experience in watching native birds I never associate them with ferns. This is to me the more strange, when I remember that the Maryland yellow-throat nests in the very heart of the odoriferous skunk-cabbage.

In the depths of the woods now there is an almost monotonous wealth of green, and we hail a contrasting color with pleasure. Even the trunks of many trees have a tinge of green, except the birches, which are often purely white, and many decked with fluttering ribbons of pale gray bark. Leaving my seat among the ferns for a more open space near by, one

"Wherein the warblers whistle many a tune
Hid in some leafy hollow, late in June,"

here I came upon an islet of color that was a veritable treat. The topmost twigs of a post-oak sapling bore glossy leaves of a deep maroon and scarlet. Constantly the passing bees hovered over them, and, with a loud buzz of chagrin, were off like a flash. It was mere color, not bloom, and offered no sweets to them; but an abundance to my sense of sight, seen, as it was, surrounded by an ocean of green leaves.

And how like the hum of summer seas is the murmur of the wind through the dense foliage. To add to the likeness, the twittering swallows chirped cheery "*peet-weets*," so that, with my eyes closed, I saw troops of sand-pipers tripping on the sand, and chasing each receding breaker on the beach.

But perhaps we can best realize the beauty of vegetation, other than trees, by standing on the edge of a marsh. There is needed the deep black peaty soil and constant moisture to give that perfection to vegetable growth which is so attractive. In the reach of swampy meadow where I linger longest in my rambles, for nature is there a wondrous picture-book, there are clusters of arums worthy of the tropics, and reedy growths that tempt certain warblers that I find nowhere else. The docks, pickerel-weed, and arrow-head here reach perfection, and every leaf, if you scan it closely, will be found a marvel of beauty. It is far too common to look at such objects collectively, and pass through life knowing but the bare fact that leaves are green.

June 19.—In the meadows, this evening, there are apparently thousands of green frogs in every ditch and pool, so great is the volume of sound that fills the air. It is a steady, uniform rattle, occasionally ending in a loud *chuck!* but the cessation is for a moment only, when the ringing rattle is resumed. There is heard with it, at times, the deep bass of the bullfrogs, and it is a pleasing accompaniment. It may strike one as strange to call the cry of the bullfrog pleasant; but this depends upon the occasion and the time, for there are times when it fits admirably with the united voices of frogs, birds, and insects. It is with this frog as with the little red owl. Lowell has justly remarked that the screech-owl, despite his ill name, has a cry that is "one of the sweetest sounds in nature."

The toads also sang until past midnight. They, too, seemed to be all in the meadows, while through the day I find them plentifully in every one of the high, dry, dusty upland fields. More careful observation of this has led to the fact that directly after sundown a large number of the toads go to the meadows and remain until daybreak. A greater abundance of food, I suppose, is the impelling cause of this migration, if such it can be called; but why, I have asked myself, do not these upland toads, that sleep all day, stay in the meadows? Surely there is room enough and quiet enough to enable them to sleep comfortably. I am tired of guessing, and until a toad can be taught to rise and explain, it will probably remain a mystery.

My old toad, that for years has had cosey quarters near the kitchen door, I find goes nightly to the meadows. I followed it yesterday from the doorstep to the tall weeds at the foot of the hill. As it slowly hopped meadow-ward, taking a nearly direct course, it called out at every third or fourth hop, and seemed to wait for an answer. I should have liked to sit up until he came home, to see if he really made a night of it, but concluded the value of the fact not equivalent to the exertion demanded.

In the habits of the catbirds that have lately nested near the garden gate I have thus far noticed a uniformity that leads me to believe that these birds whistle "good-night" at 8 P.M. The yellow-breasted chats, however, repeat their "bon nuit" at even a later hour, and often talk in their sleep the night through. Then again, the pretty indigo-bird says "good-night" at sunset, but, forgetting it, repeats it every hour from then until sunrise, when it whistles "good-morning" as freshly as though it had had an undisturbed night's rest.

I have wondered, at times, if this may not have been one of Thoreau's night warblers.

Lately, as I was about to enter the house, long after dark, an unseen warbler, hidden in the pines, shrilly asked, three times in quick succession, "Where-did-you-get-it?" and then, "Where-*did*-you?" but before I could reply, he was silent as the sombre pines in which he sat dreamily.

June 30.—With what care and circumspection a mammal walks, whether by night or day! At all times, it has its wits about it, and considers not only the actualities but the possibilities of the moment and the place. I was much impressed with this, as I had the opportunity this evening of seeing a mink saunter. Judging from the direction whence it came, it had been surveying the poultry precincts, in anticipation of a midnight raid; at any rate, it had no pressing business now on hand, and was leisurely sauntering towards its home. I stepped aside in the nick of time, to watch, and no stump was more noiseless than myself. I scarcely winked, but, crouching in the angle of a worm fence, I had for my pains a good view of His Carefulness, as he approached. "As he approached," did I say? Well, he stopped as if shot when ten paces off, and stared; it may be five seconds, it may be ten, and then, without my distinguishing a movement, the mink was gone.

This ended my sight-seeing for the day—for the month. As the melancholy thrush rounded off the remnant of the day with song, I turned my steps homeward; but oh! so reluctantly; for however kindly nature might lengthen out these closing hours of June days, there could come no surfeit of their sweetness.

July 1.—Fireflies, this evening, were unusually abundant, and of two very different species. The little yellow flash-light was that one common everywhere, and now seen dotted over the upland fields. In the meadows were streaky blue-lights that rose up from the rank grass, and sailed away over the bushes, like cerulean comets.

The glittering fireflies gild the gathering gloom very fitfully, and it would appear that, unless the atmosphere is moist, they crawl upon the leaves of low bushes, rather than fly much. This, at least, is true of the "blue-lights" in the meadow, a species which I have never yet seen on the upland fields.

The purpose of this flash-light, whether short and dazzling, or prolonged and less illuminative, is still a matter of doubt. It has been suggested that it was to assist it to see in the dark, to enable it to find its companions, or to frighten off its nocturnal enemies. None of these suggestions have been demonstrated; but that it is a common means by which these beetles seek their own kind is the most probable. Occasionally the numbers of these "lightning-bugs," as they are popularly called, is phenomenal. On several occasions, and always preceding a rain-storm, I have seen them so numerous in tangled thickets that the place was really lit up by them, and roosting birds were roused and bewildered by the flickering light. Such instances brought to mind what travellers have recorded of tropical species of fire-beetles, and the lines of Southey are very applicable:

> "Sorrowing we beheld
> The night come on: but soon did night display
> More wonders than it veiled; innumerous tribes
> From the wood-cover swarmed, and darkness made
> Their beauties visible; a while they streamed
> A bright blue radiance upon flowers that closed
> Their gorgeous colors from the eye of day;
> Then, motionless and dark, eluded search,
> Self-shrouded; and anon, starring the sky,
> Rose like a shower of fire."

July 3.—Whether the warmth of the days, or much mechanical labor, is the cause, I do not know; but rambling has suddenly grown distasteful, and I am content with the garden and the pasture-lot beyond. Have they any especial attractions now? None that I know of; but July is not an active month in animal life, and when we doubt the presence of such creatures as we desire to see, then one incentive to ramble is gone; but, on the other hand, idleness prompts to mischief, so I have been experimenting with the king-birds that are nesting in the strawberry apple-tree.

These king-birds are excessively saucy. Not a crow or blackbird can come near but that they rush out and peck at it and scold, much to its annoyance. Why they never turn and punish these impudent fly-catchers I cannot imagine. Their petty attacks upon larger birds do not really indicate courage, for they are so active on the wing that unless directly pursued they can dodge such birds as they follow and snarl at. I have not disturbed those nesting in the apple-tree, although they are at times a veritable nuisance, but I undertook to retaliate for the innumerable attacks upon crows and grakles.

Purchasing a gaudy red-and-yellow bird-kite, made in China, as I judged from its appearance, I waited until the wind was fresh, and then sent it flying over the meadows, in full view of the nesting king-birds. How they scolded! "A hawk so near them, indeed!" they seemed to exclaim. "That is too much," said paterfamilias to his mate, and away he flew, mounting the air, several yards above my very peaceful but agitated kite. As the king-bird swooped down, I gave the string a violent pull, and thus the kite seemed to be darting from him. This emboldened him, and, screaming louder and louder, he swooped nearer and nearer. Now was my chance. Seeing that he was confident of victory, I waited until he swooped once more, when, instead of jerking away the kite, I cut the string. The wind carried it towards the king-bird, which, unable to check its downward progress, plunged headlong through the gaudy paper covering. Frightened nearly to death, down he came, almost to the ground; then, recovering, he bolted westward in a bee-line, and, when last seen, was like a grain of shot in the distant horizon.

Not until late the next day did I see that valiant king-bird; and I doubt if he ever attacks a red hawk again.

July 4. — The translation of birds' notes into plain English is sometimes possible, I have thought, when the birds' actions are a clew to their utterances. This was suggested early to-day by the excitement among the house-wrens, caused by the popping of torpedoes. At every explosion they jumped straight in the air, and scolded in no unmeasured terms when they came down. They scarcely believed the noise to be dangerous, but were not sure whether to tarry in these parts was quite safe; but then, there were their young, and could they be left unprotected? Poor wrens, they had to put up with the racket all the morning, and vent their spite on the dog, at whose ears they darted now and then, and snapped viciously, but taking precious good care not to come too near. I have said the wrens scolded, and upon this point there will scarcely be any disagreement; but can we not go a little further, and classify the utterances of other birds? There is quiet satisfaction in the gentle pee-wee's voice; and who that hears the half-suppressed chuckle of a blue-jay but knows that he has dined at the expense and sorrow of some pair of nesting birds, unable to drive off the murderous intruder. It is the boast of one who claims to have been successful. Yes! but how? Ah! that is another matter, which we will not discuss. A murrain seize all blue-jays that come to my woods in early summer! Then consider the crows. Do we not only need to hear them, to guess their state of mind? The quarrels, the planning, the cry of alarm, the assurances to their timid young; all these utterances are widely different, and can no more be expressed by the syllable "caw" than can our language be said to be the letter "A." It has been said of both rooks and crows, that they hold courts of justice. Let me match this by saying that I once saw a crow "spouting poetry;" at least, it expressed a great variety of sounds, and accompanied them with gestures of the head and wings. It certainly had the appearance of poetical declaration. I afterwards learned that corn soaked in New Jersey whiskey had been placed for that crow, in a field near by.

The cool weather of late has not quieted or driven off all the tropical birds that venture here in midsummer. The humming-birds, for instance, are active and high-tempered, as usual. Their nesting is now about over, and they have more time to pick a quarrel, which they do on all available occasions.

The difficulty of finding the nests of humming-birds is not to be wondered at, when we remember how nicely they are saddled to the upper side of horizontal branches; and usually the limbs of trees that have knotty excrescences, in appearance much like the nests themselves. Still, the cunning of this bird is apt to be one-sided. After effectually hiding the nest, so far as our unaided senses are concerned, they often publish its whereabouts by unwise actions. If you chance to draw very near they lose confidence in their judgment as to the site selected, and dart, first at you, and then towards the nest, until you are actually led to the very spot.

When the eggs are laid, the female sits closely and is looked after by her mate, who brings her food at times, and occasionally takes her place. The following, clipped from a newspaper, is something very remarkable for a humming-bird to do; and why she did it does not seem at all clear. A humming-bird, generally, can cover her nest very well, and the foliage near by always affords a moderate protection:

"In front of a window where I worked last summer was a butternut-tree. A humming-bird built her nest on a limb that grew near the window, and we had an opportunity to watch her closely, as we could look right into the nest from the window. One day there was a heavy shower coming up, and we thought we would see if she covered her young during the storm; but when the first drops fell she came and took in her bill one of two or three large leaves growing close to the nest, and laid this leaf over so it completely covered the nest; then she flew away.

"On looking at the leaf we found a hole in it, and in the side of the nest was a small stick that the leaf was fastened to or hooked on. After the storm was over the old bird came back and unhooked the leaf, and the nest was perfectly dry."

Quite recently an acquaintance, living near me, has published the results of his observations on the breeding habits of our humming-bird. They are strangely different from my own. He writes, the female alone constructed the nest, receiving no assistance from the male bird, who did not show himself from the day the nest was commenced to that when the young birds left it. And also, that during violent thunder-showers the parent bird did not sit upon her nest, and the unprotected young escaped destruction by thrusting their needle-like beaks through the sides of the nest, and grasping the bottom with their long, sharp claws.

On the contrary, I have never found a hummingbird's nest where the female alone took care of the eggs and young. The male bird was always about, and ready to show fight, even when I came too near the nest.

If the nest usually is abandoned during storms, then the "pinning on" of a leaf, as quoted above, is not so marvellous. Few ornithologists, I imagine, however watchful, are likely to see the occurrence repeated.

July 6. — During the night there was a typical shower, with the midsummer accompaniment of heavy thunder and flashing lightning. The latter was very sharp and blinding, and seemed to rattle among the trees, some of which were struck. Such a storm, if any such ever does, ought to have greatly disturbed the birds, and ruined many a nest; but this morning I examined a considerable series, and found scarcely a trace of injury, and no case of abandonment. Song-sparrow nests on the ground were not flooded. The earth about them, and the arrangement of their materials, were such that the water flowed on each side, and left the nest intact. Nests of the brown thrush, too, which are sometimes on the ground, do not seem to suffer from sudden showers. Is it because they have a bulky, loose understratum of coarse sticks, which permit the water to flow by without disturbing the fine lining and the eggs or young?

Is it not probable that birds take the subject of storms into consideration in constructing and locating their nests?

It was the same with a white-eyed greenlet's nest, and the several second-brood nests of thrushes, catbirds and fly-catchers, that I visited. Not one was materially injured; yet several contained young birds. The trees wherein they were placed were violently disturbed, and it was evident the branches had been lashed in such a way as to dislodge both leaves and small twigs; yet no nest was displaced. Would not, in such a case, a bird be able to retain her place, and support the eggs or young, so as to prevent injury thereto? The orioles do this, I know, and only by such a means could the eggs be protected, during very high winds. Of course, with nests as pendent as those of the Baltimore oriole, the motion and consequent danger increase with the length of the nest.

July 9.—I had a talk with Miles Overfield to-day, and have since been on an exploring expedition. To think that for all these years there has been a mineral spring in the mucky meadow, and I not know of it! The truth is, no one can thoroughly exhaust the treasures, even of a hundred acres.

"Draw a line," said Miles, "from the tall pin-oak in

the corner, out into the meadow, a couple of hundred yards, leanin' a little towards the house, and another from the squatty sassyflax tow'rds the canal, and where they cross, if you'll look sharp, you'll find the grass sort of brown and rusty-lookin', and there's the spring."

I followed Miles's directions, which were sufficiently clear, and there, sure enough, was the spring — now, indeed, all a treacherous semi-quicksand, but the traces of the mineral water were unmistakable. I dug a little hole, and waited for the water to settle; then, dipping up a cupful, drank it. Phew! Had the birds' eggs laid in nests about this meadow since the glacial period rotted and remained in this spot, then the flavor of the water could not have been more suggestive of sulphuretted hydrogen. Nevertheless, being told that it was wholesome, I drank another cupful of it. "A gallon of it won't hurt you," Miles had remarked; but I remembered that I was very well, and took no more in anticipation of future illness.

This spring puzzles me. The water is a degree warmer than that of a much larger one of sweet water, two hundred yards distant. There, a great volume of water wells up, clear as crystal and cool as any of the foot-hill springs. Around on every side is a level reach of marshy meadow. Were these two springs a mile apart, or among rocks, I would think nothing of it, for some four miles distant is a sulphur spring; but here, on these meadows, built up of mud and gravel hundreds of feet in depth, it is natural to look for a uniform character of the water. If the source of the sulphur is the distant range of hills, then why should not the water in so long a journey have mixed with that from other mountain spring-heads? If the source of the sulphur is in the meadow, however deep down, ought it not to have been exhausted long before now? Can we conceive of a source of this mineral, or any combination, generating sulphuretted hydrogen in quantities large enough to last for centuries, yet not impregnate every spring within a mile or two, since they all bubble through a loose mass of sand and coarse gravel?

Perhaps this spring has some virtue yet unrecognized. It is to be hoped so; but it need not be the fabled water that perpetuates youth. The songs of birds, the beauty of flowers, the companionship of animate nature, prevent the naturalist from growing old, except in years.

July 16.—Even so early as this there is seen a hint of the coming autumn. The young red-wings are strong of wing and are already flocking. Red-winged blackbirds come in flocks—a few remain all winter—and depart in clouds rather than flocks, if I may use the term. To see a hundred or more now, in the middle of the month, suggests that the wealth of bird-life is diminishing. This is true. A scarcity of food, it may be; or impatience to return to their winter homes. Whatever the cause, there is now a comparative scarcity of birds, and this will become more marked as the season advances. Thank fortune! other forms of life cannot get away so easily, and half the afternoon I have been playing with snakes. There were a pair of them, both garter-snakes; one cross and stout, the other, slender and amiable. The temperaments, as given, never vary a particle. You never find the short, thick species otherwise than ill-tempered; nor the slender one other than gentle. I took them up in my hands, and tried to explain to them, by action, that they had nothing to fear. The amiable serpent was soon convinced, although willing to depart if I would permit. Not so the other. Every caress was met with a bite, or an attempt, for the creature's teeth could not get through my skin. Letting the slender snake wander at will, I set about taming the ill-natured one; but after a good two hours' trial, it still was unwilling to be controlled in any way, and I let it go. Turning about, what was my surprise to see the other, within a few feet of where I had been sitting. I stooped to pick it up, and it offered no resistance, but seemed to be pleased with the attention. Placing it gently upon the grass, I stepped forward a few paces, and, looking round, found that it was following me.

It is a curious phenomenon in the psychology of serpents, that this marked difference in disposition should occur in species of the same genus. These two garter-snakes are very abundant and do not differ in any discoverable feature in their habits; yet the difference as pointed out is noticeable to the most casual observer.

Occasionally individuals of ill-tempered species have been known to be amiable. I was lately told the following incident: A gentleman noticed an enormous black snake lying stretched out at full length on the top rail of a fence, sunning himself. Approaching closely, he surveyed his snakeship carefully, but made no attempt to molest him. A few days later he found the same snake on the fence, as before, and approached a little nearer. This continued for a couple of weeks, when the snake permitted itself to be gently stroked about the head and body; and from this time an intimacy sprang up between the snake and that gentleman which lasted for several years, when the snake suddenly disappeared.

A curious feature of this case was that, even when accompanied by the gentleman in whom the snake had so much confidence, it would never permit a stranger to touch it. If they persisted, it would dart to its underground retreat.

My own experiences with black snakes are quite limited, but that they are cunning, and therefore intelligent, I have no doubt. A chance remark of Heckewelder's, in his work on "Indian Nations," seems to indicate that the Indians had long been convinced that it was a cunning serpent, and I am disposed to accept their testimony in such matters as essentially correct. Heckewelder says the Indians gave to Gen. Wayne the name of "Black Snake," because they say he had all the cunning of this animal, who is superior to all other snakes in the manner of procuring his food. He hides himself in the grass, with his head only above it, watching all around to see where the birds are building their nests, that he may know where to find the young ones when they are hatched.

Assuming this to be true, we have here an instance not only of cunning, but of a very excellent memory.

This seems incredible, but Mr. Romanes, in his volume on "Animal Intelligence," remarks that snakes "are well able to distinguish persons, and that they remember their friends for a period of at least six weeks." If, therefore, a tamed snake can remember a person for six weeks, there is nothing very remarkable in its retaining the localities of birds' nests for a shorter period; for between the building of the nest and hatching of the eggs less than half that time elapses.

Of the eleven species of snakes found about home, it is sufficient to say that my general impression is that they are cowardly but cunning. Blessed with acute hearing and sharp sight, they use both of these faculties to the best advantage; so that, while harmless as doves, as serpents they are wise.

July 20.—It was a pleasant change to be on Crosswicks Creek to-day. The whole character of the country was radically different from that where I am accustomed to ramble, yet, being but two miles away, one can scarcely call it "foreign parts." Of all that I saw, nothing proved more attractive than a half-dozen beautiful kill-deer plovers, that tripped over the sandy shores of the creek, just ahead of the boat; tame enough to let us see them very plainly, and sufficiently confident to pursue their food, while they kept an eye on us. When a bird is so wild that it will only watch us, as we stare at it, then it is as uninteresting as a stuffed specimen. What were these birds after? Why were they there? Such are the questions a practical naturalist asks, and delights in determining, howsoever difficult the task.

Just what the little kill-deers were feeding upon I cannot say, but I found that, like woodcocks, they buried their bills deeply in the sand, and left rows of holes over its surface, often as regular in appearance as those encircling an apple-tree, and made by the little woodpecker. I suppose it will be claimed that I should have shot one of these birds to learn the character of its food. This I always intend to do, but defer until the next time; hoping in the meanwhile to find out by other means. And I did get a clue to the matter. A mass of the wet sand was allowed to trickle through my fingers, and I found mollusks, crustaceans, and undetermined small fry in it, all of which would be acceptable to the plover's palate.

This plover is comparatively rare now, and is a creekside and river-shore bird; yet, half a century ago, these birds appeared yearly, in abundance, as early as March, and frequented the upland fields even more than the meadows. They followed the ploughman at his work, and, running along the newly turned furrow, gathered up what insect larvæ were exposed. Then, later, they nested in these same fields, and their cheery *kill-dee, kill-dee*, was a familiar and pleasant bird-note. Now they are gone. How are the fields changed, that they should visit them no more?

In a pebbly shallow, where the waters were nearly at a standstill, I was delighted to find a pair of stone-catfish, shovelling the pebbles with their broad, flat noses. At times, a flat stone three or four inches square would be found, and under this one or two would work their way, and there remain for several minutes. These fish seemed to find food on many of the stones, and nipped and tugged at objects that offered some resistance. I found these objects to be small mollusks, known to conchologists as Ancylus. These fish had also eaten other shells in abundance, as proved by an examination of their stomachs; for after tiring of watching them, a skilful dip of a hand-net landed them in the boat.

It was here, just as we were about to return home, that I saw a fish-hawk under peculiar circumstances. The bird flew over at a considerable height, and then, suddenly turning, sailed slowly downward towards the creek. We checked our course in an instant and waited. The hawk alighted at the very edge of the water, and, wading in a few inches, searched the bottom carefully, as it appeared to us. We remained "stock still" for fully five minutes, watching him, yet the bird did not find anything to eat, and then, without a sound, walked to the shore, spread his wings, and was gone. Had it been a heron or a bittern, there would have been nothing strange in all this, but it was not hawk-like, even fish-hawk-like. Then, what do these birds eat but fish? And do they ever go a-fishing on foot?

The fish-hawk, or osprey, is one of the very few birds whose appearance, in spring, is at all regular. Along the sea-coast, it is said to regularly appear on the 21st of March; never a day earlier or later. I will not dispute it. I have known them to come to the river and Poaetquissings on that date, and never earlier; but are they never later? It has appeared to me, that if they always came on the 21st, they kept themselves hidden for a few days. It is quite certain that those who live along the sea-shore are as a rule far better observers of animal life than the benighted inland folk; and as they are positive of the fish-hawk's regular habits, let no inlander dare dispute it.

July 24.—Among the fruit-trees in the garden sat an indigo-bird that sang sweetly for a long time; but in spite of the shower of last evening, it seemed to have in its throat the dust of the past desiccated week.

How quickly our pleasant places might be converted into deserts, were rain withheld, is to be realized in summer when a dry week occurs. Nature does not store up a reserve supply of moisture, to provide against drought, and vegetation, in particular, suffers first and most. The leaves, of late, have rattled as I touched them; but now their May-day elasticity has come back, thanks to the passing shower.

A nest of white-eyed greenlets has been in sight, but out of reach, for a week past, and to-night I determined to see the contents. Young birds, by this time, of course, and ready to fly, perhaps. After a scramble through briers and some climbing, I got a view of the nest from above. The contents, a young cowpen-bird. I removed it, out of spite, and sat the shivering chick on the top rail of the fence. The silly greenlets scolded, instead of thanking me, and fed the fraud with as much care as though it had not murdered their own offspring.

It is strange that these birds should be so intelligent

and yet should be so easily fooled by the lazy cow-bunting.

July 31.—There is something delightfully cool and refreshing in the very mention of fern-clad nooks; but the coolness and all that, which wooes you thither, has a charm for a few mosquitoes and a bloodthirsty gnat, which for persistent persecution exceeds the former, so it is not always a bed of roses upon which you recline, if you seek a shady retreat among ferns.

But there are ferns and ferns; some, lovers of swamps; others, content with a little dampness, and growing where the rambler may go dry-shod. There are twenty species, at least, of these pretty plants, and I wandered into a dense cluster of the largest of them all to-day. It is the bracken, and as I stood I drew their waving tops above my head, and was completely hidden. All was deeply, darkly, beautifully green, and the rippling of the brook, near by, added to the coolness of the nook. Dry, dusty, and parched midsummer was, for the time, forgotten.

This bracken is a common fern; but several others are as prominent features of the damper parts of the woods. Leaving the bracken, I had to walk scarcely one hundred yards to find cinnamon fern in abundance. Not so stately, it is true, but yet nothing insignificant about it; and now it is seen at its best. The fruit panicle, a vigorous growth, with a curiously curled end, dotted with sporangia and clothed with a bright cinnamon-colored wool, is the more beautiful for the setting of dark green that surrounds it late in May.

There are two other varieties of this fern, but neither so common in this vicinity; for I am speaking of the flora of a farm, not a county or even a township.

Not right among them, yet not far away, are spleen-worts and shield-ferns, handsome always, but not so striking to the average rambler, unless he is something of a botanist. These common names refer to the character of the seed-growths, and perhaps those who have seen a human spleen can trace a resemblance between it and them, in the case of those ferns called spleen-worts. The resemblance is a very fanciful one. The others are more intelligibly named; but, after all, what folly it is to continue the use of such names for plants when far better ones are known to a few and accessible to all. Why not call the bracken, pteris, as the botanist does; and speak of the osmunda, asplenium, or aspidium, as the case may be. Let nomenclature be simple and intelligible, so far as possible; even descriptive, when practicable; and then let such names stand for common use the wide world over. Why professional botanists should monopolize the proper names, and the common crowd rest satisfied with meaningless nicknames or nothing, I have never been able to determine; unless it be that this common crowd, in all that pertains to natural history, either glories in its ignorance or is influenced by teachings, not yet unknown among us, that such knowledge is dangerous. How dangerous no one knows. Only yesterday, the mother of a promising youth boasted of her son's taste for natural history. "Nip it in the bud," was the advice of a—well, let us say, mistaken man; but I harbor harsher thoughts as I write the words.

Leaving my botanical thoughts with the ferns in the gully and along the hillside, I grew enthusiastic on reaching the pasture-fields. Up from the red-clover aftermath there arose a dozen or more beautiful upland plover, as they are usually called, and whistled in their peculiarly charming manner.

To hear these birds, far overhead, whistling among the clouds, is no uncommon occurrence, but they seldom visit our fields. A few miles away, in Pennsylvania, they have favorite feeding-grounds, and eastward, near the sea-coast, they deign to alight. With us, it is their custom to pass over and leave the rambler thankful even for their song and the sportsman chagrined that they see no merit in our acres.

Having botanized a very little in the morning, and given at least one bird a passing thought, later in the day, I looked for shells along the river-shore as the sun was setting. It was the abundance of mussel-shells that led my thoughts towards molluscan life. If we have not an abundance of species, certainly there is compensation in the number of individuals. But after all, the different kinds are not so very few. There are seven, if not others. Three are true unios, as I prefer to call them, for "mussel" is an ugly word; then there are two of another genus, but of same general appearance. Open one, and you will find the arrangement of the hinge quite different. There are no long, slender dentations at one side of the broad cardinal teeth; hence they are not true unios, but Margaritanæ, or pearl-bearers; but do not expect a pearl in every one you find; at least, in those of the Delaware River. Then there are two mussels with toothless hinges, and prettily called anodons, a name which would do credit to our language, and should pass into common use. These are, collectively, our largest shells. While a family likeness runs through the series, they vary considerably in outline, from nearly globular to an elongated oval; and as much in color. While many are a dirty green or brown, others are almost straw-yellow with broad bands of dark green. These are very pretty, and yet, as they lie in the water among pebbles, they do not show to advantage; so why should these colors have been evolved? Are they protective? Color is not confined to the outer surfaces of the shells; the interior is often beautiful. The purple anodon is so-called because of the rich coloring of the inner surface of the shell. Here again, the origin and object of color is a puzzling problem. Neither the animal itself, nor any of its kind, nor any associated form of life, can enjoy or be profited by the wealth of color that during the lifetime of the animal is wrapped in utter darkness. If the colors of these shells are of any use, the world has yet to learn the fact; and young naturalists need never despair of making a discovery.

Perhaps you cannot say that mussels are intelligent, yet they have a common-sense way of doing things, which is entertaining. I watched them walking about the sand this evening, and was surprised at the progress they made. Projecting their foot a short distance beyond the slightly opened valves or shells, they thrust it into the sand, and, giving themselves a jerky twist, were hinge up and valve-edge down, and so they travelled;

the foot taking a new hold constantly and pulling both the creature and his house, leaving in the sand a slightly tortuous furrow. Many were moving about in this way, yet they seemed never to collide; nor did any couple stop and talk. There are very many animals that have observable means of inter-communication of ideas, but mussels are not to be classed with them. Unios may have something in advance of mere consciousness, but it is not demonstrable.

They know, of course, when the tide falls and rises. As the tide fell, and these sands became bare, the mussels rested from their journeying and sank slowly out of sight, leaving no trace behind. I found them to go as deep as eighteen inches; and at other times—for I could not wait to see it repeated this evening—I have watched them returning, as the waters slowly crept over the sand. They came with it. No sooner was there a trace of clear water above the river-shore, than a point of shells could be seen peeping through, and minute after minute this shell kept pace with the steadily deepening waters, until the whole surface was once more exposed.

At such times, the least unusual motion will startle them, and back again into the loose sand they go, remaining for several minutes. If by this time the water has materially deepened, and they have had their fears allayed, they are less deliberate in their movements, and with two or three jumps, if I may call them so, they come again to the smooth surface of the sand.

These mussels of the river and Crosswicks Creek are not the only bivalves that are found here. If we dip up a handful of mud from the bottom of the meadow ditch, and let it pass through a fine sieve, there will probably be left a few white or whitey-brown little mollusks, that I can best describe in a general way as baby clams. Certainly, as compared with a hard-shelled marine clam or quahog, these little fellows from the meadow ditches are very babyish in size. They vary from about one fifth to one quarter of an inch in length, and a little less in breadth. We might live for a century on the very bank of a ditch, yet never see one, so secluded do they keep themselves. It is to be hoped they enjoy life; but how hard it is to realize that such creatures are conscious.

There are two genera of these little baby clams, called *Pisidium* and *Sphærium*, the former having one siphon, the latter two. To the untutored eye they look much alike, and the conchologist must be questioned, if you would know more about them.

August 2.—I am puzzled to know how the law of evolution operates in regard to the various utterances of birds. Yesterday a pair of chipping sparrows were greatly excited over the departure of their third brood. These little birds were fairly strong on the wing, and able to fly promptly, even from the ground to branches high overhead. Yet the parent birds were not satisfied, and, by a series of chirps and cries of alarm, which every bird-eating animal could readily interpret, they invited every snake, mink, weasel, and other foe of birds to hasten to the spot. Most snakes and certain mammals, and probably sparrow-hawks, are attracted by these cries of birds, and, hurrying to the spot, often seize the young which otherwise would have escaped. It is generally supposed that these cries of distress indicate that the parent birds have already detected a lurking enemy, and their anxiety overcomes their discretion, so that they too loudly caution their inexperienced young. This is certainly not always the case. Yesterday there was no foe near, but a cat was drawn to the spot, and would have remained, had I permitted it. Very often I have noticed the same thing, both near the house, when cats were brought to the scene, and in the woods, where other enemies responded.

It is not always necessary to be abroad to know what transpires in the bird-world of the house-yard. The family all know when a brood of Carolina wrens leave the nest. The old birds get so excited over it, they endanger not only their offspring, but themselves.

When once danger really threatens, to sound an alarm, as do the robins and other thrushes, is the part of wisdom; but the credit due for this amount of intelligence is quite offset by the habit of proclaiming a brood's departure, as so many birds do. This is the climax of absurdity, yet the birds seem as yet to have gained no wisdom from experience, although this has often been sad enough. It is but natural to suppose that evolution should operate in such cases, that these birds would acquire such power of discrimination between utterances that endanger and those that indicate its actual presence. The ordinary song of a bird certainly is unheeded by the lurking foes of the songster, for at such a time the bird's attention is not so wrapped in some one circumstance that it could not heed all else that transpired. If I am not greatly in error, when our sparrows, wrens, and other small birds give their young a silent send-off, there will be a large gain in their numbers. Invited destruction, at present, works sad havoc among many species.

August 3.—In rambling about to-day, twelve miles from home, but still on the banks of Crosswicks Creek, I found many snails of two or three species. Their abundance led me to institute a careful search for them, and I soon found that my cousin's hillside was far more favored with terrestrial mollusca than is the hillside at home. Why? I asked myself, and have not yet found the reason. Here, as at home, were chestnuts, oaks, birch, beech, and sassafras, rotten logs and dead leaves in abundance, damp ground and scattered springs in like manner characterizing the surface soil, and the outlook the same.

The prominent form was a true snail, that was readily recognized as to the "species," by its white, porcelain-like lip. The others were smaller, and inconspicuous, in comparison. There are six species of these mollusks that the rambler can look for with some confidence. Three of them are nearly or quite an inch in diameter, when full-grown, and so are readily seen; the others, smaller, and must be sought for with more care; but snail-hunting, let it be said, is not exhilarating. As Prof. Morse has truly stated, "certainly a more unassuming subject could not well be studied, for aside from the soothing pleasure of lying down, dorsal region uppermost, in some secluded grove, and hunting for half a day among the decaying leaves, upturning the different layers of successive autumnal deposits of withered foliage, . . . aside from this quieting pursuit, we have no stirring incidents in their life to contemplate, no frantic hops, skips, and jumps of the insect tribe, no terrible bites to dread, or poisonous stings to shrink from, no enemy of our husbandry to baffle, no giant stride or rapid speed to wonder at, for the snail is proverbially slow in every respect. When disturbed, it does not, like many other animals, struggle violently to escape, but ceases motion, or quietly withdraws itself within its shell. Even the heart, which in higher animals, when agitated, pulsates with increasing energy, in a snail, under similar excitement, throbs with a slower motion."

Two of the six true snails are known as the hairy and long-toothed species, and these are not usually found where the larger species occur. In this neighborhood they seek nooks and crannies about roots of large trees, where there is sure to be collected a considerable amount of decayed wood, in the form of a coarse powder. Into this, if it is at all damp, these little snails love to burrow.

Besides the snails proper, there are snail-like shells also to be found, but they will need more care in the search, as their smaller size renders them inconspicuous, unless, as sometimes occurs, you happen upon a colony.

One species is known as the arboreal snail, the other as the cellar snail; of the first, Prof. Morse says, "In New England there is hardly an old log by the roadside but that shelters them." Here, they are not so common, perhaps. The cellar snail must be looked for in localities such as the common name suggests. Here it is difficult to find, but that they do occur is unquestionable. "This species is not a native of this country. It has been imported from Europe to our shores through the medium of commerce. As these snails are generally confined to cellars and gardens, their eggs have probably been brought to this country on wine-casks or on the roots of hothouse plants;" this their history, as given by Prof. Morse, who adds, "a lady in Portland, in whose cellar the writer collected a great many, stated that the snails annoyed her by crawling into her pans of milk. We can well imagine an enthusiastic collector delighted in being able to dredge specimens from the bottom of his coffee-cup at the breakfast-table!"

A third form of these land-snails is very different in the form of its shell, "being ovate-conic, and not rolled in a plane." There is no marked difference in its habits, beyond the fact that they are more frequently found in large numbers. Thus, on the last day of May, in a limited spot in the meadows, were hundreds of them, of all sizes, apparently sunning themselves.

I have noticed none doing so very lately, but our pretty checkered snail has no fancy for an approach even to an anhydrous condition, and migrates to damper localities, as the often-mentioned midsummer drought begins to assert itself.

Such processions of these pretty snails always remind me of how slight is one's ability to find any small creatures, when scattered through the woods. One need scarcely expect to capture more than half a dozen in an acre of woods, and yet, from some leafy hollow of half that area, which, in the eyes of a snail, has for months been delightfully damp, often a hundred or more will issue forth together, directing their course towards the nearest water, either a bubbling spring or a moist bed of fern-embowered mosses.

It would be inconsistent to add one word to our local weather-lore, having held it in such profound contempt for years; but when snails are seen migrating from dead leaves to green moss, expect a continuance of dry weather. I purposely say "expect," for I have known the one incident not to be followed by the other.

August 7.—We have had a series of hard rains, gentle showers, pour-downs, Scotch mists, and wet fogs. It ought to have washed the dust from the birds' throats, but it has not. The clear ring of a June morning is wanting.

The most noticeable bird-features of the present are the flockings of various species. The bobolinks of last May are now russet-coated reed-birds, and associated with them are numbers of last spring's orioles, with much the same colored plumage. Are the orioles deceived by this, and think the reed-birds are their cousins, near or remote? The flight of the two species is quite similar, and many a sportsman, eager for the first "reed" of the season, has brought down an oriole, to his disgust.

August 8.—The wild cherries are ripening, and the robins are happy. They devour every cherry with evident relish, and twitter their satisfaction between each morsel swallowed. As to the pits, they rain down upon the grass, and before winter the ground will be well strewn with them. On the hillside, these fruit-stones sprout in May, and, if not browsed by the cattle, form a dense thicket, waist-high, by early autumn. The rapidity with which a country may become covered with trees, if left undisturbed, is realized when we see that what, last summer, was smooth grass, is now a plantation of cherry sprouts. Startling as it may seem, it takes but three years to have a cherry grove, with trees ten feet in height. After that their growth is slower; but a decade is only needed to convert a farm into a forest.

After the cherries come the purple berries of the poke, and the robins again have a feast. These berries are so full of juice that the ground beneath the bushes is sometimes stained by it, and the muscles of the birds are darkened with it; yet, although the fruit is poisonous to man, it does not affect the birds; but, on the other hand, people have suffered slight toxic effects from eating freely of poke-gorged robins.

August 10.—A half-cloudy day—"warm, cool, and pleasant," as Uz Gaunt would say—I was out early for a long ramble. Following the hillside, and raiding the meadows at times, for some supposed treasure, dimly discerned from a distance, at length I found myself in a village. A brief encounter with a fool made village-life distasteful, and I hurried back to Crosswicks Creek, which here tarries to move the machinery of three mills, and then moves on, unconscious of the blessings it has bestowed upon mankind. A way to do good, by the way, which mankind should imitate. The creek here had one merit, not common to all its bends, there were numbers of beautiful trees upon the banks—elms, liquid-ambar, hickories, oaks. Let him be pitied who cannot enjoy a perfect tree, and here were some that grew up among the Indians, and looked upon white men as strangers. This was a pleasing thought, and I was painted and feathered, and paddled a canoe, while I rested under the shade of a spreading white oak, gazing with unwearied eyes over

> "Meadows trim with daisies pied
> Shallow brooks and *Crosswicks* wide."

There were wanting towers and battlements, but high overhead, "bosom'd high in tufted trees," were warbling greenlets, that sang as sweetly as ever did any

> "high-born maiden
> In a palace tower,
> Soothing her love-laden
> Soul in secret hour
> With music sweet as love, which overflows her bower."

Whenever a philosophical rambler comes to a tall tree, he should feel it desirable to pause and make its acquaintance. If the trees cannot be said to be sociable, they, at least, do not immediately make known all their merits; and to tarry an hour in their shade is to learn much that would not be expected when hurrying by. Then, be it remembered to the credit of the trees, they do not begrudge their shade; the traveller is welcome always; but when we ask for a cup of water at the neighboring house, how often is it given with a feeling of fear that we may bite a piece from the cup's rim. I have often been tempted to do so.

When homeward bound, I gathered a handful of meadow bloom. To specify it botanically I am sorry I cannot, but I can be intelligible, perhaps, while yet so ignorant. There was scarlet lobelia and white feathery bloom of sweet odor, and snowy globes from the elder; primroses, and bits of pink, purple, and red from among the tall grasses in the meadow. As a gathering of bloom, it was rich in color, sweet in fragrance, and dainty in outline—so much so that I was charmed with it, and scarcely felt my ignorance of botany, a subject that should be in the range of every countryman's knowledge.

Birds again in plenty! and how little seems needed to make any place complete, if there be birds and birds! Even should they quarrel, we are entertained, and rush through tangled briers and over quicksands to see which whips. I have seen more than one wildly excited mortal following a pair of fighting humming-birds, through trouser-tearing thickets; yet they would grow indignant were they invited to a cock-pit. There is a difference, I suppose; but, after all, is it so very great?

Of all animal life, startling and strange as so much of it is, there is no one form that is so marvellously inconsistent and unfathomable as a human being.

Soon after reaching home, and while dining, suddenly the windows rattled, then the house shook, and every one stared at his neighbor. Each demanded of all the others, "What is it?" and no one thought of an earthquake until it was over; but such it was. It lasted ten seconds, and it is astonishing how much may transpire in that brief time. How rapidly, for instance, we thought. Once a thing of the past, I ran out of doors, in hopes of a repetition of the phenomenon, so as to have a more satisfactory experience of the sensation which a mild earthquake produces; but no second quaking occurred. Going to the meadows, I found no water spilled from the ditches, and the happy-go-lucky fishes were moving about as unconcernedly as ever.

After it had been thoroughly discussed, we all concluded it was as much of an earthquake as we cared to experience, and unlike John Gilpin, if another occurs, may we *not* be there to see.

August 12.—Again, this morning, I heard the charming whistling of the upland plover. The birds were high overhead and flying westward, as usual. It is curious that I never see them flying eastward, and, as they must necessarily come and go across the state, why should they be silent on their eastward trips; do they pass over in that direction only at night?

When pasturing sheep was much more usual than now, the golden plover was, during this month, a common bird on our closely cropped fields. They were sure to be found where the sheep were grazing, and it was often sorely vexatious to the gunner that, manœuvre as he would, he could get no shots, on account of the proximity of the sheep. The plover, if flushed at all, would skim the ground, about as high as a sheep's back, and twist in and out among them, until beyond range, when away they would go, with a shrill whistling laugh of defiance.

But these birds have years ago sought fresh fields and pastures new.

Crows, as all the world knows, are cunning birds, and they are excellent judges of watermelons. Of late, they watch the patches very carefully, as they have sometimes been outwitted and captured; but when the coast is clear and they have the field to themselves, how systematically they work! Their part of the melon is the seeds, and they consider the flavor of them to be in proportion to the thrifty and plump condition of the fruit. They know, too, when the melon is ripe; for then the seeds are full-grown, oily, and delicious. The farmer boasts of the "thirty-pounders" and larger ones even, of which he has so many. He slaps his trousers pocket and hears the jingling of the dollars he is to get. Has he not rags, tin-pans, and a scarecrow in the patch? He can rest easy; his melons are safe; Monday, they will be ready to pick. But Saturday is more convenient to the crow, and, with sentinels posted, in a stray bird or two enter at a time, and plug these noble melons for their seeds. The little ones are all ignored; the green ones passed by; the melons ripe on Monday are the crow's favorites, and on Saturday he gathers his portion. Ask no favor of the farmer on Monday morning.

As a matter of fact, the seeds of a small melon are as good as those of fruit ten times the weight, and are more easily reached by the crows; yet they always, I believe, destroy the largest melons. I have observed this very frequently, and, as a loser by their depredations, speak from unpleasant experience. Still, I am a friend to the crow.

Katydids are singing to-night for the first time. This I record as my experience; but others have heard them for a week past. It is very strange. I am a professional listener. My business with nature is to catch the firstlings of every phenomenon, but I never do it. I have never mentioned hearing a bird's song or an insect's stridulation, or caught a glimpse of an early snake, or carried home a first blossom, but that some one claims to have been ahead. It was so to-night, with the katydids. I heard them for the first time this season, and the whole family assure me I am late in the matter, late by a week; yet for the past fortnight I have been listening for them. It is discouraging, to say the least.

First or not first, there is to be frost in six weeks, or a week earlier. Such is the common belief, and generally it proves true. There is sure to be a little frost in September, but it is so very local it leaves no impression upon any frequented spots. No growing crop is likely to be injured. Some extra-early riser may spy it out in some low-lying swamp, and he duly reports it. Generally it is thin ice by the time it reaches the village paper; when, in fact, what little there was is gone before sunrise, and the average mortal would never expect such a thing had been. I have heard it said the most trying droughts are when it rains every day; and so with the early September frosts, they come often during the hottest weather.

A curious whim, too, about katydids is that you have but to put your hand against the tree on which one sits, while he stridulates, and immediately the pea-green musician is silent. My practical grandfather used, in this way, to quiet all that were near the house, before retiring. He did cause some to quit their racket, as I remember the matter; but long before the old gentleman was asleep they were singing again. He thought not, but was it not because the sound was less distinct in-doors, and hearing less acute, as sleepiness came on? With him, imagination met the requirements of the case, and confirmed him as to the efficacy of the remedy. Scores of experiments, of late, do not tend to confirm one's faith in the matter. If the trees are very large, the mere fact of touching them is insufficient, and a hearty kick will often do nothing towards stopping the noise. A decided thrill must be sent through the tree, which, being felt by the insect, quiets it for a time. The old notion of an electrical influence being exerted cannot be verified. Judging from my labors of last summer, nothing short of blows from a sledge-hammer, frequently repeated, will keep the creatures still; but then, how long would a tree stand such hammering?

August 17.—At sunrise, and for two hours after, there was a dense fog covering all the meadows, and a pale, creamy fog half veiled the uplands. Nature was quiet.

Without waiting for the air to clear, I walked to the elms that overhang Poaetquissings, at the great bend, and there hunted for shells until my back ached. Did I find any? Shall I say hundreds or thousands? If it did not take too much of a day, I could gather a million.

Not in a great variety, it is true, but in individuals, literally countless.

These mollusks were elongate and twisted to the right; oval and twisted to the left; flat and rolled on themselves, like an old-fashioned ginger-cake. They crawled over the stems of the lilies, the projecting trunks of the trees, stones, mud, dead leaves, and even came a little way out of the water, at times, although strictly aquatic animals.

These shells were not beautiful, and I can scarcely say why I hunted them so eagerly; unless to be able to determine just how many kinds were to be found. This I by no means accomplished, but was content to have a fine series of three genera, which were found in one limited spot. It is hard to describe their differences, except by giving anatomical details; so suffice it to say, I had Limnæas that were twisted to the right, and Physas, twisted to the left, and Planorbes, that were flat and curled like a watch-spring. Collectively we can call them "water-snails."

"These snails have the power of crawling or floating along the surface of the water, the creeping disk being just level with the surface and the shell hanging beneath. When they wish to sink, a portion of the air contained in the lung-cavity is expelled, and a slight clicking sound is heard accompanying this movement."

I had almost forgotten a fourth form. From blades of broad grass that were waving in the current I gathered a quantity of little shells, that had no twist about them, but were more like little bowls turned bottom upward. They are water-snails too, but let us say Ancylus, and be done with it. The naturalist has no special right to the use of these names, to the exclusion of the contemplative rambler, who also loves to see these creatures.

Having reported the result of my collecting to the schoolmaster, he bestowed upon me such a pitying smile. "And didn't you find any Goniobases, Valvatæ, Melanthos, or Lioplax?" he asked, with a frown or a look of disgust. Find them! I'm glad I did not. Had I known the probability of encountering such creatures I should have stayed at home.

The schoolmaster cooled; his disgust became sympathy, and I learned that these startling names were of other water-snails, pretty and innocent as those I had gathered. They are not found, however, in Poaetquissings; the water is too quiet, the bottom too muddy. It needs a river-bank stroll or a row on Crosswicks Creek at low tide. Then we can find them also, perhaps as abundantly as I found the others. And a word here. If you show a friend a river-snail, do not shout Goniobasis in his ear; break it to him gently.

A mid-August day is apt to be a lazy one. What birds I heard sang only in the most listless manner. One fly-catcher, in particular, drawled out pēē and postponed the wēē until cooler weather. It even raised its wings at times, to dart after a fly, concluded it was too hot, and sat still.

The bobolinks are now reed-birds, and flocks of them are gathering on the reedy meadows that line the west bank of Crosswicks Creek. The seed of these tall grasses is not yet ripe, but they find a substitute, I suppose, and never go hungry. The marsh-harriers know just as well as does the gunner that the birds are there, and to-day several of these broad-winged hawks were dipping over the reeds, beating their tops, that the frightened birds might show themselves. I do not believe they gain much for their trouble, as the cover is too dense and easily entered for ever so large a falcon to catch so small a finch. Such sights are said to be indications of the close of summer; and yet we have had but a part of summer weather, as yet; and it may be weeks before there are chilly nights, that quiet the hum of insects, bid the frogs and toads cease their drowsy monotones, and favor us with a leaf-painting frost.

The swamp rose-mallow is now in bloom, and the prettiest spots are where the congregated white and red blossoms bedeck the scene. Here is an admirable instance of where distance lends enchantment to the view. These flowers are not pretty when closely examined. They are coarse in texture, rude in arrangement, harsh in coloring; yet, collectively and from afar, they equal the frost's best efforts to variegate the forest.

A cool, wet summer has the advantage of preserving the foliage until September. To-day I could count nine distinct shades of green on the hillside, which spread out as a beautiful panorama before me, as I sat on the edge of the marsh. It was living two lives in one to sit there. A turn of the head was only needed to pass from forest to fen; and two more dissimilar aspects of nature, yet so close together, could not be conceived. Of the two, the marsh or mucky meadow was the more attractive. The dense growth concealed so much that piqued the curiosity. Every unfamiliar sound suggested some strange creature, and I anticipated monsters lifting their heads above the reeds, as the sea-serpents sometimes do for the benefit of a favored few. I half-dreamed of monstrous serpents, gigantic turtles, and elephantine batrachians; recalled the wondrous beasts of tertiary times, and with their images, as restored by the genius of Cope, before me—fell asleep. Perhaps for half an hour; possibly for but a moment, but I can realize, in thought, how finally I did come to my proper senses with a bound, as my dreams seemed about to prove true. A booming bittern, that had been napping near by, arose from the marsh with a "barbaric yawp," that shook me with more vigor than the petty earthquake of a week ago. Did that unseen bittern give the turn to my thoughts, by its presence, when I had taken my seat by the edge of the marsh? Experiences suggestive of such a fact are of so common occurrence that I half believe it. Half believe; for wholly believing anything we cannot fathom is scarcely a wise thing to do. It is easy to learn, but a task to unlearn, and to reconstruct our modes of thought.

The flicker has ceased to be a woodpecker. I found him to-day running over the closely cropped meadow with as much ease as ever a robin possessed. He was chasing black beetles, and, ever and anon, overturned chips that were likely to harbor them. After a meal of a dozen or more (Phœbus! what digestion!) off he flew to a tall hickory, and forthwith flicker was a true woodpecker again.

From this time until frosts have driven the crickets into winter-quarters, the flickers will depend upon these insects for food. I believe I have never seen any other of our woodpeckers run about on the ground. If the country should become treeless, this bird might remain, and would only be required to build its nest, like a sand martin, in a cliff, to be perfectly at home.

Where the bank of Poaetquissings Creek suddenly rises to form a pretty knoll, that adds much beauty to the intervale, there have been muskrats or raccoons digging with vigor, and there is now loose earth from the summit to the base. Poking into it, I brought a beautiful stone gorget to view; then an arrowhead, and another, and another, until, thanks to the burrowing mammal, I had a series of weapons, ornaments, and implements that sufficed to recall the life-history of the unfortunate Indians that once possessed the land, gave to Poaetquissings its name, and lived happy lives, if our old historian was not mistaken when he said this creek is by nature supplied with everything man can desire.

August 31 was beautifully bright and clear, and so it should be. All through the night it rained with sufficient violence, I thought, to wash all nature away; but when I awoke, at sunrise, I found everything as I had left it, but cleaner. Every pebble in the path was free of grit; not a vestige of dust on any leaf, and by some means, I know not what, the flowers of yesterday had not been battered or their colors washed out. Rose-mallow in the meadows; golden-rod along the road; a cluster of crimson sumac on the hillside, and scattered patches of color everywhere, greeted the eye. "Summer, this year, means to leave a good impression, for to-day she abandons us," I remarked to the winds. A Carolina wren heard me, and yelled indignantly, "No, she doesn't! No, she doesn't!" "Yes, she does," I replied, and the excitable wren grew more indignant and emphatic; and half that morning screamed, as it flew along the hillside, "No, she doesn't! No, she doesn't!"

CHAPTER XI.

SEPTEMBER SUNSHINE.

My first ramble for the month was on the 12th. As I passed down the clay-pit road a red squirrel stopped and stared, sang sibilantly for ten seconds, and concluded the utterance with a sharp twang, like the snapping of a fiddle-string. This, I thought, was made by stamping its hind-feet on the bark of the tree; at least a movement of the limbs accompanied the sound. Then the sibilant noise was repeated, followed by the trembling legs and the abrupt twang! The whole performance was far more like the sound of machinery than any caused by an animal, either vocally or mechanically.

It would need a botanist to determine the time of year, judging by the surroundings. The animal life certainly has, as yet, assumed no autumnal aspects. I can find nothing to intimate that in a few weeks, perhaps a few days, there will be a chilly northwest wind, and then a frost. What preparation is being made goes on very secretly.

It is five days since I was last on the meadows and took a hillside ramble, but five days can work a great change. To-day the first of the large hawks made its appearance. High overhead a pair of red-tailed buzzards floated, with apparently motionless wings, for hours. They described gigantic circles without the quivering of a feather, but why keep this up so long? I am positive, careful watch having been kept, that this pair of hawks hovered, circled, and floated, if I may use the expression, from seven in the morning until after four in the afternoon. If they left their elevated outlook at all it could have been but for a minute or two at most, and in so short a time could have captured and eaten no food. Do September hawks never get tired or hungry?

In the course of conversation with a conservative naturalist, ten days ago, I expressed the opinion, which I have long held, that salamanders needed no tails. My friend dissented at once. "If they do not need them," said he, "they would long since have lost them." It was, I admit, one of those assertions man is so often heard to make, and then labors hard to recall it. Aquatic salamanders, of course, need their tails quite as fully as do fishes, and terrestrial species only were in my mind when I spoke.

Two years ago, when studying three species of land salamanders, or semi-aquatic ones, I was surprised to find so great a number with lacerated tails, or that had lost a greater or less portion of the member. During the months of April and May, whenever opportunity offered, I watched the dusky and red "water lizards," as the farmers call them, and while I could not discover that the tails of the creatures were of any use, I did witness many incidents that showed they were frequently the direct cause of the animal's death or maiming; and also that scores of them, with but mere stumps of tails, were as active, as well conditioned, and, to all appearances, as happy as any of their longicaudate brethren.

My first effort was to determine what animals were given to nipping the caudal appendages of these inoffensive salamanders. In this endeavor I soon became discouraged; but such a feeling only increases one's desire to know the truth, and I continued to watch. It was not long before I found that these creatures were constantly biting each other's tails; and this is one reason why so many are found with their caudal appendages in a mutilated condition. At times an adult salamander will completely detach the tail of a half-grown specimen. Subsequently I was fortunate enough to find a meadow mouse with the tail of a dusky triton in its jaws. The frantic efforts to escape on the part of the batrachian resulted in the tail giving way, and the mouse had but a meagre breakfast if this was all he ate. I think, from this fact, that as all rodents are eminently carnivorous, that mice and squirrels are also largely the offenders; but, to even a greater extent, the amputation of tails may be attributed to the hundreds of turtles which, during the summer, leave the creek, often going far inland to deposit their eggs. The mud turtle, the stinking turtle, the painted and the spotted species, all will seize any salamander that crosses their path; and, from experiments in an aquarium, I am confident that the quick movements of the salamanders very generally result in their saving their lives, but at the expense of a greater or less portion of their tails.

And, again, only look at a dusky salamander as he scuttles away from you, and hides under a stone! The chances are nine in ten that the stone will conceal only his body, and there he remains, in fancied security, with two inches of tail in broad daylight. Let a turtle see and snap at it. What is the result? Why, in most instances, the salamander will hold on like grim death, and the sharp jaws of the turtle cut off the tail; but if the captured creature looses his hold, then the turtle makes a meal of him.

Having learned so much of the miseries of a salamander's life, and being satisfied that the smaller the tail the less the woe, were I to become one of these creatures I should choose to be three inches of timidity rather than five of fearfulness. To further satisfy myself that these tails were of more harm than good, I captured a hundred or more dusky salamanders, and endeavored to learn to what use they put their tails. This was an utter failure. Were they a guide in running? I instituted an elaborate series of races, and those whose tails I had amputated generally made the better time; on the principle, I suppose, of having less weight to carry.

Finally, I amputated the tails of all my captives, and only four per cent. succumbed to the operation. The others were soon set free, and some are even yet in full health and vigor, and neither suffer fear of attacks in the rear, nor show the least disposition to be jealous of their elongated brethren, with whom they associate on the most friendly terms.

It was for these reasons that I spoke so disparagingly of salamanders' tails, and suppressed the reasons themselves, through fear of the Society for the Prevention of Cruelty to Animals.

Let me here add reference to a kindly criticism of the same remark, published some months after the above was written. My critical friend says the assertion of the undesirability of tails, so far as salamanders are concerned, is unsubstantiated. If he will bear in mind that I meant only the terrestrial species, I feel sure that the substantiation given above will satisfy him. I have recently repeated some of my experiments, and it is a lucky salamander that has its tail reduced to a minimum.

This, too, is a fitting opportunity to refer to the subject of regrowth of lost limbs and other portions of the body of a salamander. I have not found such reproduction to occur with the regularity that is claimed. Certainly, in the case of amputated tails, it is often more than a year before this regrowth occurs. I find it stated in Packard's "Zoology" that "experiments made in Europe show that the legs and tail of the axolotl, as of other larval salamanders, may be reproduced. We cut off a leg of an axolotl the 1st of November; it was fully reproduced, though of smaller size than the others, a month later. The tail, according to Mr. L. A. Lee, if partly removed, will grow out again as perfect as ever, vertebræ and all."

In the hundreds of experiments I have made, I am positive a very large proportion remained tailless from two to twelve months, and all that I have found that have appeared as second growths were never more than one third the original size of the lost member. And so it has been with amputated limbs. No regrowth took place in many cases, and often, when it did, it was but a mere fleshy outgrowth, with not sufficient strength in it to take the place of the original limb. If experimentation in this direction could be kept up for a century or two, I doubt not but that, at least, a race of *tailless* terrestrial salamanders could be produced.

A student of nature needs good ears as well as eyes; and when, after long practice, he can identify the innumerable sounds that he hears—name to himself the owner of every voice—he has acquired the faculty second only in importance to sight, in thoroughly enjoying a country ramble. To-day, September 21, autumn really begins, and as I entered the woods the first bird-notes heard were those of a characteristic winter songster, the crested tit. Then the complaint of the nuthatches sounded among the hickories. This, the meagre list; but the day was hot, dry, and dusty, as have been each of the twenty days before it. A third bird-note would have been remarked upon by many—a most monotonous chirp or squeak—but it was, in fact, the alarm-cry of a chipmunk, that, watching every movement, uttered its quickly repeated warning a dozen times to every rod I progressed. The cries of small mammals have not received the attention of naturalists as they should have done. My attention was recently called to this in watching a pair of meadow-mice. Now, when one of these lazy creatures is picked up it will give only a faint squeak, that, in all probability, you will not notice. But the pair I have mentioned proved that they can speak loudly when occasion requires. They were busily engaged among the dead leaves, nibbling at some particle of food, I thought at the time. Presently one of them ran off a distance of five or six yards, and commenced rummaging among the leaves, as it had been doing. Possibly they were in search of some particular object. It certainly appeared so; but, whatever they were at, the one who had been left by its mate presently stopped its search, stood upon its hind-feet, and gave a shrill, bird-like call, which was plainly audible for a rod or more. The mouse that was called to straightway stood up, as the other had done, replied by uttering the same sound, and then hurriedly rejoined its mate. Of all our mammals, probably the moles are nearest to being mute, yet they, too, can utter a faint squeak, but I suppose seldom do so voluntarily; perhaps only when roughly handled by man or dog.

He who doubts that fish have some intelligence, and perhaps a language, should have been with me to-day. I passed over one of the bubbling bottom-springs in Poaetquissings, and lingered long to watch the great number of fishes that had congregated in the clear, cool waters. There, for a space of some five yards square, there was nothing in the water save the fishes; but all about them was a dense wall of water-milfoil and other aquatic plants. The fish were accustomed to the boat, and moved to and fro leisurely, from side to side of the weedless space, or were stationary. Suddenly a large roach dashed into the midst of them, and instantly every fish was still as a stone. The roach hesitated but for a moment and was gone, and with it vanished every fish in that open space. The others, somehow, learned of danger from this roach; and, as it proved, none too soon, for no sooner had the many small fishes disappeared than a dozen large white perch made their appearance, and roamed about the clear space above the spring, evidently in surprise or disappointment. As plainly as a man might startle a crowd by a cry of "fire" or "murder," that roach informed the fishes that were gathered in the clear waters below me that they must seek safety by flight.

If such incidents are explained as we would explain similar ones occurring among men, they are wholly intelligible, but otherwise they are not. Stress has been laid upon memory and experience as the mental conditions explaining certain acts of our fishes: that a few cyprinoids, seeing one of their number chased by a pike or perch, and perhaps seized by it, would remember the fact, and ever after, when seeing a fish evidently avoiding a foe, would themselves seek safety by flight and concealment. If so, then fishes are far more intelligent than even I consider them to be, and, whether it accords or not with the conclusions of others, makes them far more intelligent than are batrachians.

Any animal that profits by experience is intelligent, and no one need wonder at its acts, any more than one need wonder at those of a human being.

It is the beginning of the fourth week of the drought. Not a returning warbler that should be tarrying here before going south has deigned to appear. Scenting the dusty, dried-up country from afar, have they passed over in the night? These have been so clear that the starlight would, of itself, show them the courses of the rivers, which are all the guide they need. As Thoreau has suggested, an elevation that gives a general idea of a river's course or the trend of a mountain range would meet every requirement of a migrating bird.

Deep in a tangled thicket of greenbrier and blackberry I heard an unusual humming, late this afternoon, and, after a good deal of rough climbing, determined the cause. By some happy chance, three years or more ago a peach-stone had fallen in this thicket, sprouted, and grown to a tree; all so quickly that none suspected its presence. Even the bloom must have been of a quiet color, as no one seems to have seen it. At all events, this unobtrusive tree was now well loaded with rich, yellow peaches, small, but of excellent flavor; and above every peach were humming bees and whirring wasps, that stood guard over the fruit and enjoyed an occasional taste of its sweets.

At no little risk, but without mishaps, I gathered many peaches, with the righteous intention of taking them home. The line of peach-stones lying in my path tells a sad tale of how those good intentions came to naught. I was eating the last one as I passed through the yard gate; but is it not something to my credit that I left many more upon the tree, and straightway published my discovery?

The frequent occurrence of the unexpected is an exhilarating element in country rambles. I do not believe those peaches would take a prize at a fair, or be popular in the market, but I hold to the strong adjective "delicious." To gather peaches in such a manner is to enjoy them at their very best; and when, after a tiresome tramp over a dusty field, one comes upon such juicy growths, his surprise and delight will render his palate uncritical, and ready to say of such fruit, "delicious." For me, it was far preferable to the mussy slices, gritty with sandy sugar and slippery with cream, that are offered on many tables and accounted a luxury of the season. They may be a luxury, but not so spirit-reviving and restorative generally as the unlooked-for fruit that overhangs the path of the weary rambler as he nears his home.

Every peach that I may pluck in the future will recall the peaches of to-day. Wild peaches, wild plums, wild grapes, eaten in the woods, or along the shady banks of Poaetquissings, trifling experiences of wild life though they may be, still make, for me, the artificial life of to-day stale, flat, and unprofitable indeed.

September 24.—How very common is dreaming and somnambulism among animals, and particularly among birds! One might imagine that such restless birds as wrens would be most disposed thereto, but my observations have not verified this natural supposition. Catbirds are not only great dreamers, but often execute somnambulistic dances on a tight twig. Were it not for the great difficulty of watching birds during the night, I believe many curious circumstances might be recorded, some of which would prove valuable to students of animal psychology. Thus, besides the instance of the catbird, wood pee-wees will sometimes sally out into comparative darkness, and snap their beaks at imaginary insects. Humming-birds will dart from their perches, and, hovering in space for several seconds, as though before a flower, will then return to the identical spot they left. What mental condition is it that enables them to do this? I look upon it as the greatest mystery in animal psychology. Not always, however, are these somnambulistic performances free of danger to the birds. I once saw a purple grakle pitch from its perch, as though pursued by a hawk, and, striking the branch of a tree, fall to the ground with its neck broken. Crows, also, often perform the most curious antics when asleep; and even the more staid woodpeckers run two or three times around the trunk of the tree in which they are roosting, and then quietly resume their slumbers.

Although so abundant and prominent in the mammalian fauna, particularly now and later, the rabbit seldom attracts my attention. I trap them, of course, in proper season; but they seem, even then, more like domesticated than wild animals. In my rambles now, I see them dart by, or, scenting danger, stand well up, lift their long ears, and then speed away, until they find close cover. While yet in sight, one naturally gazes after them, but once out of sight they are equally out of mind. A consistent naturalist should try to become as enthusiastic over a rabbit as a mink or muskrat, but, in this, I imagine, most signally fail. A "cotton-tail" is as near a nonentity as any creature well can be. Why? Because they are, or appear to be, stupid; for Uncle Remus's "Brer Rabbit" never wanders as far north as

New Jersey. In the early summers I often find their nests. The litter of four or five are always without their dam, and one only wonders why dogs or rats do not find them oftener. They are always where people are surest to go, if in the woods at all; and never are so hidden as to have any chance of escape from the schoolboy or his prying cur. Rabbits provoke by their unparalleled stupidity; they never exercise one whit of ingenuity, but ever and forever trust to luck. Perhaps, in this matter, they resemble many people far more than some of our wiser mammals.

But I did see an exhibition of pluck and common-sense on the part of a rabbit, this day, and I am half led to cancel what I have written. An eagle has been frequenting the hillside since August—that is, he has been reported to me, from time to time. To-day I saw him for the first. While comfortably resting at the foot of a tall tulip-tree, and leisurely scanning the meadows, a rabbit very deliberately came towards me, hopping over the short grass, and occasionally looking back, as though in doubt as to whether it was being followed or not. In a moment a shadow crossed the rabbit's path; and with one great leap, none too quickly made, the terror-stricken creature reached the ditch and crouched in the soft mud underneath the overhanging banks. It was certainly safe, for the time being. Almost at the same instant down swooped the eagle, and struck the ground within a foot of where the rabbit had last paused, when it made its leap for life. Once on the ground, the eagle gave a searching glance immediately about, and then saw me within ten paces of him.

A look that I shall never forget, an angry cry of disgust or astonishment, and up the bird rose, with but one movement of the wings, until he was beyond the tree-tops. It was a rare opportunity, and I was thoughtful enough to take advantage of it; and if my eyesight was not defective at the time, the eagle certainly made use of its wings by a quivering motion of the feathers, which seemed to open and shut, and not by a uniform motion of the wings as a whole. Are there muscles in the wings that will enable an eagle to do as I thought this one did?

The rabbit knew when to leave its hiding-place, but was so chilled and stiff, from tarrying even for a minute in its wet quarters, that now an eagle without wings could have overtaken it. I tried to do so, and was moderately successful. Just as I put forth my hand to seize the creature, it gave a frantic leap into the briers near by, and my efforts were repaid by a thorn-stuck thumb. So one rabbit, at least, that I have seen, showed some common-sense, in an effectual endeavor to avoid being captured. Not very much, to be sure, but still a little.

Seeing a fish-hawk fly over, with a monstrous chub in its talons, I wondered if these birds find fish sleeping, or are always quick enough to catch them when wide-awake.

In the article "Ichthyology," by Dr. Gunther, in the "Encyclopedia Britannica," 9th edition, that author quotes Aristotle to the effect that fishes "sleep like other animals." If so, could not a fish-hawk find such slum-borers, at least, at times? But do fishes sleep like other animals? He who wanders along a sluggish creek or any still water, in pursuit of them, knows full well how seldom they are caught napping; and it is a difficult matter to say when a fish is asleep. Certainly, they do not give just such evidence of it as do mammals or birds; and while in a physiological sense it is true, the statement, as it stands, is somewhat misleading.

Fish that habitually or occasionally rest upon the bottom of the stream might readily go to sleep, and no one suspect their condition; but this is not true of fishes that never rest in this way. How do they sleep? Take so restless a species as the little silver-finned minnow. It must sleep, it seems; but how? Do the fins that preserve the upright position of the fish move involuntarily, just as we breathe without being conscious of the effort? If so, then such sleeping fish would be drifted by the current and be hopelessly exposed to many dangers. This, therefore, cannot be true; and yet these fish cannot go into quiet waters, for here they perish in a short time. If, on the other hand, their entire muscular activity is kept at its maximum, and they can still sleep, then it is slumbering in a manner quite unlike that of other animals.

Of such fishes as I have observed, while they were confined in aquaria, there did seem to be a listless condition at times, coupled with a lack-lustre expression of the eyes, which suggested sleep. This was the more noticeable when I aroused them, for the eye suddenly lighted up, and was very different in its general appearance from what it had been.

Fishes, are, I believe, unlike other animals, in that they sleep with great irregularity, and in their ability to go an indefinite time without any slumber or rest whatever.

September 28.—The pits of the ant-lions, to-day, were very abundant in the thin grass on the edge of the terrace. The little engineers had excavated their circular pits with wonderful nicety, and the grass was gray with the sand thrown out. I teased the occupant of one pit for some time, by dropping a seed of giant hyssop into the depression, and no sooner had it touched the centre of the conical pit than the ant-lion seized and threw it out with great force. My astonishment was very great to find that larger seeds were thrown out with proportionately greater force, as shown by the increased activity of the animal. It seemed to test the weight of the objects I dropped in, and sent them spinning to such a distance that they could not roll back again. By great good luck I caught, at this time, a little black beetle not larger than a pin's head. This I disabled and then let slowly roll into the pit. The ant-lion seized it at once, but not finding it available as food, or disliking the flavor, first gave it a tremendous shaking, moving it back and forth with a vehemence that evidently shook out its life, before it received the final toss which sent it an inch or more beyond the outer rim of the pit.

I tried yet again to tease this ant-lion, by suspending a good-sized ant by a fine thread, just out of reach, yet so near that in its struggles it rolled the sand down to the centre. This was thrown back for a time, but soon became an intolerable nuisance, and the enraged ant-lion emerged, and, seizing the suspended ant, gave it one toss that sent it far beyond the pit. But the thread controlled its motions, and in a second it was back again, aided by a little movement that I gave it. The ant-lion again seized it, and, apparently realizing the situation, gave it a jerk which tore it from the thread, and then dragged it out of sight, beneath the bottom of the pit.

Do not accord to ants and bees all the intelligence of the insect world.

September 30.— Wandering southward, along the hillside, interest centred in the absence of usual occurrences and sights. The drought has even affected the flocking of certain birds, for the scattered companies of grakles and red-wings are poor apologies for the autumnal gatherings of thousands, that are so marked a feature of the meadow landscape in September.

Speaking of flocking blackbirds, I have wondered if it were true that the pin-feather birds bring up the rear, in all large flocks. I have often been told so, and market gunners say they always fire into the end of a flock, because it contains the young birds, and these *sell more readily as reed-birds!* How good a thing would it be if English sparrows could be made palatable by some cunning of the cook's art. I have made trials, but these foreign disintegrators of equine ejecta were bitter, bitter, bitter!

But if the flocking red-wings miserably maintained their old-time reputation, the bluebirds did not fail to preserve theirs. From stake to stake, along the zigzag worm-fence, they seemed to be carried by the breeze rather than to be flying, and each, as it floated, bubbled over with music. Dear as the warbling bluebird is in spring, cheery as is his presence in midwinter, it is in the hazy September mornings that we see him at his best. A score of his kind associate to bid farewell to summer, and sing their regrets with touching eloquence; or is it that they are welcoming the coming season, sounding its praises with becoming unction? Be this as it may, the bluebird is an all-important feature of our early autumn, and chimes well with the snappy flavor of golden pippins and the mellow richness of the yellow peach.

As I look back on the past four weeks, what a beggarly array of birds for sweet, sunny September! Not half a dozen warblers! This, the month that should have brought the birds that nested even in Labrador—that has brought them by the hundreds, every other year for the past twenty—this month, none!

In the pale moonlight have they passed by, or, knowing how the summer sunshine has lingered, have they delayed their coming? I can scarcely think the latter to be true; and so sad and silent has been the month, I trust none like it will come again.

Animate nature, here, has not yet wholly accustomed itself to droughts; and the glory of this month is surely not maintained, when it proves to be nothing more than a desiccated August.

CHAPTER XII.

AN OCTOBER DIARY.

OCTOBER 1.—The first bit of color to be seen, as I entered the woods at sunrise, were the purple asters, that, like a fallen sunset cloud, lay tangled among the dwarfed bushes by the wayside. The beginning of October, this, and it should be cool and snappy, and marked by a thread of hoar-frost on the topmost rails of the worm-fences—some of this should be, yet it is all wanting. Asters clustered in nooks along the hillside road and offered the only contrast to the dingy green of this fifth week of the drought.

A little later, however, I chanced upon a thrifty growth of crimson poison ivy reaching to the very top of the tall sassafras, a tree over sixty feet in height. This was, indeed, a wealth of rich color that could not fail to charm the rambler. Why is it that this vine has such a predilection for these trees? I find it prefers them, not only in the woods, but along the creek, where but few of the trees are growing. In the course of my morning's walk I found twenty-seven vines growing upon trees, and all but six were wrapped about the stately stems of the sassafras. Does this hold good elsewhere?

It is a whim to gather a walking-stick at the outset, and leave it at the garden-gate on my return.

By the end of the month I shall have good kindling for the frosty November evenings, when the andirons will come into use. To-day I choose a stout stem of the giant hyssop. How oddly shaped it is! Accurately square, and with sharp, projecting angles, it is possibly safe from the hungry cows that nibble at every growth at this time of year. The text-books are careful to state the fact of the stem being square, but give us no reason why it is so? Is such a fact past finding out? Still deeper in the woods, color-hunting as I walked, I came upon gum-trees with an abundance of berries, the robins and flickers associating very good-naturedly, as they fed upon the sour fruit. Collectively, they numbered more birds than I had seen in a week, and even their monotonous chatter was not unwelcome. It seems a little strange that the flicker, or pigeon woodpecker, which for eleven months is insectivorous, should be so fond of these sour berries. It is not attracted merely by wormy berries, as I have tested. The fruit is eaten as such, and not as insect-traps.

The meadows at sunrise, and even now, an hour later, lay hidden in a fog. Not a thin mist that moved with the wind, but a tough, tangible, semi-liquid cloud. Once or twice each year I see just such; bathe in them, and therefrom date my malarial aches and pains. From the brow of the bluff, to which this fog did not ascend by several yards, that part of the landscape usually filled by an expanse of meadow now appears as a placid lake, with here and there a projecting rock; for such the tops of the nearest tall shag-bark hickories appeared to be. I walk to the sharply defined edge of the mist, sharply defined as air is from water, and place my ear at the surface. All is deathly still. Whatever sound was heard falls from above; not a tremor in the fog-bound area of the meadows I know are before me. Down deep into the cloud I go, but there is nothing to be heard even then, and little to be seen. Every twig is dripping, cold, and clammy. Such an atmosphere could scarcely attract even a water-bird, and I caught no glimpse of any songster. Again upward into the more cheerful air and sunlight, I was met by a Carolina wren, that whistled cheerily "You wretch you," "You wretch you," following it with complaining chirps because I had encroached too far into its domain. Finding a cosey seat at the root of a tall oak, I sat quietly; the wren looked me squarely in the face and then whistled "Right welcome," "Right welcome," twenty-nine times, without stopping. I was greatly honored by this attention, and I trust, not unduly grateful.

No sooner had the bird left me to my own devices, than two chipmunks come running rapidly towards each other, and, meeting directly in front of me, stop suddenly. I could hear not a word they said, but I saw them put their noses together for a second; after which one drew back, scratched his left ear, and whistled. His companion barked, and both, turning about, retraced their steps as rapidly as they had come.

He who doubts that these creatures can talk with one another should have seen them.

When nearly at the garden gate, on my return, I saw the first great flock of red-wings of the season. They passed as a cloud over the sun, throwing down wide dashes of shadow. Each chattered to its neighbor, and their united voices, as the birds flew over the trees, sounded strangely like hail falling through the leaves. I half held out my hand to catch the ice-drops.

October 2.—This is the first respectably rainy day since August. When the rain, at last, does come, plant-life promptly responds; but not so the animal world. Tired of waiting for a shower, the birds generally wander to within the nearest rain-belt. Of course, our small mammals cannot migrate to this extent, but they do have a curious habit, during these "dry spells," of leaving their summer homes and taking up temporary abodes in swampy nooks and about bubbling springs. Even field mice will leave the uplands, at such a time, and settle by the ditches. There they come in contact with the resident meadow mice, and jolly rows occur at times. Indeed, I have known a regular pitched battle to be the result. When it comes to a contest between the feral "domestic" mice and the true meadow mouse, the former seldom hold their own, in spite of their greater agility, but are usually driven off. On the other hand, when an army of upland meadow mice intrude upon the quarters of their cousins in the lowlands, then the result is undeterminable, for the individuals cannot be distinguished. It is, however, war to the knife, and many are killed.

The milder-mannered white-footed Hesperomys are less affected by dry weather, but still have no fancy for a practically anhydrous condition. It may, of course, be merely a coincidence, but is far more probably a deliberate change of haunt from the uplands to the meadows, brought about by the excessive dryness of the earth; for often there is no appreciable moisture even at a depth thrice that of their deepest burrow. At such a time, these creatures have one other means of escaping the discomfort of a drought—they can æstivate, or become torpid during the excessive heat; just as they would hibernate under certain conditions, during winter. Such an occurrence is probably very rare in this latitude, as compared with hibernation; but that many a poor mouse has been picked up, or trodden under foot, in midsummer, which was supposed to be dead, but was simply in an æstivating condition, is unquestionably true.

While rambling about, I have found certain limited spots which were overcrowded with field mice; but find no reference in the books to the migrations of these mammals, if, indeed, they come in one body to such places. Something strongly suggestive of collective migration I have but once witnessed. It was late in the month of June. No rain had fallen for three weeks, and the upland fields were dusty, the surface soil was hot to the touch, and the grass was as brown as well-cured hay. Passing along the brow of the bluff, shortly before sunrise, my attention was called to a black mass moving in a wavy line towards the meadow. I at once thought of a large snake, and hastened to overtake it, but it proved to be a column containing perhaps a hundred of wild house mice, each one running slowly in an irregular way, sometimes singly, sometimes two abreast. At my near approach they scattered and successfully hid themselves; but confidence being restored by my remaining quiet, they recollected and, at greater speed, hurried to the meadows near by. They were evidently influenced by excessive dryness of the upland fields; but they cannot reasonably be supposed to have anticipated the drought that followed. Even a house mouse is no fool, but it is an injustice to intimate that it ever poses as a weather-prophet.

October 3.—The rain continues, and by this time has washed the dust from the throats of the robins, which are now singing as merrily as of a " bright May day in the morning;" but I fail to see or hear another bird. Nearing the creek, sparrows are heard, and some unrecognized songster warbles a few sweet notes that are quite new. What an experience! How the heart leaps at novelty! For an hour I stooped among low bushes, and craned my neck to scan the topmost branches of tall trees. High, low, and through intervening space, but to no purpose. Something, somewhere, sweetly sang, and I was forced to give up the search and go away unsatisfied.

Poaetqnissings is vastly improved, I find, by the rain. The broad lily leaves and upright growths of splatterdocks have been gray for weeks, and now are cheerfully green again. The creek itself, heretofore too lazy to carry off the scum that flourishes in midsummer, now bears it riverward in haste, and the broken shadows of overhanging elms darken the waters from shore to shore.

It is strange how far-reaching is a drought in its effects upon bird-life. The many herons even stay close to the river, and Poaetquissings is absolutely deserted. The rain of yesterday and to-day has remedied all these defects, and again I find the great blue heron winging its way up the creek, and the little green ones are here, and everywhere. A bittern, too, I have heard booming in the maple-swamp hard by. Kingfishers are chattering, crows are cawing; fishes leap above the water, and nature, keeping time to the patter of the rain, makes Poaetquissings her beautiful self again.

October 4.—Still dull and rainy, but the birds sing notwithstanding, and even the gray squirrels barked and chattered, as I sought their haunts at sunrise; but I am thrilled and my pulse leaps at the sound of a belllike note that vibrates for just a moment in the tall hyssops in front of me. I looked for the musician that pipes on the single reed, but could not find him. Safely hidden in some little cranny, it is by chance alone that I am likely to discover him. Urged by my hopes, I sat down in the clump of weeds, remaining long, and as quietly as the stump on which I sit. Then, to mock me, every bird in the neighborhood set up a chatter. An inquisitive jay screeched to the full extent of its powers; this startles the crows, and they caw incessantly. So the sounds are diffused abroad, one creature exciting another, until even the house-dog barked and the hens cackled—and I alone was still.

The birds then seemed to take the hint and silently busied themselves with securing a breakfast. To be sure, one inquisitive titmouse came within a foot of my face, looked at me sharply, and went off abruptly, with a knowing twitter meant only for me. Soon came another of its kind, chirped "good-morning," and was gone—but still that bell-like vibration was not repeated. Had I imagined it, after all? I was about to come away, and, half-rising, was suddenly startled by the shrill peep! that surely came from the bushes near by. I looked in every direction, scanned every leaf, but nothing visible could have uttered it. I rose to extend the search, and instantly the note was repeated. "Where is the creature?" I exclaimed, and, shading my eyes to see more clearly towards the rising sun, I touched a cold object on the rim of my hat. I took it in my hand, with a startled movement. It was a Pickering's Hyla that I had brushed from the hyssops, and had borne all this while so near me without suspicion. I have seen men look for their spectacles, which were the while resting upon their foreheads; and this was much the same thing. This little tree-toad, which is a diminutive frog with disks on his toes, and an arboreal batrachian, is not abundant with us, its place being taken by the exceedingly abundant peeper, or Savannah cricket. Their vocal powers, however, are so admirably developed that they make up for want of numbers by their ringing notes, that, heard among the trees, give one the impression of many chirping birds. This note is unlike the harsher "kweep" of the Savannah cricket, or Hylodes, and the two will never be confounded, when both have been heard and recognized. It is a difference readily appreciated, when the two are compared, but not easily described. It may be said that the Hyla has a short, clear, bell-like "peep!" the Hylodes a harsher, more prolonged "kw-eep!" Although the true frogs have practically ceased their singing, it is no uncommon occurrence to hear the rattling green frog, or *clamitans*, and the burly bull-frog clack and rattle for an hour or more, if the weather is fairly summerlike. The spotted fellows are done croaking. Even by pinching them, you can seldom force a protesting squeak. There was no dust to annoy, and dozens were found far from the water, active as in midsummer, and, as I believe, hunting small grasshoppers.

Both the spring and pickerel frogs are gathered in company about the pools, for never is the one seen without the other. This constant association might lead one to suspect that here was a case of dimorphism; for, except in the matter of color, the two species are really one. The minutest details of the habits of a spring frog would equally well apply to the pickerel frog; and it has been labor lost to discover a difference of habit between the fellow with two rows of spots and him of four.

October 5. — The country is now at its best, glowing, as it does, with the freshness following a two days' bath. The low shrubbery and grass are decked with dewdrops—nature's matchless jewels. With a hope of finding some novelty, I seek the least-frequented nook on the farm, thinking its fauna would be all astir, and the tamer, it might be, for that I had been absent for a month. Reaching the tangled corner where my neighbor's fence is supposed to be, but which the wild growth renders somewhat problematical, the brilliant crimson of the gum-tree's foliage at once strikes me as the prominent feature of the spot, so far as the eye is concerned. If there could be but music with this, I thought — and straightway a Carolina wren, up from some leafy depth, mounted a dead branch of an oak near by and whistled "welcome" in wren-like fashion. Except for us two the place seemed deserted. The moaning tree-tops, waving in the wind, the crisp clatter of dry leaves as they fell singly on the thicket below, the hum of a few bees fretting for the absent flowers, were the only sounds that disturbed the quiet of this long-neglected nook. Desirous of better luck, I gazed searchingly through the trees, hoping that something was as quietly watching me as I was hunting for it; and it proved so. As is often the case, when disappointment began to tell heavily, I saw move slowly a short distance an object that seemed unlike the mere wind-tossed trembling of leafy twigs. Drawing still nearer, I readily recognized it. There, in a tall gum-tree, largely overgrown by a fox-grapevine, sat a small raccoon.

Probably no one of our few remaining mammals has figured more extensively in recent literature than the raccoon, and none is more accurately known, perhaps, as to its habits; and yet, when I chance upon one in wild woods, and see it going about its business, in an unconcerned way, it is pretty sure to attract my attention and check my progress. This was the case to-day. While scarcely larger than an opossum, with habits not more fraught with danger from men or dogs; good climbers and excellent burrowers, raccoons seem steadily to have lessened in numbers, until now one is rarely seen in this vicinity. One would think that, being far more intelligent than either the opossum or skunk, they should have outwitted man as readily, and so have held their own, even in thickly settled districts; but they have not. Here is a case where theory and fact are at loggerheads. Foolish creatures, like opossums, thrive, while cunning 'coons are forced to quit or die.

When Kalm, the Swedish naturalist, was travelling in New Jersey, a century and a half ago, these animals were fairly abundant. His description of their habits, as he observed them then, holds good to-day; but what does he mean by asserting that "the raccoon is frequently the food of snakes"? What manner of snake, even in his time, could have managed to swallow a raccoon? To-day, snakes are sometimes the food of raccoons, and possibly this is what Kalm meant to say.

The young coon in the vine-draped gum-tree was wholly undisturbed by my presence, and simply stared without winking, as I gradually approached. When within a dozen paces I saw that its chaps were literally dripping with gore. There were no feathers at the foot of the tree or caught in the tangled undergrowth, and no bits of fur; but drops of blood were spattered everywhere. The poor thing must be wounded, I thought. Hoping, therefore, to put the creature out of its misery, I planned to reach it; but as I had no gun, I could only climb. This failed, but, as I was looking up the straight stem of the tree, the coon moved a little upward and outward, as though determined to keep the space between us unchanged. The ease of its movements did not suggest a wound or a weakness from loss of blood, and I was again at sea in the matter, but only for a moment. Scattered about the vine were single grapes and bunches of two and three. A beggarly show for grapes; but then their size made up for lack of numbers. Each grape was black as anthracite, a perfect sphere an inch in diameter. Such grapes! No wonder the raccoon had jaws dripping with gore; no wonder the leaves below were spattered with purple blotches. Every grape was nigh to bursting with the richest of ruddy wild-fruit juices, crimson and blood-thick. My little 'coon was an epicure, I thought, and deserved his liberty. I left him unmolested, with many wishes for his welfare, hoping no dog or hunter might find him. Perhaps, two months later, if he raids upon the hen-roost, I may change my mind, and then be willing to hunt him myself beneath a full moon, when this same bare tree and leafless vine are mantled deep with snow.

While letting the raccoon depart in peace, I could not so readily betake myself from the luscious grapes. Their odor, of itself, called for critical inspection, and I own to a governing passion for what odors, as well as sights and sounds, my rambling grounds offer. Nor was the flavor less enticing. Nature's best effort, with her present surroundings, it would be ungrateful to belittle. I ate heartily; stained my hands with the ruddy juices, and carried away with me a full realization of how good a thing may be within our reach, unseen and unsuspected, enjoyed by the lower animals—so called. Lower, indeed! but happier in their better knowledge of the man-neglected nooks and crannies of the wildwood. It is no mean experience to end an October ramble with cool grapes, a cluster of hazel-nuts, and the rosy cheek of a spicy apple.

Leaving the hillside, on my return homeward, I passed along the main meadow ditch, and was delighted to find a star-nosed mole. Its branched snout and long tail at once distinguished it from the other species found here; for we have three of them, and these are even generically distinct—one a *Scalops*, another a *Scapanus*, and the one found this morning a *Condylura*. These moles cannot be confounded by the most careless observer, although I once did hear a man say of one, " It's too small for a rat and too big for a mouse. What is it, any way?"

The star-nosed mole that I had found had no apparent business on the surface of the meadow, and no prying cur had dug him out of his subterranean home, for the ground was everywhere intact.

So closely do these moles keep to their burrows that many people have never seen them, even where they are really abundant. In my meadows, I generally find that the burrows open into the ditch banks below the water-level, or but an inch or two above the water's usual height. Into the water, therefore, with little or no disturbance, these moles can plunge, on occasion, and swim off without being noticed. It is probable, however, that they seldom do take to the open water; for when surprised in their tunnels, they usually, I think, retreat to that portion of the burrow most distant from the ditch bank. Such, at least, has been my experience in observing them. Were it not for the destruction to meadow pastures caused by star-nosed moles, they would be about the most inoffensive of our mammals. As it is, they often cause a deal of mischief, which is usually attributed to muskrats. During the spring freshets the waters fill the mole's burrowings and loosen up the soil, so that when they have wholly subsided the ground settles, yields unduly to the tread of the cattle, and the sod cracks. A rain ensuing enlarges every crack to a gully and a little land-slide then follows. It takes but few such seemingly trivial occurrences to ruin an acre of pasture-land.

The winter habits of the star-nosed mole merit considerable attention, the more so in that my inferences have been challenged as very incorrect. After a trivial matter of some twenty years' familiarity with these animals, I have ventured to state that they dwell in complicated burrows, and at some point in their tangled tunnellings these moles make commodious nests, formed of a good deal of fine grass. Here, indifferent to freshets, they remain all winter, and, as they can lay up no food, sleep, I suppose, through the entire season. The fact that they are unaffected by being submerged during the spring freshets is an interesting one. So far as I have examined their nests, there was nothing to show that they were water-tight, and I think that the animals must have been thoroughly soaked for from forty-eight to seventy-two hours, the ordinary duration of the high-water. If through any cause the period of submergence was prolonged, it is probable that it would prove fatal to the moles.

Now it is objected by Dr. Merriam, that it would be "a very easy matter for these semi-aquatic animals to betake themselves to higher ground when driven from their usual haunts by freshets; and this is exactly what usually takes place, as I have ascertained by personal observation;" and my friend adds, "in the Adirondack region, where snow covers the ground for five or six months of the year, the star-nosed mole does not hibernate. At the approach of winter it sinks its galleries below the depth to which frost penetrates, and still finds an abundance of earth-worms, which at all seasons constitute a large share of its food. When the snow has attained the depth of a metre or a metre and a half, as it commonly does here during January and February, the frost gradually leaves the ground, and both moles and earth-worms again approach the surface. The moles sometimes burrow up through the snow; and I have captured them while running about on a stiff crust, through which they were unable to bore in time to make good their escape."

In reply to my friend's criticism, I have stated that it was probable that these moles closed their burrows in such a manner as to exclude the water; but I take it back. The fact is that the star-nosed mole is rather an aquatic animal than "semi-aquatic," as stated by Dr. Merriam, and is better adopted to prolonged submergence, even when fully active, than an otter or a muskrat. It is certainly true of them that they coil up in a corner of their burrows and sleep through a freshet, not keeping dry at the time, either; and when winter has "set in," they do not see fit to follow earth-worms at indefinite depths, but sleep; being in March or early in April "thin as snakes," instead of "sleek as a mole."

But let us consider, for a moment, the star-nosed moles of the Adirondack region. Dr. Merriam says they sink below the frost line and there pursue earth-worms, coming nearer the surface after the snow is three to five feet deep. Now, is it not probable that, at such a depth and under such circumstances, there would be so little atmosphere that the mole could not retain the activity necessary to follow earth-worms? I believe so, and am forced to conclude that the activity claimed for them, under such circumstances, is an assumption. It would be very strange if this mammal should in all respects be the same in its habits, in two regions so different as the Adirondacks and Central New Jersey; but that it is a difference as wide as Dr. Merriam claims, I doubt. Who is in error, let the world decide; but in my meadows star-nosed moles show no disposition to live during winter in the manner described by my friend.

The common mole is justly hated by the farmers, nor do I wonder at it. How persistently they pass through a "hill" of sweet potatoes or watermelons, must be seen to be realized. I cannot bring these farmer folk to believe that they are not after the seed or plant they have destroyed. The plant is destroyed, and the mole was the destroyer. This is enough; these moles are vegetarians certainly, so my neighbors insist, and set me down as a crank. Nevertheless, I am right. Probably, in many cases, the loosening of the soil, in planting, attracts the prey of the mole, the earth-worm; but oftener the whole matter is accidental, the earth-worms and moles passing to and fro in quite a haphazard manner. One instance, during the past summer, of the mole's unfortunate choice of locality, was amusing to me, but quite otherwise to the farmer. This mole had passed down a line of lima beans, uprooting every one, and then, turning about, moved sufficiently far to one side to strike the line of beans adjoining those uprooted, and with equal skill he passed down them, destroying every plant. Is it strange, after all, that a farmer should think beans, and not earth-worms, were the food of moles?

For several mornings, before I was fairly awake, I have heard the nuthatches in the wild cherry that stands just beyond my windows. "Quānk-quānk," calls the white-bellied species; "Tā-tā-tát," replies its ruddy-bellied cousin. The two seem to be always associated. These little birds are worthy of careful study, for they have a host of pretty ways; and this habit of the two species being always together is curious. It might be thought that hybrids would occasionally be found; but I have no knowledge of such having been met with. Even in the stormiest weather, as blithesome as to-day, these birds forage without a moment's rest, and move about the trees with equal ease and more grace than mice move over level surfaces. The cracked and crannied bark of the cherry-tree was hunted in the most systematic manner, and I judge an abundance of food was found, for the birds tarried on it for fully half an hour. Indeed, I am not sure that they left the tree then, for they often persistently remain on the opposite side of the trunk, when you make a business of watching them closely, and to suppose them gone, when, in fact, they were merely hiding, would be a most natural mistake.

I believe, if I were asked to name a literally resident bird, one that could be readily found any day and at all times of day, I should, at least, think of the nuthatches. Certainly, in the past ten years, I have seen individuals every week of the year—possibly every day. Quānk-quānk—Tāt-ā-tát! I hear them now, although it is past sundown, and even the wood pee-wees sing in their sleep. In May and June one might readily suppose that these birds were wanting, as their voices are lost in the great volume of bird-music that resounds through the woods; but they are here, nevertheless, and gather up insects with the same assiduity, and repeat their monotonous song with the same painfully monotonous regularity as in autumn or winter. Yet, strange to say, these stay-at-homes, with all their conspicuous ways, have never guided me to their nests. Of course, they breed here; we have dead trees and nest linings in sufficiency, and all the surroundings that they require, and, too, I have seen the young, with pin-feathers more abundant than full spread plumage; but no nest or eggs. This is one of the pleasant experiences in store for me —to find a nest.

The nuthatches should have a better name with us. They have absolutely nothing to do with nuts; never hatched or hatcheted one in their lives, nor yet fooled with a wormy one, to get out the grub; but spend their days in insect-hunting, in so tireless a manner that they put to the blush the best efforts of a wren, a kinglet, or any warbler. Nuthatches never quarrel. I have watched, during excessively stormy weather, a pair of these birds running around and around the trunk of the wild cherry near my windows. Occasionally, spinning around in hot haste, they would collide, but it resulted only in a cheery chirp, a half lifting of the wings, with an "excuse me" air, and then they separated.

For some reason, perhaps easily guessed, nuthatches are annoyed by the presence of squirrels, red or gray. Not that these animals ever molest them, when they meet in trees; but they are either interfered with, at the time, indirectly, or, what is more probable, it is hereditary hatred, caused by the villainous egg-stealing habits of the squirrel. Only the other day, the nuthatches on the cherry awoke me by an unusually animated chirping. I very naturally thought of an English sparrow; but the cause of the disturbance proved to be that a little red squirrel that nests in a hollow locust near by was wandering about the cherry in an aimless sort of way, as though enjoying the rage of the scolding nuthatches; but his enjoyment proved of short duration. Tired, at last, of his impudence, the birds, with wren-like rapidity, darted simultaneously at the intruder, with outstretched necks, which meant two vicious stabs from their sharp beaks. The squirrel squeaked and winced, but stood his ground. Again the birds darted at him, with like results. It was too much for him. The birds made the fur fly, and he flew with it.

There is another little tree-climbing bird that is seen both winter and summer, oftener alone than in company;

but not unfrequently is associated with the two nuthatches. It is the brown tree-creeper. A bird of another genus, differing in many ways from a nuthatch, yet in its habits essentially the same. In like manner, it searches every nook and cranny of the bark of trees, for insects, and chirps a whole-souled "tweet-tweet" whenever any super-luscious morsel has been found. This leads me to recall another fact. A simple chirp is not the entire range of the creeper's vocal powers. They can sing sweetly when they choose, but are too busy, or do not choose very often.

Perhaps, less than any other bird, these creepers are affected by extremes of heat and cold. I remember seeing them in full activity during one of the hottest days on record. When, in the sun, the thermometer ranged from 110° to 115° Fahrenheit, and all animate creation was at least resting in the shade, these tree-creepers were running full tilt about the trees, and as often on the sunny as the shady side. Then again, when the thermometer stood at $-12°$ Fahrenheit, and with a cutting northeast wind blowing, these same creepers were not only busy in their searching for insects, but once one of them sang as merrily as though it were a May morning. The bird is a marvel in more ways than one.

Bats are unusually abundant this evening. Perhaps they are looking for winter-quarters more anxiously than for insects. While standing in the shadows of my three beeches, I tried to count the creatures as they passed. It was evident, in this case, that figures might lie. Every one of these bats darted in and out in so erratic a fashion that the first, second, and last might have been the same individual; so I gave up counting, when once I saw, as I think, half a dozen darkly limned against the sunset sky. There are four species to be found along my hillside: the brown, red, black, and dusky. The first two mentioned are common; the others are less so. Even if we have but a single specimen, it is never difficult to determine the species, and learn his long Latin or Greek name. Sometimes this proves vastly easier than to handle the fellow with safety to one's fingers. The little differences of color, in the wings, teeth, and even in their ears and cheeks, are safe guides. For those who do not care to be thus particular, but are interested in a very general way, there lies no difficulty in recognizing a bat. No other mammal flies; not even a flying squirrel. Then, they are not overloaded with a multitude of meaningless names, as are so many of our birds. To be sure, one obstinate old man, who fishes in the meadows every day in the year, and catches next to nothing, says they are "flittermice." I asked him if a house mouse was the same thing without wings.

"Jus' 's like's not," he grumbled.

Everybody else says a bat is a bat, and we can afford to ignore the crabbed old angler.

Much as bats have been written about, there seems to have been no attention paid to the degree of intelligence they possess—for I suppose they have a trace.

Have they a voice? Can they be tamed? Are they cunning? Some of the sub-tropical species are said to scream; but never a sound from any of our four bats, save a clicking sound, which is a uniform noise, made I know not how, but certainly not with the teeth, although it gives that impression invariably to the listener. The mouth is always widely opened when the sound is uttered, and if the jaws were rapidly closed and opened, the movement could be seen. Not depending on sight, I have placed a strip of thin paper in their mouths, at the time, but it was not perforated. It is, therefore, a guttural, not a dental, click.

Can our little bats be tamed? Romanes, in his volume on "Mental Evolution in Animals," gives an instance of a large bat in the Mauritius, which was both tame and intelligent; but the little bats in New Jersey do not appear to ever become so, however kindly they are treated, or however young they may be when the taming process begins.

In studying the habits of our few remaining mammals, I have always found that the character of the voice has much to do with the degree of the creature's intelligence. The animal need not be noisy; but if it is able to utter a considerable series of quite different sounds in quick succession, then the more pronounced are all the characteristics of the animal, and its cunning will be quite apparent. For instance, it is commonly supposed that a rat merely squeaks; but it has really an elaborate series of utterances, some of which are quite musical, and no one who has suffered " a plague of rats " can doubt that they are very cunning creatures. Even mice are more cunning than is supposed, but they suffer in comparison with rats, in this regard, because of their excessive timidity. Let a mouse feel assured there is no danger lurking near, and it will readily prove itself no fool.

Probably no law can be laid down in this matter of correlation between voice and intelligence, but the fact, as stated, still remains, that a many-voiced animal will be found to be more intelligent than a, comparatively speaking, dumb one. So far as I have been able to determine, our bats are practically voiceless. I have found them under all circumstances, summer and winter; when the sexes were together, when apart; when the females carried young, and when, childless and alone, they pursued their ceaseless rounds for insect prey, and never yet have I been able to detect any sound that could be taken as evidence of their voluntarily making any noise, excepting that uniform clicking, when they are captured.

It is natural, on the other hand, to suppose that so active an animal should be cunning or intelligent; but nothing indicative of it has come under my notice. I have tried in every way to tame them, but they successfully resisted every effort. They would never take food from my hands; and insects forcibly placed in their mouths were instantly rejected.

I would be glad to know if ever a little brown bat had an idea flit through its diminutive brain. Perhaps such an occurrence is common enough, but what external evidence have we that it ever takes place? They take excellent care of their young, it is true; but all is done in such a mechanical way that the whole appearance was that of a machine rather than of living, conscious beings. Years ago, I detected evidence of common-sense on the part of a butterfly, and have ever since had hopes of equal good-fortune in the case of bats— have had these hopes for twenty years, and still have them.

Of all our mammals, bats are the most sensitive to cold, and avoid exposure to it with the greatest care; and yet I find that the little red bat is very late in retiring for the season, and reappears with great regularity early in February. Their actions at this time indicate that considerable food is to be had—that flying insects are abundant. While this bat's ordinary habits do not differ noticeably from those of the other species, it is apparently less sensitive to low temperature, and needs but the least encouragement to arouse from its hibernating sleep. It is also less crepuscular in habit than the others; but I do not know that this fact has any bearing upon the irregularity of its hibernation.

Bats disappear in November or December, immediately after the formation of ice, but do not seem affected by a mere succession of hard frosts. As insect-life is not materially affected by the first few frosts, there does not seem any reason for their withdrawal from active life, and therefore it is not surprising that even up to Christmas bats should be seen flying, at sunset, in considerable numbers. When the steady cold of an average winter fairly reaches us, bats hibernate in two ways. If they resort to the ordinary shelter of a hollow tree, or similar locality, that is considerably exposed to the wind, then many individuals cluster together; and contact is mutually beneficial, for the torpor of hibernation is not rapidly, but rather gradually acquired. Such clusters of bats, if disturbed immediately after gathering together, are as resentful as when captured during midsummer; and not until three or four days have elapsed do they become insensible to disturbance. If this be very violent, and the creatures roused suddenly, a curious condition of aimless activity ensues, but lasts for a short time only, and often ends in death.

On the other hand, I have very frequently found solitary bats in curiously out-of-the-way places, where they were so protected that they could not have suffered from the severity of the season, however intense. In such cases the torpor was never profound, the temperature of the body but little reduced, and the heart's action almost normal. For instance: a single dusky bat slept, or hibernated, as described, for thirteen weeks in the attic of my house. It clung to a nail driven into the wall of the chimney, and was protected by a piece of woollen cloth hanging from a beam above it. The chimney retained a little of the warmth derived from the three smoke-flues which passed through it, and which were in constant use during the time. This bat could be taken down and hung up as readily as an inanimate object, yet clearly showed that it was conscious of the disturbance to which it was subjected. Once I brought it into a warm room, when it revived, in thirty minutes, and flew about the apartment, but not with a very steady, well-directed flight. When taken again to the attic it responded to the effects of the lower temperature by resuming its former position, after a steady to-and-fro flight from end to end of the attic for nearly an hour. The bat seemed to be wholly aware of the position of the nail in the chimney, and, when wearied of its flight, turned to it directly, and, folding its wings about it, seized the nail with a tighter grip, and hung, head down, as it had previously done. In two hours I went to it again, and found it as indifferent to handling as before.

October 6.—Although the thermometer reached 80° Fahr. in the shade, I took an upland walk this morning, to see if the "old-barn" apples were ripe. They should be, according to the ancient rule; but my grandfather never could tell why these apples were never ready before the sixth of the month.

> "Tenth month, sixth; or clear or dull,
> Of old-barn apples, pick a barrel full;
> But leave it longer, ere you gather them,
> And they are rotten, core and stem."

To be sure, now that the old barn is gone, these apples do not seem quite the same. It really needed the shade of the old building; the moaning of the wind through its loose weather-boards, and the smell of the hay within, to bring out the full flavor of the fruit; which, after all, was nothing to the stranger. It is just ten years since the barn was removed, and the tree has been dying slowly ever since. The traditional barrelful measured scarcely a peck, and these were sorry specimens of the old-time fruit; nor were they ripe, my grandfather's rhymed rule notwithstanding. They need at least one stinging white frost to finish the ripening process, and that is yet to come.

While I sat on the top rail of the bars, at the corner

of the field, I spied Miles Overfield coming towards me. "Straight as an arrow, active as a sparrow, tough to the marrow," so he described himself, and, although over seventy, it is true of him. Miles has always lived in the neighborhood; can turn his hand to anything in the way of farm-work; spends as few days at labor as possible, and always has just enough for his very few wants. He knows everybody living, and knows of their parents and grandparents, unless they are recent comers; and these he cares nothing about. That a farm should go out of the possession of the descendants of the original settlers he looked upon as half criminal, and bemoaned the number of such instances that had occurred in his time. "The world was just about right when I was young; why couldn't it stand still?" This was a common remark with him, and I always replied "Why not?" to please him.

Miles Overfield was usually looked upon as a bore by my neighbors; but this was because they were strangers in the land, as he looked upon them, and, of course, did not sympathize with him. I was not; and so became the chosen one to whom he would talk by the half-day, provided I was willing. It was never necessary to ask any questions. But give him a hint and he took up the subject without any preliminaries; always carrying his hearer from the present to the past, to "when he was young," and the world perfect.

"Eatin' old-barn apples, eh?" Miles remarked as he came to where I sat, and, without waiting for any reply, continued: "Powerful sorry the old barn's gone; miss it more than any one thing about here. You see, nigh sixty years ago, father and I did the thrashin' for your grandpap—Uncle Josie we called him—and we had the thrashin' every winter, till father died. Seems to me we must have hammered one floor clean through; yet I don't remember any new one. But the fun was to knock off at noon, and go out in the old orchard. The nigh field was an orchard then, and this old-barn apple is a seedlin' from it, and all that's left to show apples ever grew here. That old orchard—let's see; there were Winter Pearmains, Vanderveers, Summer Priestleys, yellow as gold and with a twang of their own, Cat-heads, that your grandmother used for dumplings always, Michael Henrys, Hollowcores, Red-streaks, Sheep-noses, and a big tree of Soursweets. These were my bait for rabbits always; for you see I'd a notion that rabbits might differ in their tastes, so I'd take a Sour-sweet and cut a piece so half would be one taste and half t'other; then the rabbit was sure to be suited. No, you don't see any such orchards nowadays. Why those trees were big. You couldn't get your arms around some of them, and they towered up like trees in the woods; and then sometimes, when a big limb would die, a black log-cock, such as hasn't been about for fifty years, as I know of, would come out of Long Swamp, and hammer away at it, till you'd think a man was choppin'. There are no such orchards now, and, sure as shootin', your modern apples don't come up to the old kinds. Why, man alive, when you'd open a barrel of Bellflowers, you could smell 'em all over the house."

"Are there none of these old apples left?" I finally got a chance to ask.

"Left? yes; but they've lost their flavor. Now and

then you find an old tree in bearing; but the vigor's gone and the apples only have the look of old times."

"But talking about the old barn," resumed Miles, after a brief pause, "reminds me how different it is now from what it used to be, as to the quails. When father and I would be thrashin', in winter, the quails would come down from the swamp every afternoon, about an hour before sunset. They came just as regular as clockwork, and we always calculated on just one more floorin' after the quails came. These quails stayed up in the swamps all day, but had a notion of roostin' in the gully; to keep clearer of varmints I suppose; for weasels and such were common enough in those days. However, come they did; and your folks, when boys, used to have a great old time in trappin' them. They hadn't a gun, and couldn't shoot so near the building, any way; so, after thinking it over, your father planned a dead-fall out of a little side-door of the barn. He and your uncles tied a long string to a figger-o'-four set of sticks, and sprinkled a little grain out from the door, and a deal more of it under the door. The string ran through a knot-hole in the barn, and the boys scrouched down and peeped through, waitin' for the quails. 'Fore long a lot of 'em came, and began pickin' round like chickens, and some ran under the door. The boys pulled the string, and, by cracky! they got seven or eight of 'em. Well, now, it was a sight to behold, to see how those boys carried on. They didn't know which way to turn, and kept up such a racket that it brought their father down from the house, to see what was the matter. Well, it sort of tickled him too, to see the quails; for bein' old Quaker stock, he thought a deal of good livin', but didn't say much. Fact is, good livin' seems to be a sort of understood necessity among Quakers, which they practise but don't preach. But the boys didn't see it in the same way at all. They'd just as lief stuck to plainer meat, and carried out a plan of sellin' the quails to Ben South, up at the tavern; and didn't feel so sure of sixpence apiece, if they got into the home kitchen. I don't remember how it turned out, but next day they were at it again, and just at the same time down came the quails; but when they got up to the trap, they ate all round it, and then one old bird flew up on the door and whistled 'not quite,' and away they flew. How father laughed, and the boys somehow wandered off, without sayin' nothin' to nobody. After that, we could only catch quails by hair snoods."

When Miles concluded his narrative I endeavored to turn his attention to other matters, by a bewildering broadside of point-blank questions.

One of these was concerning wild turkeys.

"No, I never saw wild turkeys about here; but they were common, in my young days, up in the mountains; but I've often heard my father say that when he was young, along about 1800, the turkeys often came out of the swamps and ate the young corn; sometimes doin' a good deal of damage; but they were so much hunted that they took to the big woods, up in the mountains, and left these parts."

"Then in the Indian times, I suppose, they were common," I remarked.

"Must have been, from what I've heard. Father

once told me that he was out near Cat-tail one Christmas, and some Injuns came to the house where he was. They got to banterin' one another about shootin' and huntin', and one said he'd kill more turkeys before mornin' than t'other Injun would, and so, about noon, they went into the woods. About sunrise, next mornin', one of the fellows came in with six old gobblers, and the other Injun followed with only two. They sold 'em then and there; but it turned out the six gobblers belonged to one of the neighbors, and the Injun had picked 'em, so you couldn't tell they were tame."

The moon fulled on the fourth; the fifth was a warm autumn day, and this, the sixth, is simply summer returned. To be sure, the leaves are falling; the poison-ivy is crimson, the maples yellow, and gum-trees of every hue—still, the great mass of foliage, as you look over the country, is green. On such a day the autumn flight of home-returning warblers arrived. Perhaps they travelled wholly by moonlight, or were guided by some unrecognized power, for there cannot be traced a positive connection between the phases of the moon and the migration of birds. If bright, clear nights are followed by a great accession of birds in the morning, it seems very probable that the migrants travelled by night; but certainly birds do not always wait for the moon to suit them, and often arrive when it is very cloudy; or can it be said that they flew above the clouds? If so, how could they know just when to drop beneath them? Yesterday not a warbler was to be seen along the hillside. I looked for them, morning and evening, but in vain. To-day, an hour before sunrise, many of the trees were crowded with them. There was a multitude of black-throated blues, beautiful spotted ones, and others of duller coloring. From the north and west, down the valley of the river, I suppose, these little birds came as a cloud, and happily chose the tall pines about the house for a resting-place. Still, it cannot be said that they rested much. All were active as in spring, evidently unwearied by their journey, and were themselves in all respects save song, for scarcely one deigned even to feebly chirp.

The nuthatches and their accompanying tree-creeper did not take kindly to the warblers in such vast numbers. They remained nearer the ground than usual, venturing only to the lowest branches; but when a warbler came that low, the nuthatches pursued it in hot haste, and sent it flying to its kindred in the sky-parlors of the pines.

At the close of day I watched these myriads of restless birds for an hour or more, and when it was almost too dark to distinguish them, a great chirping, twittering, and shrill whistling was set up, and more suddenly than this commenced, these warblers took flight, mounting upward, I thought, for I could not see; and then, as a few favoring rays of light lit up the southern horizon, I saw minute black dots, for a moment, against the pale gray clouds, which were, I doubt not, these southward-travelling birds. They evidently intended to travel by night, as they had done on the previous one; but surely they took no rest while they tarried in the pines; and this ability to remain constantly active for so long a period is, to me, far more wonderful than any feature of the habit of migration.

Much to my surprise I heard and then saw a spotted sandpiper. It came from over the fields and flew towards the river. I very much question if the elaborate songs of some of our birds are always those that are most enjoyed. Delightful as is bird-music to the contemplative rambler, those notes, however brief, which call up some pleasant spring morning of long ago will ever rank highest in his estimation. To hear the first "peet-weet" of these spotted sandpipers in April is one of those delightful experiences which make for me a red-letter day. Hearing it, I am thirty years younger and abroad for the first time alone. The creek seemed vastly wider then than now; the trees, taller; the flowers, brighter; the turtles, monsters; the stately herons, veritable giants, and the restless "teeter" that startled my timid footsteps, as I ventured to the water's edge—that bird was, indeed, a wonder to my untrained eyes, that as yet had learned to know but the sparrows in the garden. I have heard all of our birds since then, but no song, however elaborate, charms as does the first spring notes of the spotted sandpiper.

Unlike the great family of wading water-birds that haunt the sea-coast and frequent the shores of inland rivers, the "teeter," as I early learned to call him, is well content with the most meagre of pools, ditches, and temporary puddles of rain-water. Indeed, it can slake its thirst with the dew and take kindly to the highest and dryest of upland fields. It at once becomes a land-bird, if it chooses, without apparent effort, and is cheerful withal. I have seen it perch upon fences and tops of dead trees with all the grace and ease of a hawk, and thread its way, in and out, among tangled bushes, with all the skill of a sparrow-hunting shrike. Then, suddenly longing for its old-time haunts, it would rise to a considerable height, and with steady, snipelike flight, wend its way to the nearest water, and straightway become as aquatic as any of its cousins. I am not quite sure where I better like to see these birds, in the upland or on the meadow. Beautiful anywhere, at ease under all circumstances, there is pleasure in watching them wherever they may be. They lend a charm to the river-shore, the weedy banks of creeks, or wooded slopes that guard the forest brooks; but with greater interest, perhaps, do I watch them as they curve, with pendent, pointed wings, over upland fields, skimming the waving grain with the same grace that marks their progress over rippling waters.

As there are some inland birds that have become essentially aquatic in their habits, so this little sandpiper is now more than half a land-bird. It offers us an admirable opportunity for studying that profoundest of all matters in biology, the origin and instability of habits; for these, like specific differences, cannot be asserted as fixed. No bird, no creature, be it higher or lower, but is something different from its ancestors of a few centuries ago. During the past summer, as for ten years past, a pair of these sandpipers have nested in a weedy corner of a dusty field, and have been as truly land-birds as the song-sparrows, with which they were much associated. Even during the annual summer drought they stuck closely to their nest, and if they or their young suffered from want of water, they kept the matter to themselves. They raised two broods successfully, and the bird that I saw this evening was probably one of the parent birds, leaving its upland home for the last time, until the early flowers and warm sunshine of April tempts him back again.

October 7.—It by no means follows, because I have seen no coots during the summer, that none were here. I think it strange, of course, for I have been thinking of late that nothing escaped my notice, inasmuch as I have seen so much; but this is one of those unfortunate blunders, common to all mankind. I find my brother-naturalists are all inclined to overrate their powers of observation. The truth is, if one's mind is on objects of a wholly different character, coots might be directly in one's path and not be seen. Looking for arrowheads, one morning, I was startled by a shrill "Look out!" that a neighbor kindly shouted. Looking up, I saw an escaped bull coming towards me. Since then I am never sure that I have seen everything that was to be seen in the course of my walk. Had that bull been of a peaceful disposition I might have passed him by without knowing it. To-day I did see a half-dozen wild geese flying down the river, and so, at the very outset, was prepared to see water-fowl of all sorts, if such were about. This explains the fact that no sooner had I reached "Birch Point," on Poaetquissings, than I saw a coot—for me, the first coot of the season. It stared back, as though I was the first man of the season, for it uttered a cracked cackle of derision, and, diving suddenly, disappeared. Not for long, though. I had excited the bird's curiosity, and back it came. On the opposite side of the creek, of course, but where it could see me plainly enough. Then, as it floated on the still waters, it took me in from top to toe, again laughed derisively, and disappeared. I waited for half an hour, but the coot failed to return.

Coots, or "crow-ducks" as my neighbors persist in calling them, are curious creatures. They never give one, in this locality, sufficient opportunity to study them; coming and going, as they do, in the most erratic manner. I am moderately confident of but one fact concerning them: they migrate at night; and at such a time, if they choose, can fly with great rapidity. Some years ago, while spending the night upon Poaetquissings, for the double purpose of studying certain fishes and the night herons, I was, at one time, considerably frightened by a coot. While experimenting with a lantern in illuminating deep water, that I might observe the fishes, a body, falling directly from above, struck the water within a few feet of me, with the force of a cannon-ball, and disappeared. It was after midnight, dark as pitch, and in as lonely a spot as any in the county. I was more than merely startled, I was frightened; but consoled myself directly that the falling object was probably a meteorite, and a second was not likely to follow; and while slowly gathering my scattered senses, I was again shocked by a sudden commotion beneath the surface, the disarrangement of my illuminating apparatus, and extinguishing of the light in my submerged lantern. Hastily lighting a little bull's-eye lamp, to determine the cause (and to effect my escape, if matters grew worse), I found that my submarine illuminator, the careful work of weeks, had been struck a terrific blow by a coot, that tore away a gauze netting and shattered the glass globe. The coot was a prisoner, and I learned something of his nocturnal habits, to be sure; but the fishes, that night, escaped a searching investigation, to which I had planned to treat them.

October 8.—Not unlike the coot in its methods, but less graceful, perhaps, and so less attractive, is that little brown-gray diver that has just five local names, all meaningless, and four indelicate and objectionable. Three of these names indicate that, for some strange reason, this bird has been coupled with popular ideas of the infernal regions, and one of them associates him with Inferno's principal occupant. I have often asked the old fishermen why they called this diver by such foul names, but could never get a satisfactory reply. There certainly is nothing, either in their manner or appearance, that savors of devilry, unless it be that they scare the herring away from deep pools, as I have heard it asserted of them. Such a habit might prejudice the fishermen.

As the little brown diver, like the coot, comes and goes with such irregularity, I have gathered nothing of interest concerning it, beyond the fact of its cunning and that it can stay under water a much longer time than is generally supposed. Whether life is sustained by any process of skin respiration as in frogs, I do not know, but suppose not; still the fact remains that the birds have been found tangled in nets, and brought to the surface uninjured. The length of time they were thus imprisoned could not be determined, beyond the fact that it was much longer than any usual voluntary submergence.

On questioning certain observing old fishermen, who had taken these divers from their nets, I found the impression to prevail that all the divers, loons, and the coot took down a volume of air under their wings and remained beneath the surface as long as this lasted. This absurdity was their means of explaining the phenomenon of their remaining so long out of sight, after diving, coupled with the fact that they were so often taken from nets, in which they were presumed to have been entangled for hours.

The statement, often made, that these birds will stay under the stern of a boat and follow it for an indefinite time is certainly true. These divers, associated with ducks, will, when startled by the discharge of a gun, hide in this way; at least all the circumstances point to the belief that they were afraid of being shot at, and instead of flying or simply diving, only to reappear, they took this means of escaping further notice. This is a rather startling statement, but is rendered less so when it is remembered that they can be made very tame, and soon learn to distinguish between those who feed them and strangers. This brings it quite within the bounds of possibility that the diver is as cunning as he has been represented.

October 9.—This is the first typical autumn day. It is cold, not cool, and, but for a high wind through the night, there would have been frost. To-morrow, if the wind falls, there will be an abundance of it—a carnival of needle-points that will cause one's face to tingle, if out before sunrise, and bring the red leaves of the maples, in a reluctant shower, to the ground. I anticipate waiting but one day longer, before the shady wood-path will be carpeted with crimson and gold, and the rustling of the fallen leaves, as I walk to the creek, will do fairly well for the death-song of summer.

But what of to-day? The wind chilled even the blue-jays, and the woods were silent. In quiet nooks along the banks of the creek the crested titmice whistled, perhaps because their toes were cold, on the principle that small boys whistle when their fingers are numb. The prominent feature of the morning was the remarkable abundance of spiders' webs. Geometrically arranged webs were on all the fences, and every available projecting limb of a tree supported one. The grass was starred with dewy circles of gossamer, and even the nooks, crannies, and corners of woodpiles and brush-heaps were tenanted with spiders, whose banner-like webs spread over every entrance to their dens. I saw no insects anywhere. Not a web was disturbed, save by the crowding dewdrops waiting for kindly sunbeams to return them to the clouds. This at sunrise—but as the morning wore away, and insect-life was warmed into activity, there was a marked change, and, before noon, every spider had broken its fast. Insects were tangled in every web, and the spiders, at noon, were not aroused by fresh victims becoming entangled therein.

Except the turret-building spider, so common in certain of our upland fields, these creatures, as a class, have not been closely studied, so far as to determine the differences in their habits. In a very general way they are the same—they spin lace webs, in which insects are caught, and these the spiders feed upon—so far, so good; but there is a great mouse-colored spider in the garret, as large as a mouse, I believe, of which I long to know more. She is big enough to be a bird-killer, such as Bates describes in his incomparable "Naturalist on the Amazons," but finds other food, I suppose, in the garret, that suits as well. I have never been able to find her hiding-place, nor seen her feeding upon any animal. She darts across the floor, occasionally, and once I cornered her, but, am free to confess, I had not the courage to do more. Her abundant eyes shone with such fiery indignation at being disturbed, and her general attitude was so threatening, I held back. She showed fight too plainly to be misunderstood; but I have no reason to believe could inflict any serious injury. Certainly mere size is no indication of it. I have seen this mammoth spider twenty times, and, unless there are more than one in the garret, which I very much doubt, she is fully ten years old, and still living. This, of itself, is an unusual circumstance. Speaking of the ages of these creatures, Emerton remarks: "Blackwall observed nine moults in *Tegenaria civilis*, a spider that lives several years. Many species, and among them some of the largest, live only one year, hatching in the winter, leaving the cocoon in early summer, and laying eggs and dying in autumn. . . . Some species are found adult at all seasons, and may live several years." From this it would seem that spiders are generally not long-lived, and my garret specimen is an exception to rule. I hope to learn her whole life-history before another year.

A rattling, noisy kingfisher finally disturbed the quiet, and I followed his flight, up stream, till he alighted on a projecting dead limb of an overhanging elm. Here he sat, watching for small fishes, with one eye on me, I suppose, for as I changed my seat to get a better view, off he darted, with a repetition of his disagreeable screaming rattle. I have no disposition to question the conclusion that every habit and peculiarity of an animal is derived through some evolutionary process, and all with the result of a survival of the fittest; still I cannot but marvel that such discordant cries should ever have been evolved, and of what use they now are is past finding out.

Fairly attentive to each other, as are mated kingfishers, it does seem as if they would be more amiable could they speak in pleasanter tones; for in their subterranean nests, or near them, indeed, whenever together, they rattle and scream with all the harshness, although less loudly, than when alone, busy at fishing.

The kingfisher that I had lately seen and could still hear, far up the creek, recalled one of its kind that years ago I experimented upon, as to its bump of locality, as the phrenologists call it. A pair had burrowed into a clay-sand cliff near the creek, and were constantly seen going to and fro between their nest and the stream. During their absence I filled the opening to the nest with a ball of clay, and obliterated all traces of the original opening. I then made a hole in the cliff, just three feet to the left of the nest. The whole act was but the work of a moment and I was out of sight, I think, before either bird saw what I was at. I had but to wait for a minute before one of the birds came back and was making a bee-line for the nest. Although flying at a high rate of speed, it stopped suddenly in mid-air when within six or eight feet of the bluff, gave a shrill cry, presumably of disgust, and turned away. It sailed along the bluff for a few yards in each direction, but took no notice, apparently, of the hole I had made. Then it flew back to the creek, as if to survey the cliff from a distance, and then returned to the very spot where I had been at work. Supporting itself both by claws and wings, much as a chimney-swift holds to the bricks near its nest, the kingfisher used its bill as a shovel and soon removed the ball of clay. It entered the nest, remained about one minute, and flew away towards the creek. Joining its mate there, it told her, I suppose, of what had happened. At all events, neither came back, but in a few days made a new nest, half a mile away.

One of the charms of a country ramble is the possibility of a wholly unexpected occurrence, a sort of gathering grapes from thistles. I lately read that a foolish woodcock flew directly to the doorstep of Delmonico's. A friend, not long since, captured a lovely ring-snake in town, as it was crossing the pavement; so I, to-day, wandering in the gully, watching the robins feast upon chicken-grapes, saw a crow act the part of a humming-bird, and act it well. Something, I know not what, away up in a tall oak, was found by the crow, but could not be reached. It climbed above, below, and around it, but all to no purpose. That unknown something was safe, I concluded; but the crow was not so readily convinced. Baffled in every other way, the bird took a short outward flight, turned, and, maintaining itself in humming-bird-like position for several seconds, at last secured the coveted morsel. Then it sought the nearest perch, held the object, about the size of a hen's egg, a moment in its beak—and swallowed it. It was evidently a dainty tidbit, for ere the crow took flight it chuckled to itself in a very meaning way.

That crows are cunning all the world knows; but I have never seen the fact more clearly demonstrated than by the bird I saw this morning.

Equally intelligent, probably, is the following, which I take from my note-book: The crows had assembled on Duck Island, in the Delaware River, and were busily engaged in running along the edges of the sand-bars, exposed at low tide. Every few moments one of them would rise up to a height of fully fifty feet, carrying a mussel in its beak, and flying inland, to a distance of one hundred yards, would let the mollusk fall on the meadow. Usually the force of the fall was sufficient to break the shell. The crows, as soon as they had let fall their burden, immediately returned to the island and bars, and gathered more mussels. This was continued until the returning tide made mussel-hunting impracticable. In no instance did the crows carry the food they were gathering by their feet; a method said to be adopted occasionally by these birds. There is one fact with reference to this mussel-hunting by the crows which is, I think, indicative of greater intelligence than the mere fact of lifting an object and dropping it in order to break it. This is, that all the mussels so dropped were left undisturbed until the returning waters made further fishing impracticable, when the birds hastened to feast on the results of their intelligent labor. Marvellous as it may seem, these crows recognized the nature of tides, and, knowing their time was short, made as good use of it as possible.

The crow is, beyond all question, the most intelligent of our birds, more so, indeed, than the average parrot.

CHAPTER XIII.
AN OCTOBER DIARY—CONTINUED.

OCTOBER 10.—The predicted frost has come. Not in uncertain patches that needed a glass to detect them, but as a generous gift to everything that looked upward to the star-lit sky. Before sunrise I heard a song-sparrow rejoicing, " Good, good, good, autumn's coming."

It was charming to hear the meadow-larks this morning. From the top of a tall oak that stands alone in the fields an old bird whistled, "I see you—you can't see me," and I could not. The cunning bird knew well how to arrange himself with reference to the surrounding leaves, and, with perfect security, whistled to his heart's content, and with just a suspicion of banter in his tones. Nearer and nearer I drew towards the tree, and still he sang, "I see you—you can't see me." Finally I reached the long shadow of the tree, and the lark probably had this as his guide, for, once there, he arose directly upward from the tree's topmost twig, and, as if to ridicule my eyesight, whistled with redoubled energy, "You can't see me;" but I did, and heard him so plainly that the music of his early morning song still lingers clearly in my memory, so clearly that I have but to close my eyes to see again the field, the tree, the rising sun, and the lark.

The meadow-lark is one of several birds that are usually considered as migratory, but which are strictly resident in this neighborhood. Indeed, I have always classed them among our winter birds, because it is from autumn to early spring that they sing most frequently and become most prominent among the birds seen during the rambles of this time of year. I would not have it understood that they are silent during summer, but then they are lost in the multitude, from not possessing sufficiently strong features of shape or song to attract particular attention. Curiously enough, these birds are not partial to our meadows as formerly. The great majority of all that I have seen of late years have been in the upland fields, and no longer do I find them in flocks. A dozen at most, and these scattered, is what one usually sees, and oftener a single pair.

How often I have been told that the swallows gather in force in some good convening ground, and, after discussing the subject on the 10th of September, depart on the 11th. It is an old woman's story, which I know dates back to the seventeenth century in my own family, and, like nine tenths of these sayings, unfortunately indestructible, it is absolutely false. Not even a hard frost sends them off. At least, I saw thousands to-day— just a month later than they should be—merry and active as in June, and I do not believe they will go for a week or more, if the weather moderates. So long as the food supply keeps up swallows are happy, and will not worry about possible cold snaps. If these come, then it will be time enough for them to go. The swallows seen to-day were not all of one species.

"How long will a wren live?" I was asked to-day. I replied, "Ten years;" for I know of one, or think so, that summered a decade in the back-yard. My friend mentioned a lame one that for nine consecutive years nested in the same place. There is probably a good deal of variation among small birds in this respect, but I have failed to gather satisfactory data bearing upon this point. I believe that the warblers, as a class, are shorter lived than the finches, yet cannot say how or when I became so impressed. But I do know of a little chipping sparrow that certainly was ten years old when it died, and probably older; and canaries are known to have lived a much longer time. A partially albino humming-bird nested in the same tree for seven summers, the albinism being my sure guide to the bird's identity.

I went nutting to-day for the first time this season, choosing the finest of the trees in the pasture meadows for my grounds, a stately shell-bark, towering up just eighty-two feet, and as symmetrical as a scissor-trimmed evergreen. The wind and the frost during the night conspired to rob the tree of its fruit, and scattered over the grass beneath were the white-shelled nuts. I stooped and gathered until my back ached, and then, choosing a seat from which I could see the tree to advantage, sat down to contemplate it. I know every tree within three miles of it this side of the river, and there is not one that, for beauty, can compare with it. The drooping elms, the enormous beeches, the commanding oaks, all bid us pause, and it is no belittling worship to bow down to them; but I yield not in my original declaration. The meadow shell-bark is the chiefest of them all. However otherwise opinions may differ, my neighbors are one with me in this. It is always mentioned with an emphasized *the*.

When, in midwinter, a year ago, the meadows were snowclad, and scarcely afforded shelter to a wandering rabbit, this splendid tree was the resting-place—the observatory—of an eagle that spent a month with us, in spite of persecution. In the early spring the branches were often black with the clouds of grakles and starlings. In summer, when every twig spread its leafy banner to the breeze, this same stately tree was the home of more warblers than all the surrounding thickets contained. The preference shown by these birds to this tree over others near by was very marked, and I believe I saw no species of warbler elsewhere not also seen upon it. In September the associated king-birds and bluebirds made it their principal rendezvous; and to-day, as it is dropping its fruit, it harbors birds of half a dozen kinds. The crows are on its topmost branches, a flicker is but little lower down, nuthatches are everywhere, a crested tit announces its presence with its clear voice, and restless kinglets chase spiders along the outermost twigs.

October 11.—The air was full of birds, mostly chattering robins, but with others fairly represented; and it was an unusual experience to hear so very much and see next to nothing. The fog, as usual, was most dense over the meadows, and when I plunged into it, bushes a dozen yards distant were no longer to be seen. Do meadow mice know that the hawks cannot see them, and so have a good time on the wet grass? I saw scores of them scampering about, and their united squeaks were not altogether unlike the chirping of birds. A star-nosed mole, too, was taking an airing on the ditch banks; but it heard me before I could reach it, and plunged into the water. They are freer of foot than common moles, and swim with grace and rapidity.

It is during such a fog as that of to-day that birds prove their possession of a spoken language. I saw a few crows, perhaps twenty, that were scattered among the tree-tops at the mouth of the gully. These birds seldom uttered the same sound twice consecutively. No two of them uttered similar sounds. They were so far scattered that they could not see each other. To me, standing beneath them, it was precisely similar to a gathering of foreigners discoursing earnestly in an (to me) unknown tongue. Certainly the loud and varied cries of each individual crow could not have been uttered for his own edification merely, as is true of the songs of certain birds; and, to prove that this view of the matter is correct, it was not long before these birds came to a conclusion upon an important subject they had been discussing; for, with a unity of movement not otherwise explicable, they all came to the ground. Unfortunately I did not conceal myself quickly enough, and they all went back again with unceremonious haste. Still, they did not take flight until after brief consultation, when they started towards the river as a little flock, keeping as near each other as practicable. Such little incidents must be witnessed to be appreciated;

but, even without their occurrence, the evidence is abundant, not merely to lead one to suspect, but to practically demonstrate to him, that crows have a spoken language.

The clear, white, icy casing that enveloped every blade of grass and twisted twig they call a "killing frost;" but what does it kill? The nights are still as noisy as before it came, so a certain range of animal life is unaffected. The grass is yet green as in midsummer. There is a sickening something in the air of August that poisons one who lingers too late afield, which is now wanting; this the frost killed, and the rambler can realize its absence. Nature otherwise remains the same. We hear no evening chorus of frogs, it is true; but even they are not altogether silent, and the toad by the kitchen door still rattles his vesper thanks for the noonday feast of flies. There is no sure guide to the effects of frost; it comes too often after nature has put on her autumn aspect to say that it is the cause of any change other than the one I have mentioned.

At the bend of the hill or terrace, among a few young native trees, I found a Lombardy poplar that has been making a vigorous growth for several summers, and is now ten or twelve feet high. Straightway I sat down to look at it leisurely. It was a tree to contemplate. Some thirty years ago my house, my neighbor's house, and my neighbor's neighbor's, east, north, and south, had a double row of tall poplars in front of them—tall, straight, dignified, unbending poplars; strict, orthodox Quakers turned to trees. As I sat looking at the tapering top of this lone tree, still in full leaf, the old front-yard of my earliest recollection came back to me very vividly. The little paling that surrounded the trees marked my playground, and beyond all was terra incognita. In later years, when I dared venture in the branches of the apple-trees in the lane, I longed to explore these poplars also, but to reach their tops, or even to near them, proved impracticable. This the wary crow-blackbirds seemed to know, for a colony nested among them every summer. How I longed to secure a nest, with its complement of eggs! Day after day those tantalizing nests, far out of reach, were watched, in hopes, by some lucky mishap, one of them might be dislodged. Still later, from some unknown cause, these poplars sickened. Dead, leafless branches for a while pointed skyward, rattled in the wind, and bit by bit were scattered over the grass; and so, in a few brief summers, these old trees were dead — not only the home trees, but those of my neighbors — and now I know of none within the range of my rambles, save the young sapling that I found this morning.

October 12.—The haze, the quiet, the soft south wind, and towering trees, still green of leaf, and ribboned with scarlet creepers, twining from trunk to twig, give this perfect day that combination of color in perfection which is the great seal of the month of October. The harsh scream of the blue-jay waxes musical at such a time; nothing seems crude or out of place. The squat, broad-leaved oaks now show the deepest green. So tough and leathery are their leaves that the late frost could not affect them. The white, pin, swamp-white, red, and chestnut oaks all cluster here, either on the slope of the hill or in the level meadow, and show the effect of frost, if that it was which changed the color of their leaves; but this sturdy *Quercus obtusiloba* laughs at all such cold snaps, and will wave green leaves until November, perhaps later, and then drop them down to Mother Earth, tough, shining, unbroken, and brown as the polished chinkapins upon which they fall.

The increasing warmth towards noon brings out myriads of wasps, that congregate on the south side of the house and of all the outbuildings. I dare venture into no sunny nook regardless of them. They are not teachable, at least at short notice, as Sir John Lubbock's wasp was trained, and respect no lover of nature and admirer of hymenoptera. It is all one with them: touch, and they touch back with emphasis. I sat upon one this morning while in the meadow, and how quickly he unseated me. Now, safe from their assaults, I hear their horny heads bring up against the window-panes like rattling hail. They retire undiscouraged, and return as impetuously. Lively little battering-rams, always ready for action, never tiring of this butting process, and never learning that they cannot get in. They give us every evidence of stupidity, yet are really teachable creatures.

Cabbage-butterflies and fritillaries floated over the frostbitten grass, active as in August, stooping now and then to suck some sweet the October frost has spared; but not a flower was to be seen in acres of meadow. A more striking insect phenomenon was the myriads of grasshoppers. They weighed down every blade of grass, and yet there was not a bird in sight to feed upon them. These hoppers were not eating the grass. Had they been, not a blade would have been left by sundown. I chased a cloud of them into the widest portion of the main meadow-ditch, but all, I think, swam safely across. Not a frog or fish appeared to rise to the surface and seize one.

I pushed one well down the tall clay chimney of a Diogenes crayfish, but it promptly returned, none the worse for its subterranean journey. I placed another in the dark den of a villainous-looking spider, but it was simply ordered out, and not harmed. It would seem as if these grasshoppers have no enemies, or was it that all carnivorous creatures hereabouts were surfeited with their flesh?

Passing to another lower, weedier, wetter meadow, the number of dragon-flies was the most marked feature of the locality. A few were black as polished jet; others gray, green, red, barred, and indefinitely varied. I did not stop to count the varieties, but to learn why so many gathered in so small a space. The cause proved to be the decomposing remains of a calf, of which but little beyond the bones were left. Not a square inch of the exposed surfaces of these but was covered with the flies. I knew they were carnivorous, but not to the extent suggested by their hovering over nearly dry bones.

I was not much surprised, on a closer inspection of the remains of the calf, to see half a dozen meadow-mice scuttle off through the tall grass, for they are fonder of a flesh than vegetable diet, in spite of their anatomy; but I was surprised to find large numbers of humble-bees creeping over the ground, in and out among the bones, reaching to where the dragon-flies could not go. Tainted flesh, it would seem, has a host of admirers in many orders of the animal kingdom. On moving some of the loose bones I found beetles of several sorts, and ants, white, black, and red, and at times disturbed whole clouds of minute flies of no name known to me. What a wealth of animal life to be found in so unsavory a place! Mice, bees, beetles, dragon-flies, and minute insects by the million; all feeding quietly on the shreds of skin and tendons left by greedy vultures a month or more ago.

The threatening bank of dull gray clouds that all day long had been lying along the western horizon roused itself to action an hour or more before sunset, and, overspreading the unflecked blue sky of the morning, practically closed the day. Without further warning it rained, suddenly, steadily, penetratingly. The thickest foliage could not ward it off, and the steady dripping of dislodged raindrops was heard all through the woods long after the shower had passed by. Without a farewell ray to gild the tree-tops on the eastern slopes, the sun went down, and a gloomy night followed what so lately had been a rare, ripe autumn day, full to the brim with all of October's glories.

Gloomy out-of-doors, but none the less worthy of being studied. What of the wealth of life seen earlier in the day? How and where did it take shelter? It would be hard, indeed, to determine this in every case;

but of a few forms something may be said. The myriads of grasshoppers, strange as it may seem, cunningly sought the broader blades of grass, and, securing a firm hold on the under side, stood, head downward, comfortably roofed and safe from any ordinary rain. I found thousands sheltered in this simple manner.

The meadow mice apparently anticipate a soaking rain, and their tortuous tunnels, shallow as they are, were so arranged that the rain did not flow through them. In little, hay-lined anterooms I found several, and all were dry as chips. The roofs of these snuggeries were waterproof, and the rain was warded off from the paths that led to them. These mice were prepared for any ordinary dash of rain, but I suppose had other shelter during and after protracted storms. My studies were here interrupted by a second shower, and I was forced to seek shelter for myself, rather than look for the dragon-flies, as I intended.

The tangled clumps of wild roses, so lately rich with pink blossoms, and showing the brightest of green leaves, were, to-day, strangely different. Every leaf was in place, but marred by brown splotches that gave them an aged and worn-out look; but, to compensate them for the loss of both green leaves and pink blossoms, the seed capsules were beautifully polished and bright red. No berry-bearing bush ever shone with crimson fruit to better advantage. While I stood by a thicket of these roses, in the meadow, birds from the marshes, sparrows, blackbirds and robins came and went continually, yet not one touched the brilliant seed-vessels of the wild roses. Do none of our resident birds ever eat them? If so, their brilliant color goes for naught, unless evolved to attract those irregular visitors from the north that are fond of rose seeds the cross-bills.

I opened scores of these seed-vessels and found but one that was wormy; the seeds have a pleasant sub-acid flavor, and it seemed very strange that not a bird was there to feast upon them. Surely they are preferable to the berries of the poke and the sour fruit of the gum-tree; and yet the omnivorous crow passes them by when starving during snow-storms.

The ash does not flourish on the hillside. It grows in moderate abundance, but never becomes a marked tree. Ashes, with us, are always to be sought—never, like oaks, elms, or hickories, do they intrude upon you. The leaves of one that I saw to-day were a bright chrome yellow; the foliage of another was maroon; the leaves of a third were scarlet, and a half-dozen saplings were unaltered in hue, being brightly green as in early June. So little difference appeared in the surroundings that I was puzzled to know why there should be so great a variation in the color of the leaves. I studied other trees in this respect, but saw no difference at all equal to it.

By referring to notes, jotted down in years past, I find great irregularity in the time of the leaves appearing in spring. Of every half-dozen trees, some were late, some early; and therefore the well-known couplet,

> "The oak before the ash—there'll be a splash;
> The ash before the oak—there'll be a soak,"

suited the season, in all cases; for we had only to refer to the proper tree, later in the season, to prove that the tree was, at least for once, a true prophet.

As weather proverbs will always be in vogue, it is desirable to have some meaningless ones that are applicable to any season, and this is one of them.

The Indians, it would appear, were accustomed to cut off the ash-trees as soon as they were large enough for "basket stuff," and used but a very small portion of each. For this reason they soon became scarce, and now, in post-Indian times, as the tree is one of slow growth, the oaks, elms, and hickories have gotten the start, and are all found of much larger size than any ash-tree I have ever seen.

October 13.—Fog. How much this little word suggests to the rambler, when, up at sunrise, he finds that he can see nothing but the very nearest objects. The blotting-out of the familiar landscape is, in effect, to transport one to unfamiliar regions, and to-day the fog was so dense, and the range of vision so limited, it was like standing on a rock in mid-ocean. Still, a fog has its merits. It lends a pleasing sense of distance to the sounds heard, and muffling, as it seems, the lower tones, give the higher ones an unfamiliar character. I could hear few of the notes of distant song-birds, and recognized none of them. The scream of an impatient buzzard was unlike any sound I have ever heard, and only the fact of the hawk swooping within sight gave me opportunity of ever knowing whence came the weird sounds it uttered. Stranger than all sounded the deep-toned twittering of the grass-plover, clear as the tinkling of silver bells. Note after note came raining down from the unseen clouds above, and then, as the birds passed over, other notes, falling far out above the meadow, were barely audible to an attentive ear. Of course, the ever-present crows were noisy, often drowning the pleasant voices of dearer birds; but thrilling it was to hear the honking of bewildered wild-geese, that, having lost their way, now floundered, almost helplessly, in a sea of fog. How I hoped that they would stumble into the meadows that I might give chase! No such good-fortune, however, awaited me. Fainter and fainter were their voices, as they passed westward, towards the river. The Canada geese, at this time, are suggestive of cooler weather soon to come; but better the geese false prophets, and pleasant weather, than the converse, and premature winter.

To see the robins hurry out in their heels-over-head fashion, if not helpless from over-feeding, I plunged into a dense clump of poke, and away darted a hundred of these birds. They, too, were bewildered by the mist, and one, more reckless than the rest, flew directly into my face, so that I caught it. Its astonishment and fright robbed it of its breakfast, which, as a mass of gore, in appearance, was vomited over my breast. I let the bird go and only wished the breakfast had gone with it.

Passing into the woods, I was struck with the unusual variety of notes uttered by a company of jays. There were a dozen or more distinct sounds, all jay-like, it is true, but differing widely. I suppose that, as has been so often noticed with reference to crows, these birds were somewhat bewildered by the fog, and were discussing the subject in the only practicable way, by talking; only, instead of their ordinary clear-weather voices, this morning they seemed to have sore throats.

The spiders, of course, gloried in the fog, and all had their nets spread out to perfection. One web, covering the opening in a hollow fence-rail where a knot had loosened and fallen out, was unusually elaborate; so much so that I stopped to examine it. The web was funnel-shaped, eighteen inches in diameter at the exterior rim, and twelve inches in depth, or from the exterior margin to the knot-hole, where the owner lived. She was a dull, gray, hairy creature, an inch long, and rather forbidding in general appearance. There was no prey in the web at the time, so I hunted for the spider's as well as my own benefit. A single beetle was all that I could find, but this the spider declined to notice. A little later I found a dead kinglet or ruby-crowned wren, and this I gently placed on the web, where it appeared to be strong enough to bear its weight. The spider promptly rushed out and bit it several times, but made no attempt to move it. Then it began to spin other webs about it, in such a manner as to hold it perfectly secure. That this spider can eat even so small a bird is, I am sure, impracticable, so am puzzled to know what object it has in view with reference to it. Time will show.

October 14. — Clear as crystal, save a long line of

smoke-like fog that veils the river to the great bend and beyond. The snap in the air—I can call it nothing else—brought out the birds, as it always does, and crows cawed, jays jabbered, warblers chirped cheerily, and even the nuthatch forgot the obstruction in his throat, and every complaining "quank-quank" he uttered was not rasped, ragged, and rough; but sounded smoothly, softly, as a bird's note should.

Up in the fields, amid the long rows of corn-shocks, I lingered until long after sunrise, taking in draughts of morning air that were to keep me while I tarried in town, during the hot, dusty noon. I envied the huskers, with their pleasant surroundings; while they, deluded mortals, longed to spend their time in town.

It was the mice in the corn-fields that had called me thither, and I had not long to look before I found dozens. The short-tailed meadow mouse was there, having come up from the meadows, some weeks ago, to feed on the grain. But there is another species, so like the semi-domesticated house mouse that I am disposed to call it such, and, whether correctly or not, it is, when in the corn-fields, a most entertaining creature. This corn-field mouse, unlike the short-tailed meadow mice, does not have any runways in the stubble, but lodges among the corn-shocks, often half-way to their tops; making a nest by nibbling to a pulp the leaves of the plant. Here the little fellow will sit, and take life very easy until over goes the shock, at the hands of the huskers, when away darts the mouse, leaping like a jerboa, until it finds concealment in dead grass or other cover. I tried this morning to catch some of these house mice run wild, if such they are, but all were too quick for me. A year ago I tried to determine the species, but found no trace of various characters belonging to certain forms, such as the rice-field mouse or the harvest mouse; both of which are possibly found about here. On the other hand, the specimens examined did not quite accord with the descriptions given of a typical house mouse.

An observing old husker, to whom I applied for an opinion, said he did not believe they were the same as house mice. They were "too quick, too small, too black, too knowin'." I have no reason to believe my corn-field mouse is one not down in the books; and as I have never seen them except when the corn is being harvested, I have thought and still believe they are mice from the out-buildings that are abroad for a time, and will return to their old quarters in the course of the season. Supposing them to have been two or three months in the fields, ought we to expect a variation in the color of their fur? All such mice were apparently nearly black. As to their being "too knowin'," as my friend said, I am in doubt. It is a mistake to consider a house mouse dull; and my corn-field mice have never shown, in my presence, evidence of superior intellect.

That cunning spider has been visited again and again, but the purpose of spinning a web about that dead bird does not yet appear. I believe the fact that dead animal matter attracts flies is known to the spider, and so the bird was acceptable as a bait for them. If so, this is a wise spider. It may be, that in time, if the weather stays warm, the decomposing mass of bird-flesh will, of itself, be food that the spider will accept, but all this is conjectural.

I, to-day, tried placing a beetle grub on the web, but the spider would not accept it. It bit it, pushed it, and finally snapped the cords beneath and let it fall; then mended the web so neatly none could determine where it had been broken. This spider begins to know me from others, I think.

October 15.—The river is clearly defined, even from the distant ridge, as a steel-blue line, winding along the foot of the steep bluff; and the day is as cold as the river looks. This is the second white frost of the month. Every leaf, even every pine-needle, has its load of crystal to carry; and there is not a breath of wind to disturb them. Having to forego my morning ramble, I took in the country from "Overlook," the most commanding point of view near by. Stood there for an hour and smelt the battle from afar, wishing myself in a score of visible places; and, because I was unable to go anywhere, longed to explore every distant point in the horizon. But staying at home may be turned to good account. There were birds in abundance in the door-yard trees, and an excited Carolina wren, in the stable, whistled so loudly the terrier barked himself hoarse. Something surely must be the matter, I thought, and set out to investigate, when whish! came the wren athwart my nose, and a winter wren followed as swiftly and as near. They evidently had had a fight, and it looked very much as though the larger bird of the two was whipped. However this may have been, the Carolina wren soon recovered from the contest, and sang as usual, as though the world was his, and made for him alone.

Until this morning I have seen no cardinal red-birds for several weeks. To-day a half-dozen were in the garden, seed-hunting and chirping, but none sang. These birds have probably been summering to the north of us, and are now on their way to more temperate winter-quarters. The more strictly migratory are they as they spread northward in spring, but here, thank fortune! they are resident.

One might suppose these birds to be very conspicuous objects, from their color; yet they are not always so. To-day they glistened in the clear sunshine and were not readily recognized as birds. I tested this in many ways, and found it was really difficult to get a view of them that enabled me to be sure of their identity. They were always in motion, and seemed to keep themselves so exposed to the sunlight that lurking foes might be blinded by their brilliancy. Often they appeared to be fragments of glass in the bushes, and not beautiful crested red-birds. But at other times, as I have elsewhere shown, they study to conceal themselves.

From the "Overlook," as I call a favorable point on the brow of the terrace, where the river and meadows are in fullest view, I noticed this morning an unusual number of hawks, all flying in the same direction, south-southwest. It can hardly be said that they were migrating—there were too few of them; and very likely they changed their direction before long, and sought only the wild woods of Pennsylvania. They flew at too great an elevation to enable me to determine anything more definite than that they were hawks or buzzards; but their passing presence recalled an October migration of hawks such as I have never since, nor had I ever before, witnessed.

My attention was called to these migrating hawks (there were three or four different species of them) at about nine o'clock in the morning, and for an hour I watched their progress. I subsequently learned that they had been seen as early as sunrise, and for five hours later than when I saw them last; so they were, at least, numerous enough to require nine hours to pass a given point. How much longer than this they continued on their westward course, the growing darkness prevented our determining. These hawks were noticeable not only for their numbers, but the manner of their flight. While moving in a westerly direction, they by no means followed a direct course, but described large circles, or ellipses, each intersecting the previous one. This, of course, made their onward progress slow. A no less marked feature was their constant screaming. Every bird seemed angry at all his fellows, and scolded each in turn, as it came near. On the other hand, there was no actual quarrelling.

The weather was sufficiently warm to-day to bring out a few flies, and some of them were attracted to the kinglet on the spider's web, that had so far decomposed as to throw off a decided odor. The spider sat near the entrance of her den, not at all concealed, and darted upon every fly that became entangled in the web. Large flies, that by hard struggling might escape, were seized with lightning-like rapidity and benumbed by a bite, and then the spider left it, to wait for other large flesh-flies that might come. In this way a dozen were caught by noon, and then, for some undeterminable reason, the spider snapped the web supporting the dead bird and let it fall upon the underlying fence-rail. The web was not immediately repaired.

Although there have been two hard frosts, the ferns that grow upon the south hillside are neither dead nor drooping. I worked my way through a dense cluster that was nearly breast-high. Pausing a moment to hear the repetition of an unrecognized bird-note, I noticed a pale yellow spot in front of me, that appeared to move slightly, in a life-like manner. If an animal, it certainly had no color-sense, sitting, as it did, in so exposed a position. Or is it possible that it has no enemies and needs no protection? Drawing nearer, I saw the "yellow spot" to be, as I surmised, a Pickering's Hyla, and tried to catch it with my hand. It was too quick. It gave a vigorous upward and onward leap, alighting on a distant fern frond. I measured the distance afterwards and found it to be just three feet. This trivial incident suggested how readily such creatures, if timid, can elude our search.

For months I had one of them in a Wardian case, and it was undoubtedly the most voracious of all the allied creatures about us. Its digestion was perfect, and marvellously rapid. It always was ready for another fly, however many previously had been given it; and yet, a fast of two weeks seemed to prove no inconvenience. In one instance, it had a prolonged nip-and-tuck tussle with a great black horse-fly, larger than itself. It ultimately disabled the insect, but failed to accomplish the often-attempted act of swallowing it. A month later, I offered this same Hyla another fully as large, but which was deprived of its wings. After many efforts, this wingless fly was partially swallowed, and the Hyla remained with widely distended jaws for nearly an hour, when, with one mighty effort, it rejected it, and has not since been disposed to eat other than common house-flies. Never, I believe, has this little fellow "peeped," since I placed him in the case.

October 17.—
"A cloudy west and a sunny east,
That rouses the bird and sends home the beast,"

fitly describes this morning; and if the couplet quoted is not poetry, it at least has the merit of being true. From dawn to sunrise, and the short twilight, of our October days, is worth more to the naturalist than all the mellow sunshine of the intervening hours. The novelties are only to be seen then, and the best efforts in every direction are far oftener witnessed then than at any other time. Creatures whose presence would be wholly unsuspected, if we were never abroad except hours after sunrise, are often seen in the early dawn; not so much because these animals prefer this time of day, but because they know that man, their arch-enemy, is less likely to be encountered. One of the most striking instances of this fact of which I have knowledge is that of a pair of raccoons that took up their abode in a hollow apple-tree not two hundred yards from a farm-house. Here they lived all one winter and spring, and only by mere chance were they discovered during the summer. So systematic had these 'coons been in all this time, that not even their young were seen; and yet these cunning creatures feasted on my neighbor's poultry quite frequently, and in thus outwitting both dogs and men they certainly offer convincing evidence of the power of "close calculation" on their part.

The evening proved quiet and eventless. As I walked down the lane I saw a single apple on the top of a tall tree, and after throwing ninety-and-nine sticks at it, it came down of its own accord. It was stale, flat, and unprofitable.

The tree that bore it was full of bloom in May, and one worthless apple the result, in October! If I do them no injustice this is like some people I have met. Full of blushing promises in the spring, and autumn passes with but one poor performance, or none.

Turning to the woods, I heard what I took to be the last katydid of the season. It gasped, or rather rasped, "Katy" a dozen times, and finally accomplished one melancholy "did." The poor thing had grown old, and these last efforts may have been complaints that it was forced to await the summons of another frost before it joined its kindred.

How seldom one thinks of the possibility, not the inevitability, of growing old! Yet, taking a retrospective view, as I lingered in the lane, it did seem as though the years were shorter than formerly, and the elasticity of youth was growing less and less; so that it cannot be long before my song, too, will be shortened, syllable by syllable. What further might have been thought upon these doleful subjects can never be known. My unwilling cogitation was happily interrupted by the looked-for owl, which heralded his approach by a wild too-whoo-oo, that was music to my expectant ears. This owl was of slender build, with wide-spread, tapering wings and a generally hawk-like movement, as it sailed with speed from tree to tree and bush to bush, as though looking for something it had lost. I had hopes of cultivating its acquaintance, but it would not. Every attempt to follow proved a miserable failure.

The rapidity with which the gray squirrels make their nests of dead leaves and twigs is something marvellous. In a single night the work is often done, unless they subsequently add a little finer material for the lining. To-day I saw a large, globular leaf-nest near the top of a tall oak, which I know was not there yesterday. I was then examining every twig of this same tree for a little warbler, that eluded all my efforts, and I could not have overlooked so prominent a mass of leaves as this nest. No one squirrel could have done this work. It is the result of joint labors of three or four, and, unless they can work in darkness, must have been, even then, accomplished rapidly. How they secure these leaves against winter's winds is not clear, but they are always intact at the close of the season. To be sure, the twigs are not dead and brittle when gathered, but this does not explain altogether how they interweave them so that few, if any, become dislodged.

Flying squirrels, also, build such nests, and I have known one to harbor seven squirrels during the winter. In this case, the leaf-nest was in a tree that had a large cavity in the trunk, at the base of the lowermost branches. This capacious retreat had been discarded, apparently, because it had been found too much exposed to storms; and squirrels have yet to learn how to construct a door. To avoid being drowned out, the large leaf-nest I have mentioned was constructed. The family occupying it was less nocturnal in habits than any I have seen. They were sure to leave home before sunset; and twice, on cloudy days, I saw them frisking about at noon. Constraint seemed exceedingly distasteful, or were they afflicted with the common complaint of insomnia?

October 18.—Snow-birds in abundance. In them we have evidence of autumn in earnest. It is late for their first appearance, and probably there have been dozens skulking in the bushes for weeks past; but, to-day, early in the morning, they rushed through the dripping leaves of the black oaks, for it was raining; and these birds were singing, too, a plain but pleasing melody.

Burroughs, in ever-delightful "Wake-Robin," asks: "Who has heard the snow-bird sing?" I have, and not only to-day, but all the past autumn, winter, and early spring. They are never mute, with us, but sing longer, louder, sweeter than usual just before a snow-fall. Not so long before that their song can be taken for a weather-sign, but at that half-hour before the first flakes appear, when the woods are always painfully silent, unless these birds proclaim the glad tidings, "the snow is coming." Indeed, the song of this bird may be fairly well expressed by the words, "Snow's coming, 'tis, 'tis, 'tis."

With the snow-birds, this morning, there were a few white-crowned sparrows, singing their peculiar songs. The former—Juncos, as I call them—seemed to exult over reaching the dear old hillside again, and even quarrelled with the robins that still thronged the poke-bushes, gum-trees, and grapevines. They certainly did not appear to have been on any long journey, and probably, like many warblers, have been coming south by very easy stages.

A gentle rain, such as that of this morning, is stimulating to bird-life. The few warblers that I saw were constantly chirping, and one Maryland yellow-throat sang vociferously. The crested titmice were noisier than usual.

Crossing the pasture lot, I was serenaded by rival song-sparrows, one perched upon the garden fence, the other on a tall mullein stalk. The effect was fine. The birds followed each other antiphonally, uttering nothing in concert; so I took it, they had made me umpire to determine their merits as songsters. I, at least, acted fairly by listening for a long time, and when, at last, they flew away without hearing my decision, I bowed politely, hoping by so doing to give each the impression that I thought him the victor.

My fence-rail spider has renewed her elaborate web, and, I thought, recognized me. I was duly careful not to annoy her or her house in any way, simply "took a look." She showed her cunning in one way, admirably. The leaves of an overhanging branch were in a position to make a trough, and conducted a little stream of raindrops directly to the opening of the spider's den proper, or nest. To rid herself of this annoyance, she had gathered a small leaf, and placed it in the web so as to catch the water and carry it to one side, where it did no harm. The more I see of my friend, the more convinced I am of her cunning. I use this word as it would be applied to a person. It is precisely the same sort of mental phenomenon.

The spider recalled the ant-lions, and I found their pits pretty much obliterated by the rain, except such as were directly under the bottom rail of the fence. Were these purposely placed in this sheltered spot? I have never been able to detect any design in the locating of these pits, and often have found them where it was most unlikely any prey would come, yet the ant-lion is a sensible creature, in some respects, as we have seen.

The afternoon and evening were cool, and the former windy. Not a bird of this morning was to be found. What has become of them? Perhaps nothing in the whole range of our home ornithology is more of a puzzle than the sudden appearance and disappearance of birds. As I stood on the hillside this morning, it is safe to say there were a hundred within a circuit of five hundred yards, perhaps twice that many birds; yet this evening, before sunset even, standing in the same spot, I saw none, and, taking much the same walk, still neither saw nor heard a single individual. Every bird had left the neighborhood. During very stormy weather, particularly in winter, I have found many birds that had sought shelter and were as unlikely to be seen by the average pedestrian as the burrowing mammals; but this is not the case during days like this. The birds are not in the cedars, nor in hollow trees, nor in caves. They evidently have taken wing, moved to do so by some common impulse, the character of which cannot well be determined. Birds of different species, and of very different habits, are never seen, as a mixed company, to move off like a flock of blackbirds, but drop out of sight and hearing, one by one, gradually, and in an hour or more, it may be, a crowded clump of trees will be absolutely deserted. To-morrow morning every bird may be back, or as many others may have taken their places. It is pleasant to remember these birdless interims are of short duration. This may seem a very trivial matter, and one of no possible interest, but it is a fact in the history of our resident birds, the "true inwardness" of which we have yet to learn.

As athwart the hillside's wooded slope the lengthening shadows slowly crept, the last rays of the sun warmed the varied colors of a host of trees, and made of the extended bluff a brilliant panorama. The maples were scarlet, crimson, and maroon; the tulip-trees yellow; the sassafras and gums purple; the birches gray, and all else green as in midsummer.

October 19.—The skies, early this morning, were pearly with mist; the ground silvered with frost. The sun barely asserted himself, and the trees cast but uncertain shadows over the meadows. It is the third of these magnificent white frosts, and an earnest but not wholly effectual effort of the season to silence the katydids, crickets, frogs, and salamanders. Of course, an overbrave individual, now and then, will pipe his regrets at the death of summer; and in the Indian summer of next month many will chatter "I told you so," thinking spring has come again. These are the deluded creatures that form the laughing-stock of their kind. Probably every class of animals possesses such.

The third white frost, and now, persimmons are ruddy, wrinkled, and ripe. It is strange this fruit should have remained so long neglected. To be sure, there is needed some instruction in the art of eating it, but this can readily be obtained by application to the average country boy living in persimmon districts. All that is required, really, is to use your tongue and lips, and keep your teeth out of the way. A wise persimmon eater I once knew took the precaution of placing his teeth in his pocket before commencing operations. The fact is, the fruit resents being bitten, and invariably wrinkles one's mouth into every conceivable shape when treated to a crushing bite.

That the persimmon is capable of being greatly improved and made a valuable fruit has often been remarked, but no one seems to have started the improving process. I have long since learned, however, that there are persimmons and persimmons, and while some are really worthless and painfully astringent, even after many frosts, others, after a nipping frost or two, are really delicious.

My talkative neighbor, Miles Overfield, has noticed this fact, too, and when questioned about it this morning, said, "The best p'simmons grow on dry ground, and some say the trees must be mixed with oaks to get their top flavor. I know the best trees about here grow that way, and the 'possums know it too. The big p'simmon-trees 'long the line fence 'twixt you and next place always has a 'possum or two in, in the full of the October moon. I've taken one or two there every fall so long as I can remember."

"What other animal eats persimmons, or does any bird?" I asked, when Miles stopped a moment to catch his breath.

"Not that I know of. Perhaps a blue-jay might eat the seeds, or a starvin' crow, in a snow-storm; but I never saw the like."

Not because a few long straws were lying conveniently near, but for purely biological purposes, I took the bung from a barrel of new cider. If this third white frost has not killed all insect life, then they will be sure to collect about the barrel. No insects came, and I found, on testing the cider, that if insects were still about they surely would have flocked hither—the cider was excellent. It would appear that the rule of three frosts is nearly correct, and kills, or sends to winter-quarters, flies, bugs, and beetles that have hummed and buzzed all summer.

Let the above stand as a proof of the absurdity of hasty conclusions! Here is another barrel of cider on the south side of the house—the other lies in the shaded north side—and it is alive with bees, wasps, and indefinite diptera of no names. This cider is no sweeter than the other, but it is in a position twenty degrees warmer. It is a good rule, in making any investigations as to the prevalence or absence of animal life, or in judging of the effects of weather, to have a barrel of cider on each side of the house, and only draw conclusions after all have been examined.

It needed but a short walk, to-day, after the sun was well up, to see that frost stupefies but does not kill, except some of the tenderest insects. Miles Overfield remarked, a few days ago, that wasps would not sting after the third frost. Will they not? Could my thumb testify, it would have some interesting remarks to make upon this point. Whether it is stinging or not, the effect is the same, and the thumb needs as much of a poultice. A good rule is to flatten a wasp before you pick it up—a better one is to let the creature severely alone.

As I passed through a gory thicket of half-crushed poke-weeds I was startled by a large bird flying almost into my face. It seemed to be an albino robin, as it flew; but a better view enabled me to identify it. It was a shrike. There was nothing offensive in its general appearance, but the flock of thistle-finches near by evidently thought otherwise, for they scattered in hot haste as it approached. Shrikes are yearly becoming more common, and it is to be hoped that they will wax strong enough to keep down the disgusting superfluity of English sparrows. Both the northern and southern shrikes occur here, so between them some good may be accomplished.

An interesting occurrence of to-day was the freak of a passing gust of wind, or whatever it may be called. While standing at the edge of the woods, one tree, a very tall tulip-tree, was quite rudely shaken by the wind, sending a tremor through every leaf, and bending the upper branches; yet not a leaf on any other tree stirred. The disturbance evidently came from above, and spent its force in the one tree it struck in the descent.

The hornets' nests that I have found, as yet, have all been close to the ground; a sure sign of a cold winter, it is said. This was a matter to refer to Miles Overfield, and I hailed him this evening, as he passed through the yard.

"What of the hornets' nests, this fall, Miles; are they high or low?"

"All high up, and we'll have an open winter. Never knew it to fail. Have seen a dozen, and all are on the tops of the trees."

"Well, I have seen just half a dozen, and every one was low down; one on the bottom rail of a fence," I replied.

"Ain't you a jokin'?" Miles asked, with a look of astonishment.

"Not at all," I replied.

"Well, if that's so, there's goin' to be both kinds of

winter, by spells; but I never knew the like of this; never;" and he showed that he was sorely puzzled.

This is the average weather-wisdom of my neighbors. Their convenient memories make the rules hold good in all cases, and contradictory facts are never recognized at the time, and subsequently denied in toto.

The broad quarter-mile of Poaetquissings, above the flood-gates, was perhaps, to-day, the most charming spot within easy walking distance. What the two earlier frosts had failed to accomplish that of last night has effected, and not a trace of lily leaves, pickerel-weed, arum, or other aquatic growth mars the surface of the water. Smooth as a mirror, it reflected, without a break, every tree that overlooked the creek, now in the glory of autumn coloring. Scarlet maples, yellow ashes, purple oaks, and varied birches were all faithfully portrayed. There was an unstained sky below as well as above, and my boat seemingly floated in space. In perfect silence I drifted from shore to shore. It was painfully still, as though Nature herself had died; and then, with a startling suddenness, trying even to old nerves, a kingfisher darted, with a wild scream, into the water, and shattered the mirror. But it was a welcome sound, when the shock of its abruptness passed. A stately heron, that had been dreaming in the drooping elms, flew from its perch, and waded, knee-deep, along the opposite shore. A startled pike leaped from the water; a muskrat swam with but the tip of his nose above the surface, leaving an ever-widening wedge of silvery ripples behind him. It was a strange transition from absolute silence to noisy, active life. All these creatures, of whose presence I was unaware, appeared to be waiting, each for the other, to break the spell that bound them. It fell to the kingfisher's lot. He moved, spoke, and all was set in motion.

Towards noon, when the gathering haze was tinting with old-gold the distant hills, and half the horizon was wrapped in mist, I wandered to the edge of the low-lying mucky meadow, scarcely hoping, even there, to find active life. A strange stillness brooded over all, and gave to the occasional chirp of some restless bird a weird, unnatural tone. Soon, however, I saw, far to the south, a flock of grakles that were coming towards me. I welcomed their promised presence and stood awaiting their arrival, when suddenly, from no cause that I could detect, they turned towards the river. I was doomed to be alone, and threw my stick into the tall reeds, as a relief to my feelings. Very childish this, I admit, but happily it effected what I desired. As the stick fell, up from a tangled mat of grass struggled a wee brown bird, warbling a few sweet notes. I took it, they were uttered to comfort me. Then another of these birds rose up, but barely into view; rose, sang, and disappeared. Neither flew boldly; both seemed to be unable to do so; but the heretofore silent meadow now became vocal with these sweet flute-notes in brown feathers, struggling to be free. It was the marsh-sparrows that wrought the change; and probably, of all our song-birds, no one is so little known to people generally. This arises principally from the fact that their haunts are seldom intruded upon by mere lovers of bird music. They are content with the song-sparrow in the garden, and so never learn of its cousin in the dismal swamp.

The marsh-sparrow, with us, remains closely to the wet meadows, passing a quiet, secluded life; wasting its sweetness on the desert air, if it sings for the pleasure of others—which it does not do.

When the little commotion caused by my impatient throwing of a stick in the grass had died away, not a bird was to be seen. I waited for half an hour, but neither heard nor saw one. Gathering a few sticks, I threw them into the marsh, and with like result. Here, there, everywhere, like marsh-wrens, up to the tops of the taller reeds they came, fluttered, sang, and disappeared.

These sparrows afford an instance of how a most interesting creature may be very near us, yet his presence be quite unsuspected. By a mere chance, they became the notable feature of my morning's walk.

It is stated in every ornithological work to which I have access that these birds are migratory, and in more northern localities this is true; but it is only partly true in Central New Jersey. Many come and go, I doubt not, but a goodly number remain, and add a charm to the winter scenes on the meadows. I have even heard these sparrows, during bright moonlit nights, sing while perched upon the tops of leafless twigs, projecting above the ice and snow.

Coues, in his "Birds of the Northwest," says, according to his own observations, "it is only a bird of passage in the Middle States," a most remarkable statement, considering that scores of them are in my meadows all the year round. Their song, he adds, he has never heard, and quotes Nuttall's description. This does not do the bird justice. The notes are more like those of a song-sparrow than of the field-chippy, and have that liquid character which is their greatest charm. The late Wilson Flagg does the swamp-sparrow justice, in remarking that "he sings so sweetly that the very desolation of the scene borrows a charm from his voice." But I can only go part way with Mr. Flagg. How any one can call a swamp desolate is indeed strange! The mucky meadow desolate! Is it a scene of desolation, even in October, to watch the waving of the tall reeds, as the breezes gently sway them; to hear the song of this sparrow, of which I have said so much; to watch the broad-winged harrier beat the grass, that frightened birds may rise to, perhaps, their own destruction; to mark the mighty flocks of red-wings that, as a cloud, settle on the reeds, and bend them to the water's edge; to hear the songs of half our winter birds, that now are coming from their summer homes in the North; to follow in their flight, as, with all the grace of a fly-catcher, the blue-birds sally over the reeds in pursuit of the few remaining insects? All this, and more, passed before me in the course of my walk to-day, along the grassy margin of the marsh; and never would it occur to me to call such a spot a scene of desolation. That spot is, to me, desolate, in proportion as man has eradicated nature's handiwork.

October 20.—A misty morning, at sunrise, without a trace of frost; and all quiet, both in the fields and meadows. There appears to have been a fresh arrival of Northern birds, and the fields are filled with tree-sparrows, snow-birds, white-throated finches, and some undetermined species. None sang. Why these fits of silence I do not know; but they are not uncommon. I have watched an individual bird for quite an hour, and not a single chirp has it uttered in all that time. It was a male bird, and busy seed-hunting. Female birds never, probably, go half so long without chattering, and I am led to believe that they, far more than males, chirp and twitter in their sleep.

In the upland pastures, at a later hour, there was sweet music to be heard. An unusual flight of bluebirds were resting there. The gaunt gray stalks of the mullein were each topped with a warbling bluebird singing with all its springtime ardor. As usual, at this time of the year, these birds were adepts at fly-catching, and at a little distance might readily be taken for pee-wees or king-birds. They were not migrating. So long as I can remember, they have been wintering in the warm southern exposure of the bluff near by, and in unusually severe weather seek shelter in cedars, and cosey crannies in the stacks of hay and corn-stalks. There is no noticeable accession to their numbers in spring, so I hold them to be here in no sense migratory. The statement of Dr. Brewer, in vol. i. p. 63 of "North American Birds," that "in the Middle States, with every mild winter's day, the bluebirds come out from their retreats, and again disappear on the return of severer weather," is not true. They do not appear and disappear in the way he describes. Their movements are not at all affected by temperature; and only very high winds, or unusually severe snow-storms, send them to shelter. Well can I remember one clear, cold, January day, of the past winter, when the mercury fell to $-2°$ at sunrise. From the tops of half the stakes of a long worm-fence bluebirds were singing gleefully. Not with any loss of voice, as Dr. Brewer mentions is usually the case, but with all the animation and variation of their May-day warbling. Even then, they seemed actively in search of insect food, for they sallied out into the clear air, precisely as they would do in October. If there were no insects flying, and surely none were visible to human eyes, then these birds were exercising to keep up their warmth.

There was a red sunset this evening, such as were so common during the past autumn and winter. Not only this, but the eastern horizon was a pale green, and in no direction was nature cheerfully lighted up. The sickly tints cast upon every object seemed to have its depressing effect upon animal life, and the few katydids that have survived made only painful efforts to rasp out *Ka*—and left *ty Did* to the world's imagination; but they kept up this monosyllabic effort until midnight. The crickets, however, are full of activity, even on such a night, and, wherever there was tall grass, were noisy as in summer. They stick so close to the ground and under cover that no mere atmospheric condition, such as cold, affects them.

In the hillside woods, a single Pickering's tree-toad tried to get rid of the blues by occasionally uttering a shrill "peep," but it had no inspiriting effect. No other batrachian responded. It was a doleful evening.

Was it on this account that a little red owl, at midnight, mourned in most sepulchral tones? For the first time in my recollection, this little owl added gloom to the scene. Ordinarily, I love to hear the owls, large and small; but to-night it was unwelcome. Melancholy nights, such as this, are not uncommon in autumn. I know of no reason, unless there is some peculiarity in the atmosphere, as I have suggested; but certain it is that the depressing effect is at times produced, and scarcely a creature stirs. The shrews stay in their burrows. Mice remain at home. Flying-squirrels forego their foraging. The mink, weasel, and skunk sleep the sleep of the virtuous. Life rests by common consent, and the idea of exertion is repugnant.

Ordinarily, when we wander into the woods at night, and can summon up the necessary courage and patience to wait, alone, for coming events, it will be found that there is considerable activity, even when the darkness is profound; and proportionably more as there is light from the stars, an aurora, or the moon. If the moonlight is very bright, then the activity is often curtailed, just as sunlight puts an end to the predatory excursions of many animals.

To-night it was dark, but not so dark but that the trees could be seen against the clear sky. I spent a long time in the woods that fill the gully. The absence of all evidence of animal life was remarkable. I could think of no reason for this, so held the pale green sky and lurid west accountable. Had a brisk breeze sprung up, there would have been a change at once. The insects would be first to respond, then batrachians; then birds, half roused from their slumbers, would chirp; and long before dawn predatory mammals would yawn, shake themselves, and start upon their rounds. I have known such changes to occur, and the breeze and the activity might, of course, have been a mere coincidence. Such an objection is easily urged, and bears upon its face a winning reasonableness, but my conviction of a mysterious relationship between atmospheric conditions and animal activity is not disturbed.

CHAPTER XIV.

AN OCTOBER DIARY—CONCLUDED.

OCTOBER 21.—I found a pair of magnificent emeralds this evening—small, it is true, but they made up in brilliancy all they lacked in size. Dark though it happened to be, they glistened as I had never seen gems glisten before. They seemed almost to be sources of light and to illuminate their immediate surroundings. When within reach I stopped—and they were not there. The weasel that owned them was not green, whatever the tint of those wonderful gems. This was the weasel, I suppose, that has been running at large in the cellar, and darting among the apple-barrels, when not wishing to be seen. I speak advisedly, for at times he is bold as a hawk, and ready to fight if molested. Better a weasel than the rats he preys upon, so long may he flourish!

I took my fence-rail spider a handful of flies this morning, but she was out of humor and returned me no thanks. Indeed, she did not deign to notice in any way my contribution to her larder. So far as I could discover, nothing had gone wrong with the elaborate web; and the cause of the sulkiness could only be attributed to over-feeding or injury. She sat, or, more properly, stood, in the door of her den and looked at me, but did not stir a hair's-breadth, although fly after fly, of the score I had brought, were escaping from the web. I sat down as near the place as practicable, determined to see when the spider would condescend to step out or back into the recesses of her quarters. Perhaps I sat five minutes—it seemed an hour—but nothing like voluntary movement on the spider's part occurred. Finally, just as I was about to change my position, to get a closer view, I felt a slight stinging sensation on the end of my nose, and waving my hand involuntarily before my face, I found myself cabled, in a flimsy way, to the fence and the branches of the tree nearest me. A spider, nesting in the tree, had selected my hat as the support of some new webbing, and had fastened a hundred cables to it, selecting my nose as an additional support. Regretting I had so rudely disturbed the plans of the new-comer, I rose to go; but not before I had solved the mystery of the motionless spider before me. Placing my forefinger upon it, to my disgust I found that I had been staring at the mere ghost of my friend. Something had attacked her, and sucked out all her juices; not a trace of moisture remained; she was hollow as a "locust-shell."

If the spider that had utilized my hat and nose, in spreading additional webs, had done this murder, did it also set my defunct friend in this life-like position, as a trick on me? There was every appearance of this; but not until after many similar results will I admit even any degree of probability in the matter.

There is, without doubt, no class of animals that offer a more fruitful field for study than do spiders. Their habits show a marked degree of cunning, and I have no hesitation in placing them on a level with ants in the scale of intelligence.

The evening was very warm, and the full tide of insect-life common to August appears to have wholly revived. The flies and the frost play such remarkable tricks with our theories that, before a new idea can be formulated, the frost or the flies upsets our preconception.

October 22.—No fog, save scattered remnants of the veil of mist that yesterday draped the meadows. Every indication is that of a warm south rain; and this usually does not introduce a cold wave, such as is still reported to be coming. The crows fly low, and this is a sign of rain. How strange it is, that men otherwise intelligent should believe such nonsensical sayings. Certainly more than half the time crows fly very near the ground, a few feet above the level of the fields, and just skimming the tree-tops. All through a drought of five weeks they flew as low to the ground as I ever knew them to; and so it is all winter, stormy or clear, moderate or cold, quiet or windy; but the facts have no value in the sight of my neighbors. What they have always heard they always believe; and one proclaimed to the audience, at the close of a lecture, as a settler to my "newfangled notions," that "as these sayings originated in the *good* old times, none of 'em could be *bad*." I was about to reply, when he closed the discussion prematurely by adding that "these science men can get up new things as much as they please; but they needn't try to push the old ways to the wall; there's room enough for both." He is right, there is room enough for both, and ignorance will survive for years to come. Teach the young the fallacy of weather lore, but let the older generations believe in it all, in peace. My lecture on "Weather Lore" fell flat on that audience. Every blessed one of the old folks voted me a crank, and the very few young people did not hear it, or failed to catch my meaning.

For hours the crows have been flying low, and when the day was done a rolling black cloud and a puff of wind ushered in a rain-storm from the south; and soon began the steady pour which means an inky-black night and scarcely any creature astir. It is useless to go abroad at such a time. You can see nothing and hear nothing, and what you chance to touch may mislead you; for dripping feathers and soaked fur, handled in the dark, are a trial to the flesh and vexation to the spirit.

It seems never to have occurred to Wilson, Audubon, or Nuttall that birds are gifted with intelligence like our own, differing only in degree — as a rule, having less, except in some one or two directions — while their capabilities are greater. Probably in no one way is the identity of human and bird intelligence shown more clearly than in the marked variation in individual dispositions. This has been entirely overlooked in the works of the authors mentioned, and in a vast number of instances what is recorded of a single pair of birds that chanced to come under observation is assumed to be an exhaustive life-history of the species.

What is needed is to write the lives of our birds so that the creatures may be recognized without the aid of an illustration. It can be done.

This thought occurred to me as I saw the first linnets of the season, an hour before the rain began. I thought of it again as a little saw-whet owl crossed my path, skimming the ground like a whip-poor-will. The linnets were in a flock of fully one hundred, and, as usual, they dropped from the clouds. I happened to be near the tree upon which they all alighted, and just as I saw another flock, months ago, come to the big elm in the yard, so these came directly from overhead, to the tall sassafras "on the line." For years past I have noticed this peculiarity.

Wilson, in 1808-10, and George Ord, a few years later, refer to the rarity of this bird in the neighborhood of Philadelphia, considering its appearance as only an exceptional occurrence in severe winters.

This is wholly a mistake. Linnets are as sure to put in an appearance as snow-birds or pine finches. They are not often seen as early as October, in this latitude, it is true, but why should it excite surprise, when it is the rule for them to remain until late in April? Their apparent rarity, in winter, is really due to the abruptness of arrival and departure, and unless there is much snow, they remain closely among the tall forest trees; if systematic search is made, linnets will be found in Central New Jersey from November to March, both inclusive, year in and year out. I base this statement on notes of their presence jotted down during the past twenty years.

October 23.— At sunrise there came a shower of liquid bird-notes trickling through the pines—songs that resembled the lower tones of the musical water-jars of the ancient Peruvians. They were uttered by a flock of fifty or more cowpen-birds, singing in concert. The birds sat in short rows on the branches of the pines, and did not move the while, except to slightly raise their wings and spread their tails, as the soft sounds came bubbling up to their beaks and trickled over. They are curious birds. Cuckoo-like, they build no nests, but drop their eggs, here and there, in the nests of much smaller birds. Thus much all the world knows, or ought to know; but how little besides has been recorded of them! In Central New Jersey they are not migratory. They come and go, erratically, like the robin. A week or perhaps a month may pass without one being seen, and then, some bright morning, they may be the first birds to attract our attention as we venture out of doors.

It is commonly stated that these birds are gregarious the year through; but this is, at least, open to discussion; and depends very much upon the number of birds needed to make a "flock." From March to September they are most frequently seen in pairs or trios, and quite often singly. They associate with the robins, and are constant companions of meadow-larks, whose flight, even, they sometimes purposely imitate. When the female is ready to lay her eggs, she skulks through the bushes to find a suitable nest; and sometimes does not wait until the nest is finished. During the past summer, watching a pair of white-eyed greenlets while building, I, one afternoon, saw a cowpen-bird fly to the half-finished nest, and in less than two minutes fly away. In that brief space of time she deposited an egg. Meanwhile, the rightful owners of the nest were much exercised, and held a long discussion over the occurrence. This resulted in a remodelling of the bottom of the structure, the egg being neatly floored over.

Young cowpen-birds, for a short time after leaving the nest, associate with their foster-parents; but, as the season wears away, the birds that were hatched in one neighborhood finally meet, and a flock is eventually organized, retaining its numbers until the breaking-up of winter. During the spring and early summer of 1884 I found eleven nests containing eggs of the cowpenbird, the nests being in one limited area of a hundred or more acres. In a very short time after they were able to fly these young cowpen-birds would find the company of their own kind preferable to that of the warblers and fly-catchers that had nursed them. I have never seen them with their foster-parents after the nesting season of the latter was practically over.

Another peculiarity of the bird has been wholly overlooked. During July, August, and even September, the female cowpen-birds continue to drop single eggs at irregular intervals, and, when so doing, they do not look up some deserted nest, but drop the eggs upon the ground, and then descend from their perches to eat them. This I have witnessed on several occasions.

But, to further determine the facts concerning this extraordinary habit, I have killed numbers of female cow-pen-birds even as late as September, and in several found eggs nearly ready for extrusion. They were, to all appearances, fertile.

Last night's steady rain cleared the air and earth of dust. The gorgeous tints of the autumn foliage now show to perfection. Now is the one favorable time to realize how grand a color is a bright green. Some of the trees still retain it in various shades, and it shows forth in all its beauty in the setting of contrasting tints wrought by the frost.

The promised cold wave has come. Even in the full glare of the noonday sun it is cold, and the fitful west wind shakes the trees with sudden shivering, and millions of bright leaves flutter through the air, and star the grass with flakes of red and yellow.

For exercise I climbed a chinkapin-tree after the few nuts remaining on it, and brought down upon my head the fury of indignant blue-jays. One slapped my hand with its wing as I was reaching upward to a cluster of burrs. These jays were as bold as though I was after their nest. Had I, in their fearlessness, as shown this morning, an evidence of quick-wittedness on their part; did they realize my comparative helplessness while in the tree? Probably so. No bird, I think, fears man when in a tree as it does when he is standing on the ground. They seem to know that, with his hands grasping the branches, it is highly improbable that he has a gun with him, and so approach on the part of a bird is comparatively safe. A crow would reason in this manner, I know, and the evidence favors a like intelligence on the part of other birds.

Shortly after sunset a cat-owl screamed from some distant shelter in the meadows, and the pleasant sound, borne by the wind and toned with the sighs of the tall pines, added a charm to the evening. To me it has ever been a matter of wonder that the cries of owls should be thought mournful. In a little poem by Alexander Wilson, called "The Foresters," the author speaks of

> "The hollow, quivering, loud-repeated howl,
> Full overhead, betrays the haggard owl."

To what haggard owl he refers I am uncertain, but probably this long-eared one, that, from the varied notes of its cry, is locally known as "cat-owl." Formerly it was more abundant than now, and its place in the meadows is taken by the short-eared or marsh owls. The voices of the two are quite different, and by this means the birds are as readily distinguished as when seen. The marsh-owls, as found in the meadows, offer one peculiarity not noticed by ornithologists as occurring elsewhere. They build in cavernous hollows of old trees, and not on the ground. Either this, or the young, as soon as they are hatched, leave the nest and take shelter in such hollows. I can readily understand why this should be the case. They frequent only the wet marshes, where there is an abundance of mice and of reed-birds at certain seasons. These are their sole food-supply, and the birds do not need to wander any distance from the marshes. To nest on the ground would be to expose the eggs and young to freshets, and it probably has resulted from this cause that hollow trees — the proper home of owls—have been resorted to. Either this, or the young resort, when but a few days old, to the trees. While I have never found the eggs, I have so frequently found the young that I have never doubted but that they were hatched in the hollows where they were seen.

"Sometimes a tame cat takes to the woods, and when it does it gets wilder than a wild cat," was the remark of Miles Overfield, who gave me a rambling account of his having seen such a cat. It was a strange coincidence, for to-night I crossed Poaetquissings above the flood-gates, and the scream of a cat was decidedly horricapillatory. I felt my hairless scalp to be unpleasantly ridged, and the same effect was produced on the night-herons near by, for they straightway ruffled their feathers and flew into the outer darkness. I listened for its repetition, yet half hopeful I should not hear it; and I was both pleased and sorry that the cat remained quiet so long as I tarried by the creek-side. This cat, which I know to be one that has " taken to the woods," uttered this evening probably the wildest cry I have ever heard in my rambles. Not so startling as that of a barn-owl, perhaps, but simply because it is uttered more deliberately. You have time to catch your breath; but when the barn-owl yells its wild kr-r-r-r-ick! you are apt to be bewildered by its abruptness. The sound was unlike that made by any domestic cat, varied and unmusical as their vocal efforts are, and did approximate to the cry of a cougar, as I have occasionally heard it at the Zoo.

Perhaps it may provoke a smile to refer to cats when treating of the scattered remnants of wild nature, but it can be accepted without qualification that a cat that takes to a wild life will be so essentially feral that a person, a stranger to domestic cats, would never infer the truth. Of a number of such instances I have collected careful, trustworthy data, and they all accord with what I have myself observed. Such cats become arboreal and strictly nocturnal; they haunt the remotest portions of wooded districts, and utter a cry different from any of the sounds characteristic of domestic Toms or Tabbies.

October 24.—Frost put a quietus on creation in the night. Even the crackling leaves are still this morning. Squirrels, if they move at all, step on tiptoe. A long line of voiceless crows pass over the meadows, winging their way so stilly one might think them a wind-driven thunder-cloud. The brook best shows the footsteps of the frost-king, where ranks of icy spear-points glitter in the sun. Every projecting pebble is encased in crystal, and the cheerful waters sing a rapid roundelay as they hurry by. Autumn has chosen her time and placed on view her choicest handiwork. But its beauty avails it nothing; it is fated to quickly pass and be utterly forgotten, for who that shudders in the early morning at the sight of frosted fields thinks of the matchless beauty of the ice-crystals spread so lavishly before him? Yet

I doubt if, in all nature, there are more exquisite shapes. From the clear sky the meadow-larks give promise of a splendid day, for they are silent as death if it is going to storm—so it is said; but he is not a wise traveller that has no better barometer. Grass-finches, that had shivered in their weedy caves through the long night, now rejoice at the victory of the rising sun, and sing with increasing ardor as the generous warmth stirs them to action. Bluebirds, in straggling dozens, lined the worm-fences, and a flock—perhaps a thousand—of red-wings came chattering up against the westerly breeze, and clothed the bare branches of an old apple-tree as with summer's full complement of leaves.

A half-hour in the early morning works a wonderful change in upland and meadow, and it is not well to be discouraged if, at first, either locality appears deserted.

The freshness of the day recalled the rabbit-traps of the past winter, and towards evening I hunted them up. In the tangled growth of wild grass in the orchard one was found, and, to my delight, it was occupied by a beautiful white-footed mouse. Her nest was a globular mass of leaves and long grass, as firmly fixed as the nest of a marsh-wren. It was lined with the soft, silky "cotton" of the milk-weed. The pretty creature was not alone. Three young mice clung to her teats. These were one third grown and of a dark mouse-color. She was a bright yellow-brown. The white legs and bellies of the young strongly contrasted with the dark color of the sides and back, and had they been found alone their identity would not have been so readily recognized.

Placing them in a large glass tank, I noticed their movements were much unlike those of the common domestic mouse. They did not run; they walked, and held themselves erect. Young as they were, they stood on their hind-feet a great deal, and used their fore-limbs as arms. When so doing they brought their long tails into use as an additional support. One little fellow, more anxious than the others to escape, took eleven firm steps on his hind-feet without any evidence of indecision or strained effort at balancing. It had all the appearance of the practised walk of a biped, and seemed not an unusual occurrence. This was a source of great satisfaction to me, as I had already been convinced that mice could walk in this manner, but had never had so excellent an opportunity to witness it.

The little creatures' arboreal habits have been largely overlooked. Seldom are they found except upon the ground, unless when occupying an old bird's nest; but they do at times, nevertheless, ascend to the very tops of hollow trees, or as far as the decayed interior reaches. They clamber along the sides of this cavity only, and so you may be leaning against the very tree they are in and never suspect their presence. What induces them to do so is not readily determined, but the probabilities are that they are in quest of food, and not merely seeking safety from pursuing foes. However this may be, I have several times found them in such positions, and once an abandoned leaf-nest of gray squirrels was utilized by them as a winter home.

These arboreal habits of the white-footed mice bring prominently to mind the once seductive theory, and happily now demonstrated law of evolution. This little mouse has often been noticed as occupying birds' nests built in bushes. I have found them in nests six and ten feet from the ground. To reach them, they must necessarily be expert climbers, and their skill in winding through briers is marvellous. Added to this, they now wander through the dark recesses of hollow trees, often to a considerable elevation. What such changes of habit may lead to is readily imagined, and if, as the country becomes more and more settled, these mice find their safety increased in proportion as they remain away from the ground, it is certain that an arboreal mouse may ultimately replace the present species, which now lives upon the surface and only visits hollow trees. That so great a change as I have intimated should be brought about is quite within the bounds of probability.

October 25.—There were five minutes of brightness, as the sun rose, and then a rapid overclouding of the whole sky. The prominent effect was to sadly upset the calculations of the birds, and a remarkable restlessness was noticeable. The great flocks of red-winged blackbirds, here since yesterday, were broken into little companies of a dozen or more, and no two individuals flew in the same direction. The robins were all "at sea," and even the thistle-finches found themselves without a plan. I have seen such disturbed conditions among flocking birds before, but never could I get any clew to the cause. The mere cloudiness of the sky will not account for it. An hour later the sun again shone, and the blackbirds regathered and passed, like a cloud, to the meadows; the robins sought the wild grapes, and the thistle-finches went—well, they disappeared.

The last rays of the sun to-day—a handful of golden arrows—were shot through the three beeches at 5 P.M., and the last of the roostward flying crows passed over ten minutes later. An hour afterwards the night had set in, breezy, cold, clear, and moonlit. Does an October night need anything else? I walked up through the cornfield to the lone oak in the upland clover, and, after standing awhile, I was fortunate enough to see an old grizzly opossum start on his nocturnal rounds. The exit of an opossum from his home-tree is an artistic proceeding. With only his head projecting beyond the opening, he took a long observation. Just of what, is not easy even to guess, but very possibly only of the weather. Then, placing his fore-feet on the rim of the hole, which was ten feet from the ground, the animal looked downward and sidewise for fully ten minutes. Wrapped in gray and hidden in tall weeds, I do not think he saw me. Then slipping his fore-feet down the trunk of the tree, the opossum held on by his hind-feet and tail, and in this upside-down position again scanned the neighborhood closely, or listened for suspicious sounds, or both. This was but for a few moments, and then the downward climb commenced. Once at the foot of the tree, the opossum broke into a jog-trot and was directly out of sight and hearing.

We are all familiar with the fact that rattlesnakes, prairie-dogs, and burrowing owls are sometimes found in the same subterranean retreat. Such cases of associated animals of widely different character are not so very uncommon, after all. From the same great hollow in the old oak, or from another section of it, if it is divided, this same night, and within half an hour, came a beautiful barn-owl, and directly afterwards another.

Unlike the opossum, they did not wait for preliminary observations, but sailed away in the moonlight, without a moment's pause. I tarried awhile, hoping they would return, but they did not, and being too cool to sit up until late for their reappearance, I turned my face homeward, pausing at times to listen to the notes of birds, if such they were — half-uttered cries, as though the birds were dreaming. Thinking of them as I continued my walk, I wondered if owls were ever attracted by such sounds, and so were led to the roosting-places of sparrows and tits. Let us hope not. Owls are seemingly only mouse-hunters, and as such the world should welcome and protect them.

Even yet, migratory birds are dropping in every hour of the day and night. As I passed by the maples in the lane there was a faint chirping that came from a score of throats, and seemed afar off and directly overhead. I stood but for a moment, when a flock of small birds settled in the trees, and I recognized them as pine-finches. Usually, I doubt not, birds on their migratory journey, when flying at night, do not stop until dawn; but, of course, it happens otherwise at times, as was the case to-night. All was quiet within a minute, and happy birds they, to be able to fall asleep the moment they closed their eyes.

Probably only the hot-headed tribe of wrens are

troubled with insomnia. Wrens are hatched mad. Turned out of their shells by an impatient parent, they never know anything but high-tempered activity, and die, I suppose, of sudden collapse. In the woods all day there have been a half-dozen winter wrens spider-hunting along the worm-fence; but not one of them has spoken to another audibly, nor sung a single note. Some sudden freak, to be atoned for to-morrow by a wasteful wealth of music.

Charming as are the upland fields, the hillside woods, and level meadows, by moonlight, the creek offers attractions on such a night that are not elsewhere to be found. What though ice is forming and a cutting east wind blows! There are sheltered nooks where one may stand, as cosily fixed as at home, and see all that is going on in the little world of Poaetquissings; for although but a week is left of this month, wherein the last of the summer visitants are supposed to depart, there yet remain the herons and bitterns of the past summer and half the kingfishers. The muskrats seem to love just such a night as this, and a dozen of them rippled the quiet waters, as they frolicked, uttering a peculiar cry at times which might readily be mistaken for the chirp of a bird. Take the same stand by day and every day for a month, and the chances are you would never imagine that such a creature as the muskrat dwelt in the banks of the creek before you.

Moonlight is not wholly satisfactory to man in which to view the movements of various small and timid animals; but the naturalist-rambler must not overlook the fact that, to a considerable extent, the creatures he wishes most to see are nocturnal. Curious as it may seem, very many animals are more strictly nocturnal than those which are ordinarily referred to as such. Thus we speak of owls and bats as nocturnal. In reality they are crepuscular, for they do not keep on the wing all night, unless it is moonlight; while muskrats, weasels, opossums, 'coons, and mice are often on the go from the setting of the sun until dawn. I have had particularly good opportunities of investigating this matter with reference to nearly all the mammals of the neighborhood, and found that even when, as very rarely occurs, there is an absolute darkness animals may be abroad. Of, course, however excellent their vision, for the time being they were blind, and guided solely by the combined action of the senses of smell, hearing, and touch. Rapid locomotion would be impracticable, but safe progress perfectly feasible. Animals are often trapped on such pitch-black nights, which is incontestable proof of their having left their lairs. The traps were set by lantern-light, long after sunset, and visited before the first intimation of dawn. If any one doubts this, let him wrap himself in a blanket and sit from midnight to dawn in the woods. Timid people need not try this, as they will see and hear strange creatures at the rate of a menagerie a minute; but a naturalist can convince himself that there is considerable activity in the animal world. The cries—conversation, I take it—and footsteps over the dead leaves can be heard, and the occasional leap from a tree to the ground is a movement that cannot be mistaken, although only heard.

There was an absolutely dark night, a year ago this

month, and I sat for two hours on an uneven stump to learn something—anything—of the animals I knew were in the woods. Under a cloth cover, so that it was available, but wholly hidden, was a little bull's-eye lantern. The knowledge of its proximity, I admit, was a source of comfort. Long minutes, composed of very attenuated seconds, passed and not a sound was heard, other than the wind in the tree-tops. Even this, at times, died away, and during one such interval of absolute silence I heard faint footfalls on the dead leaves. I thought of the lantern, and touched it with my foot to make sure it had not wandered off. The footsteps were then more plainly heard, and with them a faint series of squeaky tones, as though there were two animals engaged in conversation. Suddenly the sounds ceased. Had these creatures discovered me by some other sense than sight, and so were puzzled as to my identity, as I was of theirs? The suspense, on my part, became unbearable. I slowly reached for the cloth that covered my lantern. I removed it suddenly, and a glimmer of light was shed on the surrounding trees and road, displaying a pair of full-grown skunks, and then the lantern, overturned by my nervousness, went out. Would that I could have gone out with it! but it was too dark to make any movement safe. The abruptness of the whole proceeding happily proved equally terrifying to the skunks, and they fled without previously committing any revengeful act.

The last of a dozen matches proved available, and the lantern was relighted. I covered it with care, and again awaited developments. For half an hour, perhaps, I sat with folded hands. I soon found that what few sounds were heard were readily distinguishable from the noise made by wind-tossed leaves or the creaking of rubbing branches. Indeed, the hearing becomes much more acute under such circumstances, and one can more readily realize the perfection of the sense in many animals. It approaches much more nearly to the value of sight than one would suppose. But I was soon subjected to another testing of my nerves. Moved by curiosity, a pretty white-footed mouse—I suppose—nibbled at my boot, then perched upon my toes, and finally proceeded to crawl up my leg. A very slight movement sent him back, but not very far, for soon it ran again up to my lap, and as I moved my hand to touch it, gave a wild squeak and was gone.

By this time I was becoming a little more used to my situation, and honestly longed for another episode. I had not long to wait. Again I heard approaching footsteps. I thought of the skunks; but no, it was too firm a step. Was it some benighted tramp? This was an animal I did not wish to meet. Leaning forward to catch the full volume of the sound, I was sure it was the shuffling tread of a four-footed beast. This brought a feeling of relief, and, after all, it was but one chance in a hundred if it came directly to where I sat. I had full faith in the ninety-and-nine chances in favor of its passing me. But it was now very near. I was beginning to think a dozen things at once, and forgot, for the moment, about the lantern. The steps are at my very side. I can feel the animal's breath in my face, and, most unfortunately, the last step of the passing creature overturned my lantern. Again a provoking flash of light, and there, in utter bewilderment, stood my neighbor's heifer.

October 26.—Jack Frost legislates, so far as the game-laws of the hillside are concerned, and the weather suggested the setting of rabbit traps last evening, which I did. One trap in the garden, two in the gully, three along the hill, and a rabbit in every other one when the night is keen and still. This was the rule in the days of my grandfather, a century ago; but now one rabbit to every six traps, and that but seldom, is much nearer the mark. What of that? The quiet stroll to the places where the traps are placed, the setting of each, and dusting of our tracks with dead leaves, all this is to be done, and the excitement of faint expectation of a "cotton tail" is worth a good deal. The night passes; by the first cock-crow it is time to recall the traps, and just before sunrise each should be visited. There is a strange notion quite prevalent among the very old people yet remaining that a buck rabbit will lift the lid of a box-trap, at sunrise, even if it is weighted. Absurd as it is, it holds in the mind of men like Miles Overfield, Davie Shores, and half a dozen septuagenarians within a mile of home.

The ordinary reply to the question of why this is, is that they know it—had they not always heard it? Miles's father told him that "the first glimmer of sunshine would open a steel trap and let every critter go as was caught in the night," and Miles believed it, although every winter of his trapping days had contradicted the absurdity.

The probable origin is, that in colonial times, when every farm lad had his traps, this idea was spread abroad;

in order that the traps might be visited as early in the day as possible, and no time be taken from the ordinary work-day. If not this, I am puzzled to know why otherwise clear-headed men should be such fools. Such a notion, so originating, might readily be handed down and perpetuated as a superstition long after the circumstances which gave rise to it had passed away. The practical Quakers who settled Central New Jersey certainly turned everything to advantage, and were ever ready to profit, even by a little cunning of an innocent kind. The concern was only on their minds if they failed to reap every possible gain, and never that their fellow-men might possibly question the means adopted, and doubtless cunning Quakers started the story of the powerful influence of sunlight upon traps.

No night so long but morning follows; and at daybreak the fun offers of the round of the rabbit traps. The first breath of the air this morning suggested a rabbit in some one of the traps, too. There was a frosty snap in the sleepy breeze that barely stirred the pines, but which now and then whirled the dead leaves in the wood-path, as though stirred by an unseen finger. The blue-jays screamed with more than usual vigor, the chipmunks chattered, the nuthatches querulously complained, and every crow in the tall oaks cawed a warning to its fellows far afield.

First, to the quince-bush in the garden. The trap was open. Never mind, there are three along the hillside; and down through the green briers, beyond the lone cedar, where winds a narrow path, is the second trap. It, too, is open. Then to the clump of hyssop and poke; this, too, is undisturbed. Ah, well! I am having my walk, and really am not disappointed. Now along the worm-fence through the black oaks to the next trap —this is sprung. With what light footsteps I approach the trap! The lid is down. Down tight, and the weight still rests upon it. Through some unaccountable twist in the mind, the idea of seeing what is in the trap never occurs to me. I stand and wonder. Of course, the triggers were not jarred by a falling leaf, and so the trap was empty. But is it 'coon, squirrel, rabbit, or blue-jay. I lose five minutes trying to guess. At last, I stoop down and peep through a crack, narrow as a spider's web. There is nothing to be seen. I test the trap by lifting it. Yes, it is heavy, but with what? Slowly then I lift the lid and take another peep—the trap is empty. It was heavy with the weight on the lid, which I had neglected to remove. But what had sprung it? There were a few hairs on the sides of the trap. The bait was untouched, but one of the spice-wood triggers was gnawed. The hairs are scanned more closely, and prove to be those of a chipmunk, and through a knothole in the bottom of the trap he had passed into the ground and burrowed a semicircular tunnel that opens less than a foot from where the trap stood. It was all as plain as the increasing daylight, and far better than the prosy capture of a rabbit. There remain two traps in the gully, and I hasten to them, a little disappointed, perhaps, at so poor a show for the opening night of my trapping. In the gully, a narrow path climbs the steep side of the ravine, and over it rabbits are known to run, particularly when chased from the fields by dogs. Why should they not pass that same way at night, and without special purpose? At the foot of the only walnut-tree in the gully the two traps were placed, end to end, so that they commanded the path in both directions. Rather quietly I approached them, as though there might be some hesitating "cotton-tail" looking in at one or the other at this moment. When within a few paces, I can see both traps, and one is sprung. My former vacillation and worse is not repeated. I slowly raise the lid and see the rabbit. Cautiously I reach in and draw the squealing creature out, and straightway silence it. Not so bad, after all.

I met Miles Overfield on my way home and told him of my luck.

"Nothin' strange about it. You see, you go blunderin' through, and never take notice of the signs, and think you've only got to set your traps. Fact is, the rabbits are too full of turnips, and windfall apples, and cabbage leaves yet. You've got to wait for food to get scarce, and you must season your traps. It takes two good frosts to get the smell of your hands off 'em. Then like as not you baited with some apple—"

"Hold on, here," I cried; "if they went so far in the trap as to test the apple, it would be all that was needed."

"Would it, greeny? You bet, a molly cotton-tail can't be so easily fooled. They can tell by the smell, and that afore they go in. Why, young man, you've got a heap to learn about rabbits. Now, my father used to say, when he lived down on Pearson's hillside, that the rabbits never went into a trap before the truck and garden sass was all gathered; and it stands to reason;

and then, bless your soul, there's another reason. Rabbits don't turn up, in a day's walk, like they used to; and for one, I take time by the forelock, as folks say, and snared, without hurtin' 'em, about a dozen, which are in a pen now, waitin' for the law to come in, so I can sell 'em. You needn't say anything about this, but you just keep on settin' traps, and perhaps you'll catch another 'twixt now and Christmas."

As I went home, it occurred to me that I might as well give my traps to Miles. Somehow, it was evident he would have all the rabbits, and empty traps all winter would become tiresome.

I am surprised to find my observations ever fail to tally with the conclusions of the learned doctors of the science of birds; but such is the unpleasant fact. The birds are obstinate enough not to follow the rules laid down for them in the books. To-day, as I walked across the mucky meadow, stepping from hassock to hassock, I startled from the grass a dozen pretty finches, which, at first glance, I took to be swamp sparrows; but their voices betrayed them; they were sharp-tailed finches, or quail-heads. There is no possibility of confounding them with any other bird; and here, fifty miles from salt water, were these sea-coast birds, lively as crickets and happy as larks. Now, it is laid down in the books that this is a strictly marine species, a coast-dweller, and one that abhors the semi-desiccated inland. But so are curlews coast birds, yet they are killed, every year or two, on these meadows. So too are willets, turnstones, avocets, and sanderlings. All come up the river, and in this way these pretty quail-heads also come, "by spells," as Miles has it—come, stay for a day, a week, or a month, for aught I know, and then for a year or more none are seen. These sea-side finches present nothing to particularly mark them. They wander about the reeds, much as a nuthatch scrambles over trees, often head downwards; but generally stay so closely to the ground that they escape notice. It is very probable that those I saw to-day were migrating, and to-morrow may be resting along the pleasant shores of the Chesapeake. Still, seen so far inland, they are essentially a bird out of place, and the more interesting on that account. They are fearless, to a certain extent, or was it cunning? A marsh-harrier beat the bushes, just after I had passed, but not a bird was disturbed by it. They saw him coming, and quickly settled down in the grass. After he had gone, up they came, scolding, I thought, at the disturbance of their quiet, first by myself, and then by the hawk.

Nature is always quiet at noon, unless there is a storm approaching or prevailing. In recalling the fauna of the county, whether furred, feathered, or finned, it matters not, the great majority of its members sleep with greater regularity at noon than at midnight; except some birds, and these take a noonday nap. The apparently ever-active warblers, sparrows, and other little fellows are often found asleep, and would be seen more frequently than they are, were we a little less noisy as we walked through the woods. Often have I seen a titmouse with its feathers ruffled, until it looked like a gall excrescence on an oak. Often, too, sparrows, with their heads under their wings, may be surprised; and swallows rest, in long lines, on the telegraph wires. Thrushes hide in the tangled briers, and are therefore sometimes surprised by black snakes; whence the antipathy of these birds. Even wrens will be quiet at noon, for a little while; and every one of the birds mentioned will be about, long after sunset, often; particularly if the moon prolongs the day. Of course, with mammals it is different, and our night is their day. This is probably a change brought about by the increase of their principal enemies, men and dogs. I do not believe, in Indian times, the mammals found here then were half so careful to keep hidden through the day as they now are. It would seem that they have gradually acquired the knowledge of the fact that there are fewer men prowling about at night; and, possibly, fewer dogs. There is evidence, too, that the common mammals, as opossums, minks, raccoons, and squirrels, are abroad during dull, rainy days more than when they are clear. It may be thought that the mere absence of sunlight tempts them abroad, or that their prey, likewise, is more readily to be found. I can assent to neither proposition; but believe it is simply because these animals anticipate freedom from molestation. The average man does not go out in a pouring rain; or, if so, confines himself to the highways, or takes a short-cut across fields, quite unmindful of what may be going on beside him, as he hurries by. The average mammal has learned this fact, and so have I.

A steady pour-down, if there is no wind, is the time of all others for a naturalist to be about. Such a day, will teach him more and show him more than all the year's hours of sunshine put together. A rainy day in the woods—there is music in the very mention of it! What have I seen, at such a time, do you ask? Rather what have I not seen. I have seen skunks hunt in concert, rolling over a decayed log to find the rich, white insect larvæ of which they are so fond. I have seen the raccoon slowly crawl from his home among the tree-roots, and stroll towards the meadow in search of crayfish. I have seen the opossum with her pouch of young climb to the very top of a persimmon-tree, and search out the daintiest fruit that had been shrivelled and sweetened by the early frosts. I have seen the squirrels leave their home-tree, and, congregating on the wild-grapevines, play in mid-air, and execute such marvellous feats of high and lofty tumbling that the art of the gymnast, on his trapeze, was very tame in comparison. I have seen leaping that matched the flight of the flying squirrel; grappling in the air of two individuals, which descended as one body, swiftly as a falling stone, yet which separated in the proper fraction of a second, and touched the earth lightly as zephyr-wafted thistledown. This in a steady rain, when everything was dripping. Was such a time chosen because of the advantages it offered? Not a bit of it. The squirrels simply knew that men were in their houses, and dogs in their kennels, and hawks were sheltered in the cedars— at least, it was so far likely to be the case that they were willing to take the chances. The truth of this whole matter is just here. There is not a mammal in the land to-day that is not a closer student of man and his habits than naturalists are of the habits of mammals. The creatures we essay to study play bo-peep with us whenever we go abroad; and often they must merrily chuckle to themselves, when we turn homeward in despair, thinking there are no living creatures within miles of us.

How quickly the water-plants are stricken by the first autumn frosts. There are now, in the meadows, long reaches of open water, where, during the summer, nothing but a rank growth of vegetation was to be seen. The pontederia, arum, and other similar growths are now a slimy, homogeneous mass upon the bottoms of the shallow ponds, which, but a few days ago, they blotted out of sight. The waters, to-day, rejoiced that their time had come; they sparkled and danced in ripples as the breezes swept over them, and many a foolhardy bird got an unlooked-for bath by venturing too near. When there was a calm the colored leaves were reflected in the pools, and repeated this glory of the October landscape. Fish now catch the inspiration of brisk autumn days, and the silvery minnows leap continually above the ripples. In the deep pond beyond Poaetquissings, where there have been land-locked gizzard shad for many years, I saw several of these fish in a state of unusual activity. They leaped above the waves, for the water was quite rough, showing their silvery sides to great advantage. This leaping was so continuous that the thought arose that they were chased by some enemy beneath the surface; but I could detect none by floating over the pond, although, when the wind ceased, the water was very still, and so clear that the bottom of the pool, twenty feet below me, could be distinctly seen. The shad were there, quiet as possible, and unmoved by any influence without themselves. I believe they had been playing—something most fishes do very frequently.

More birds arrived to-day from the north; some to spend the winter, as the white-throated sparrows, kinglets, and a sly, evil-minded shrike; others to pass on, as a few swallows, and straggling warblers, that probably had company thus far, and must now journey alone, or wait for still tardier birds. These warblers were as quiet as mice, and had none of their accustomed springtime activity. Perhaps they thought insect-hunting would profit them nothing—but why should it not? Before their very faces wandered kinglets and tits, gathering food from every nook and cranny into which they peeped. Could they not take a hint from them? Still, they may have been too tired and not hungry. Enough to know they were here to-day—are here, this cool evening—and to-morrow will be on their journey again; or, by the clear moonlight, while the bird-world generally is at rest, will they climb to the clouds, and amid those dizzy heights pass southward, propelled by a wonderful flight-power, which, when hugging the earth, no one would suspect them to possess.

For some time after sunset I heard the steady hammering of a woodpecker in the lane, and, wondering why one place should be so long worked at, went thither to investigate. In a dead limb of an old apple tree—dead, but very hard, as it proved—a flicker was working away as though it were April and he were behindhand with his nesting. The bird had evidently been at work for several days, as a deep hole was already pecked in the limb, and I suppose the bird proposes excavating a nesting-place. This is a curious freak for the time of year, but one not unknown to ornithologists, I believe. I have notes of a downy woodpecker doing the same thing, but never occupying the hole after it was finished. Is it a weather sign? I find none in the list at hand referring to this work of the bird. Woodpecker weather-lore is not very satisfactory. We are told that when these birds leave (*i. e.*, in autumn), expect a hard winter. Fortunately, they never leave, but the hard winters do come more frequently than I fancy. Again, the list of proverbs has, "When the woodpeckers peck low on the trees, expect warm weather." The hole being pecked out in the apple-tree to-day is scarcely six feet from the ground. Is this low down or high? If I remember rightly, I saw several hairy woodpeckers to-day tapping vigorously at the highest limbs of the three beeches in the corner of the yard; are we then to have both cold and warm weather? Probably, for there never yet was an autumn or winter without both. Leaving the flickers at work, I went over to Miles Overfield's cottage, for Miles is my last resort when I am puzzled. Not that he always enlightens me, but he is sure to have some curious wrinkle upon every subject connected with local matters. Like many men, knowing very little, he thinks himself the embodiment of wisdom.

"Have you ever seen a woodpecker make a nest this time of year?" I asked, when I was fairly seated by his smoky chimney and tobacco bespattered ten-plate stove.

"Of course I have. They do say it's a sign of a cold winter, but I never put that and that together in back years to see how it was. The red-headed woodpeckers and log-cocks, that in your grandfather's time was common enough, used to be pegging away at the apple-trees all winter, and sometimes dug out big holes. I've heard as how it was only hen birds as pecked the holes, 'cause they had eggs to lay, like chickens, and made new nests to drop 'em in. Don't suppose this is quite likely, do you?"

"No," I replied promptly; and, seeing he was only talking for sake of talk, added, "I'm in a hurry, and must go," and slipped off before he realized my intention. As I jumped the garden fence I looked back, and Miles stood in his door, with a dazed look, shading his eyes from the setting sun by bending one of his horny hands over them.

October 27.—Cloudy and warm, with that peculiar something in the air that makes you look up every moment to see if it is not raining; and at times the noises you hear are certainly rain-drops on the leaves, and with confidence you hold out your hand to feel them. Such a day is fraudulent. It promises everything, and performs nothing. The unseen blight has a depressing effect upon all animal life; and were it not within the range of possibilities that something may be in the traps, I would scarcely be tempted to pass the garden gate; but I do go, and in the first trap visited is a rabbit; the second I have caught. It is but five days before the law comes in; so I'll tell nobody, and keep it.

The walk otherwise was stupid, wherever I went. Neither hillside, upland, nor meadow had any attractions. At last I detected a trace of animation in the birds. A young English sparrow, having wandered from the highway, tried to make friends with a company of white-throated sparrows. No bird ever made a more miserable failure of any undertaking. It passed from one to the other of the whole flock, and was rebuffed by each in turn. Finally they left, in a flock, for a journey across the meadows, leaving the young sparrow dejected and forlorn. It seemed to have just enough sense to know it was not wanted.

Later in the day, and for an hour before sunset, in particular, there was a return of animation, and the hillside was enlivened by the united songs of Carolina wrens, titmice, and nuthatches. It was a strange medley, curious, but tiresome, and the pleasant warbling of happy snow-birds in the adjoining fields was a positive relief. The black-and-white snow-birds, or Juncos, are now in the height of their glory. Half the fields are forests of rank weeds, and the supply of nutritious seeds is inexhaustible. It is no wonder that, whatever the weather, they occasionally break forth in song, and sing, too, in a manner creditable to the tribe of finches. Just at sunset these snow-birds flew, in a loose flock, towards the barn, and I followed to learn precisely where they went. It proved that they were roosting in the cow-stalls, ranging themselves along various beams, where they had the protection of the roof a few inches above them.

Last winter, hundreds of snow-birds roosted in the long rick of corn-stalks ranged beside these cow-sheds. Such shelter would be more to their taste, I doubt not, and I could not but wonder if these were last year's birds, come again to the same winter-quarters, and now were waiting or hoping for another rick of corn-stalks. This is improbable, I admit; but why should not birds that regularly winter here be as systematic in their comings and goings as are the summer residents? I have knowledge of the same birds coming, year after year, to the same spot; as, for instance, a cat-bird, recognized by two white feathers in one wing, which nested for five consecutive summers in the same clump of briers; and I cannot, in the face of such facts, see any inherent improbability in the other case. It is true that birds do not winter here for the same purpose, but merely are influenced by the question of a food-supply; but if this proved satisfactory one winter, the birds would probably remember it, and come again. The main difficulty is in the identification of winter residents. They are not sufficiently marked by any one peculiarity, and sing too seldom to enable one to recognize individual voices; but for all this, I felt as if the snow-birds in the barnyard were old friends, and not chance strangers, that happened here by mere accident.

October 28.—It was raining before the sun could exert his power, and, when nature became fairly visible, it was still wrapped in patchy mists that hid all the low-lying meadows and half the upland fields. Some of the larger trees, now leafless, stretched out their bare branches as though imploring help, their trunks being fog-wrapped and hid from view. With it all, it rained.

To keep up the habit of an early morning walk, and to see if there was any life astir, I passed along the hillside and up the gully; but the feeling slowly dawned upon me, perhaps it was too stormy, and I had a longing to make a short-cut across a field. Such weakness occasionally attacks one, and I gave way sufficiently to take a few steps in the field, when up sprang a covey of quails, with a thrilling whirr of their wings. I was fairly roused to action, and my walk commenced.

Peter Kalm, when travelling in New Jersey, recorded, under date of January, 1749, as follows: "These birds—quails—are numerous in *New Sweden, i. e.*, this part of the country. On going but a little way, you meet with great coveys of them. However, they keep at a great distance from towns; being either extirpated, or frightened there by the frequent shooting." What Kalm said of them then is equally true of them now; but to show how much they have had to contend with, I refer to the "frequent shooting" he mentions, one hundred and thirty-five years ago. Inasmuch as they have withstood this persecution for so long a time, it is very easy to see how readily this and other birds could be preserved in thickly settled districts, were there wise legislation in the matter.

In three days it will be lawful to shoot these birds, and, considering the number of sportsmen in every town, it is a mystery how any of the quails escape. They must know of man-proof and dog-proof swamps, wherein they take shelter when pursued. I surely hope so; for next April the shrill "Bob White," whistled from the angles of the weed-grown worm-fences, is a part of the morning anthem I would not like to miss.

The air to-night was full of moisture, but no rain fell. The moon could be followed through the misty clouds, but not actually seen. Her whereabouts looked like the reflection of a fire, far off in the cloud-world. Stranger than all, the air was full, too, of the hum of life, presumably insect-life. How I wish I could identify the endless buzzes of an autumn or summer evening! I have often gathered a roomful of such creatures as a light would attract, but not one of them would sing in my sight or hearing. These supposed insect voices heard to-night seemed to come from everywhere, but from no point near at hand. They are all from a distance, and, go in any direction whatever, the sounds come from all the others. You can never approach them. It is as easy to corner the Will-o'-the-wisp.

October 29.—Typical autumn weather again! I know not what it is, perhaps ozone, but in the atmosphere of this morning there was an abundance of "snap." One feels like running, rather than walking. Gates are not sought, nor fences clambered over. We leap them. Although so many leaves have fallen, it would seem as if they were only the plain browns that are on the ground. The green, scarlet, and golden remain on the trees. I lingered long over a clump of birches. Their straight white stems were bare of branches on the northern side, and the bright yellow foliage of the southward-reaching branches made a magnificent background. I know of no purer white in nature than that of these birches; at a little distance it is as dazzling as newly fallen snow. I did not go nearer than a furlong, as when that far off they show to the best advantage in such an atmosphere. I cannot recall looking at a birch during the summer: to-day they are comparable to the showiest maple on the hillside. Even a towering oak, now wrapped in royal purple, cannot carry off the palm. Standing in the orchard, and wholly lost to every sense save that of sight, these splendid birches broke forth in song. This is one of the charming experiences of a country ramble. These trees were full of birds, yet not one was to be seen. I saw the tree and heard the music, and to it belonged the merit of both the melody and brilliancy. He that asketh for more deserveth nothing.

It is true, indeed, that the days are now in their yellow leaf; the flower and fruit are gone; but they pass away in such a cloud of glory that it profits us to enjoy them. The worm and the canker, too, are vastly entertaining, even if devoid of beauty; and nowhere, that I can discover, does grief find place; at least in a typical October morning.

White-throated sparrows were abundant again, to-day. They are sure to come in October, sometimes a little earlier, and remain until spring is well advanced. Of all our winter birds, they are least affected by weather.

The winter may be "open" or "hard," the words locally used to express a mild or severe season; but it matters not with these birds, they are here just the same; and this fact does not apply equally strongly to any others; for, comparing year with year, the numbers of many other species vary considerably.

One can scarcely grow enthusiastic over the song of these Northern sparrows; it is too shrill and uniform, and so soon becomes tiresome. I suspect they seldom sing such songs as is recorded of them far away in the New England woods; but to-day, hearing a number of them for the first time, it was a veritable treat.

October 30.—A steady rain and dense fog were the prominent features of the day. How quickly the weather changes from one extreme to the other! With a gumcloth cape over my shoulders, I sauntered to the meadows, but all the world had gone wrong; every tree and bush was sobbing. The only birds seen were nuthatches, and these were upside-down. Why do they not get wet? The rain falls against the grain of their feathers. At all events, they appear to keep dry, and kept up, also, their usual high spirits, "quank-quanking" at every fourth hop, with mathematical precision.

I tried to outstare a chipmunk, on my way home, but it was not to be done. The little fellow never winked, and I believe I did. As I stared, I approached. This motion on my part the chipmunk saw, and he measured my movements without winking. When I was within five short steps there came a flash, like brown lightning, and the tip of a tail sinking in a hole in the ground is all that I can recall. I found that the little fellow had been sitting at the opening of his underground retreat, and so could afford to be brave.

All day long the rain continued falling, soaking every nook and corner of the fields and woods. It grew distasteful to the birds, and most took shelter in the cedars and other available spots. One restless song-sparrow tried to sing, but big round rain-drops burst upon his open beak so often he gave it up in disgust.

A few warblers congregated in the big locusts in the yard, and offered a chance to take an observation from within doors. There were black and white tree-creeping warblers, a black-throated blue, and two myrtle birds. These gave me hopes that an autumn flight of warblers may wind up the month, or be the prominent feature of November's Indian summer.

Between wind and rain, the leaves have had a poor show to-day, and far more than half are now scattered. Through the bare branches I see many nests not discovered during the leafy month of June. Some of them, too, are in positions which it seems impossible should have been overlooked. The exposure by the winds of so many nests proves the cunning of such birds as desire to have their summer retreats hidden. They certainly must study the matter of location very carefully; for it is not to be held that the whole matter is one of mere accident. I counted eleven nests to-day in the dooryard trees, not one of which I suspected as being within half a mile of the house; and I can never believe they were not purposely hidden among the leaves.

October 31.—Still dull and dismal, as a northeast rain can make it. Everywhere, the superabundant moisture makes travelling troublesome; all that we touch is cold, clammy, and repugnant. Enthusiasm needs constant pricking to keep it alive, and backward glances towards home are dangerously seductive. Still, I resolutely passed down the hillside towards the weediest pastures, anticipating nothing but possible rheumatism; but the gloom was more apparent than real, as the warblers of yesterday tarried with us, and a brave-hearted yellow-throat whistled encouragingly. Whistled nothing in particular, but merely a generous series of emphatic notes, translatable by every one to meet his fancy. I construed them into a welcome, and stood by a mammoth pin-oak taking in fresh inspiration with every repetition of his song. The storm-stayed warblers took heart in time, and they too sang cheery notes; a merry treble to the doleful bass of the dripping, ceaseless dripping, from the overarching trees.

The richest green is now along the borders of the hillside springs. An herbarium of pretty plants may be gathered from the margins of the little pools, where the water bubbles upward into daylight, after miles of subterranean flow. The frogs have learned of these spots, or have stumbled upon them by accident, and winter therein, often in such numbers as to crowd each other. Wriggling salamanders likewise find it a safe and comfortable retreat. In counting the frogs in a sunken cask, placed to collect the waters of a little spring, I made a discovery, and so forgot entirely the steady pour of the cold rain upon me.

As these springs are all concealed at this time of the year by a thick coating of autumn leaves, their presence would not be suspected except for their rich rim of bright green grasses; and when there is a deep pool in coarse gravel, or a cask has been sunk to catch the water, then there is nothing, often, to show the danger of passing that way. In their usual reckless manner, chipmunks, mice, and shrews go at breakneck speed over the ground, and sometimes, to their sorrow, drive into these leaf-covered depths. In the large cask I examined to-day were several mice and one squirrel, and on these the frogs were feeding. This was my discovery. These frogs remain active, if a food supply such as I have mentioned is available; but if not, hibernation is available to ward off the gnawings of hunger. To be sure, batrachians can fast for a long time, but probably not from October to the following spring, and keep up their ordinary summer-time activity.

The woodpeckers that built so elaborate a home in the apple-tree have deserted it; and now are equally busy, a furlong off, pecking at a dead limb of a maple. I can get no clew to their object; unless they purpose having the holes in readiness for next spring, which I do not believe.

Towards sunset, the crows as usual took their westward flight to their roosts, and flew in a disconsolate, dejected, downcast manner. Coming quite down to the tree-tops as they passed the bluff, I gave a loud shout when several were near. It seemed to awake them, as though they had been sleeping as they flew. Straightway they were noisy as geese, each scolding the other for not seeing me before, and all that passed after that rose a hundred feet or more in the thick air.

These were the last birds of the month. An hour later, dull, dreary, dripping night kept even the owls at home, and October, that was ushered in with such a wealth of light and music, had not one ray of sunshine to brighten its final hours, or aught to soothe it, beyond the moaning of the east wind in the sobbing pines.

INDEX.

Achpoachgussink, iv.
Acrelius, Israel, iv.
Adirondacks, 279.
Alder, smooth (*Alnus serrulata*), 43.
Amazons, naturalist on the, quoted, 303.
Ancylus, 221.
Anemones, 102.
Ant-lion (*Myrmeleon*), 261.
Apples, 289.
Aquikonasra, iv.
Arbutus, trailing (*Epigæa repens*), 102.
Arcella, 137.
Arum (*Peltandra Virginica*), 194, 376.
Ash (*Fraxinus Americana*), 319.
Aster, 264.
Audubon, J. J., 92, 351.
Axolotl, 251.
Azalea (*Azalea nudiflora*), 70.

Baird, S. F., 128.
Barton, Dr. Benj. Smith, 63, 66, 99.
Bass, black, 148.
Bat, little brown (*Vespertilio subulatus*), 286.
Bates, H. W., 303.
Batrachians, 63.
Bats (*Chiroptera*), 283, 365.
Bear, black, 4.
Bees, honey, 40, 316.
Beetles (*Coleoptera*), 43, 317.
Bellwort (*Uvularia perfoliata*), 70.
Belostoma, 179.

Bill-fish (*Belone truncata*), 153.
Birch (*Betula alba*), 23, 53, 384.
Birds, somnambulism among, 256.
Bittern (*Botaurus lentiginosus*), 30, 244, 270.
Bittern, least (*Ardea exilis*), 197.
Blackbirds, red-winged (*Agelaius phœniceus*), 23, 262, 361.
Black hawk (*Archibuteo lagopus*), 28.
Bladderwort (*Utricularia*), 186.
Bloodroot (*Sanguinaria Canadensis*), 68.
Bluebirds (*Sialia sialis*), 18, 344.
Bluet (*Houstonia cærulea*), 102.
Bobolink (*Dolichonyx orizivora*), 233, 242, 262.
Bordentown, New Jersey, 58.
Bracken (*Pteris aquilina*), 223.
Brewer, Thos. M., 128, 344.
Brinton, Dr. D. G., iii.
Bristol, Penn., 116.
Burroughs, John, 332.
Buttercup (*Ranunculus bulbosus*), 68.
Butterfly, cabbage (*Pieris rapæ*), 315.
Buttonwood (*Platanus occidentalis*, 33.
Buzzard, red-tailed (*Buteo borealis*), 24, 247.
Buzzard, broad-winged (*Buteo Pennsylvanicus*, 24.

Caddis worms (*Phryganeidæ*), 177.
Campanius, Thomas, iii, vii, 86.

INDEX.

Carr, Lucien, 111.
Cat, domestic, 37, 357.
Catbird (*Galeoscoptes Carolinensis*), 73, 78, 81, 91, 206, 214, 381.
Catfish, 147.
Cattail swamp, 6, 294.
Cedar-birds (*Ampelis cedrorum*), 58.
Cedar, red (*Juniperus Virginiana*), 42, 129.
Chat, yellow-breasted (*Icteria viridis*), 206.
Cherry-tree fly-catchers (*Sayornis fuscus*), 63, 88.
Cherry, wild (*Prunus serotina*), 233.
Chesapeake Bay, 90, 373.
Chickweed, star (*Stellaria media*), 42.
Chinkapin (*Castanea pumila*), 315, 355.
Chipmunk (*Tamias lysteri*), 266, 385.
Cinnamon fern (*Osmunda cinnamomea*), 223.
Colorado River of the West, 8.
Columbine (*Aquilegia Canadensis*), 69.
Conrad, T. A., 65, 69, 192.
Cooper's hawk (*Nisus Cooperi*), 29.
Coot (*Fulica Americana*), 298.
Cope, Edward D., 244.
Corixa, 175, 182.
Corydalis, yellow, 67.
Coues, Elliott, 342.
Cougar (see Panther).
Cowpen-bird (*Molothrus pecoris*), 82, 223, 353.
Crayfish, 166, 190, 316.
Cricket (*Gryllus neglectus et Nemobius vittatus*), 336.
Crossbill (*Loxia Americana et leucoptera*), 23, 30.
Crossweeksen (see Crosswicks Creek).
Crosswicks Creek, 58, 166, 219, 227, 230, 234, 242.
Crows (*Corvus Americanus*), 27, 49, 52, 144, 211, 238, 307, 350, 388.

Cyprinodonts, 149, 160.
Cyprinoids, 149.

Daffodils (*Narcissus pseudo-narcissus*), 69.
Dandelion (*Taraxacum dens-leonis*), 43, 62.
Darters (see Etheostomoids).
DeKay, James E., 139.
Delaware River, iv, vii, 2, 16, 55, 90, 157, 226.
Diapheromera, 174.
Dipper, American (see Water ouzel).
Diver, eared, 60.
Diver, little brown, 300.
Dragon-fly (*Libellulidae*), 316.
Ducks, wild, 2, 56.
Du Pratz, Le Page, 120.
Dytiscus, 181.

Eagle, white-headed (*Haliaetus leucocephalus*), 24.
Eardrops (*Dicentra cucullaria*), 44.
Earthquake, occurrence of an, 236.
Eels (*Anguilla longirostris*), 162.
Elm (*Ulmus Americanus*), 191.
Emerton, J. H., 303.
Erythronium Americana, 68.
Esquimau, 45.
Etheostomoids, 159.

Falcon, peregrine (*Falco anatum*), 24.
Falcon, rough-legged (*Archibuteo lagopus*), 24.
Falcon, winter (*Buteo lineatus*), 24.
Ferns, 202, 328.
Finch, grass (*Poöcætes gramineus*), 359.
Finch, pine (*Chrisomitris pinus*), 23, 363.
Finch, sharp-tailed (*Ammodromus candacutus*), 372.
Finch, thistle (*Carduelis tristis*), 338, 361.
Finch, white-throated (*Zonotrichia albicollis*), 344.

INDEX. 393

Fireflies (*Lampyridæ*), 207.
Fish, habits of, 23, 48, 50, 63, 253.
Fish-hawk (*Pandion haliaetus*), 63, 221, 259.
Flagg, Wilson, 343.
Flicker (*Colaptes auratus*), 244, 377, 388.
Forget-me-not (*Myosotis palustris*), 194.
Franklin, Dr. Benj., 110.
Fritillaries (*Brenthis Bellona*), 315.
Frogs, 50, 61, 204, 301, 336, 387.

Gar (*Lepidosteus osseus*), 149, 162.
Geranium, spotted (*Geranium maculatum*), 69.
Girard, Dr. Chas., 169.
Gizzard shad (*Dorysoma cepedianum*), 148.
Gnat, 223.
Goniobasis, 242.
Goose, Canada (*Bernicla Canadensis*), 321.
Gooseberry (*Ribes grossularia*), 142.
Goshawk (*Astur atricapillus*), 24.
Grakle (*Quiscalus versicolor*), 101.
Grape, chicken (*Vitis cordifolia*), 305.
Grape, fox (*Vitis labrusca*), 275.
Grape-hyacinth (*Muscari botryoides*), 69.
Grapevine (*Vitis cordifolia*), 34.
Grasshoppers (*Locustidæ*), 316, 318.
Grebe, crested (*Colymbus cristatus*), 60.
Grebe, red-necked (*Colymbus Holboellii*), 60.
Greenbrier (*Smilax rotundifolia*), 34.
Greenlet, warbling (see Vireo).
Grosbeak, cardinal (*Cardinalis Virginianus*), 23, 124, 326.
Grosbeak, pine (*Pinicola enucleator*), 128.
Grosbeak, rose-breasted (*Hedymeles ludovicianus*), 189, 203.
Gryllotalpa, 199.
Gum-tree (*Nyssa multiflora*), 265.

17*

Gunther, Dr. Albert, 259.
Gyrinus, 49.

Hawk, Cooper's (*Nisus Cooperi*), 29.
Hawk, fish (*Pandion haliaetus*), 63, 221, 259.
Hawk, sharp-shinned (*Nisus fuscus*), 29.
Hawk, sparrow (*Tinnunculus sparverius*), 29.
Hawks, 24, 36, 327.
Heckewelder, John, 218.
Hickory, shag or shell-bark (*Carya alba*), 121, 265, 312.
Holbrook, John Edwards, 139.
Honeysuckle, wild (see Azalea).
Hornet (*Vespa maculata*), 339.
Humming-bird (*Trochilus colubris*), 142, 211, 236.
Hyatt, Prof. Alpheus, 183.
Hyla Pickeringii, 271, 328.
Hyssop, giant (*Lophanthus nepetoides*), 265.

Indian relics, vi.
Indians (see Lenâpè).
Indigo bird (*Cyanospiza cyanea*), 91, 206, 222.
Infusoria, 15.
Iroquois Indians, 34.

Jack-in-the-pulpit (*Arisæma triphyllum*, 69.
Jacob's ladder (*Polemonium cœruleum*), 69.
Jay, blue (*Cyanura cristata*), 54, 210, 270, 314, 321, 355.
Juncos (see Snow-birds).

Kalm, Peter, 109, 111, 117, 127, 274, 382.
Katydid (*Cyrtophyllus concavus*), 239, 330, 336, 345.
Kingbird (*Tyrannus Carolinensis*), 208.
Kingfisher (*Ceryle alcyon*), 270, 304.
Kinglet, ruby-crowned (*Regulus calendula*), 322.
Kinglets (*Regulus satrapa et ca lendula*) 18, 54, 377.

Lark, horned (*Alauda Alpestris*), 31.
Lark, meadow (*Sturnella magna*), 308, 359.
Larvæ, insect, 20.
Least bittern (see Bittern).
Lee, L. A., 251.
Lenâpè Indians, vi, 16, 34, 37, 111, 235, 294, 320.
Lily, pond (*Nymphæa odorata*), 194.
Limnea, 241.
Linnet (*Ægiothus linarius*), 23, 31, 352.
Lioplax, 242.
Liquidambar styraciflua, 235.
Lobelia, scarlet (*Lobelia cardinalis*), 236.
Log-cock (*Hylotomus pileatus*), 7, 379.
Lord, John Keast, 21.
Loskiel, Geo. H., 112.
Lowell, J. Russell, 205.
Lubbock, Sir John, 315.

Maltese cat, 37.
Manteese Indians, vi.
Maple (*Acer rubrum*), 39, 55, 335.
Marsh-harrier (*Circus Hudsonius*), 243.
Marsh-marigold (*Caltha palustris*), 69.
Marsh-wren, long-billed (*Cistothorus palustris*), 93.
Marsh-wren, short-billed (*Cistothorus stellaris*), 98.
Marsh-wrens, 88.
Maryland yellow-throat (*Geothlypis trichas*), 48, 203, 333.
Melantho, 242.
Meneick, iv, v.
Merriam, C. Hart, 278.
Migration of birds, 22, 254.
Mink (*Putorius vison*), 48, 59, 206, 346.
Minnow, silver-finned (*Luxilus analostanos*), 260.
Minnow-mud (*Melanura limi*), 72, 159.
Minnows (see Cyprinoids).

Mole, common (*Scalops aquaticus*), 279.
Mole, star-nosed (*Condylura cristata*), 23, 276.
Mole-cricket (see *Gryllotalpa*).
Morse, Prof. Ed. S., 230.
Mosquito (*Culex damnosus*), 48.
Mouse, harvest (*Ochetodon humilis*), 39.
Mouse, house (*Mus musculus*), 37, 269, 323.
Mouse, jumping (*Zapus Hudsonius*), 63.
Mouse, meadow (*Arvicola riparia*), 59, 269, 316, 318.
Mouse, white-footed (*Hesperomys leucopus*), 269, 359, 367.
Mullein (*Verbascum thapsus*), 344.
Musk-rat (*Fiber zibethicus*), 22, 59, 200, 364.
Mussels (*Unionidæ*), 153, 201, 225.
Myriophyllum, 173.

New Jersey, 14, 25, 54, 257.
Notonecta, 173, 175, 182.
Nuphar pumilum, 51, 194.
Nuthatches (*Sitta Carolinensis et Canadensis*), 53, 54, 252, 280, 295, 322.
Nuttall, Thos., 196, 343, 851.
Nymphæa odorata, 51.

Oak, broad-leaved (*Quercus obtusiloba*), 315.
Oak, pin (*Quercus palustris*), 315.
Oak, post (*Quercus obtusiloba*), 203.
Oak, red (*Quercus rubra*), 315.
Oak, swamp-white (*Quercus bicolor*), 315.
Oak, white (*Quercus alba*), 315.
Opalina ranarum, 138.
Opossum (*Didelphis Virginiana*), 37, 48, 337, 362, 375.
Ord, George, 352.
Oriole, Baltimore (*Icterus Baltimore*), 73, 80, 91, 214, 233.
Oriole, orchard (*Icterus spurius*), 91, 214.

INDEX. 395

Otter (*Lutra Canadensis*), 47, 59.
Overfield, Miles, 8, 214, 337, 368, 371, 380.
Owl, barn (*Strix pratincola*), 331, 357, 363.
Owl, cat (*Otus Wilsonianus*), 356.
Owl, great gray (*Syrnium nebulosum*), 53.
Owl, marsh (*Otus brachyotus*), 356.
Owl, red (*Scops Asio*), 346.
Owl, saw-whet (*Nyctale Acadica*), 352.
Owls, 47, 205, 346, 365.
Oxalis, 194.

Packard, Prof. A. S., 71, 251.
Panther (*Felis concolor*), 6, 37, 358.
Pectinatella magnifica, 182.
Pee-wee (*Sayornis fuscus*), 63, 83.
Pelecoris, 178, 182.
Penn, William, 37, 111.
Perch (*Perca flavescens*), 148.
Periophthalmus, 149.
Persimmon (*Diospyros Virginiana*), 336.
Philippine Islands, 149.
Physa, 241.
Pike (*Esox reticulatus*), 147, 155, 162.
Pike, Nicolas, letter from, quoted, 139.
Pine-finch (*Pinicola enucleator*), 23.
Pisidium, 14, 228.
Planorbis, 241.
Plover, kill-deer (*Oxyechus vociferus*), 63, 219.
Plover, upland (*Bartramia longicauda*), 237, 321.
Ponctquissings Creek, iii, iv, v, vii, 18, 23, 24, 26, 28, 29, 31, 32, 35, 37, 43, 44, 45, 46, 50, 52, 54, 147, 151, 155, 178, 182, 183, 194, 245, 269, 364, 376.
Poke (*Phytolacca decandra*), 234.
Pontederia, 51, 194, 376.
Popihacka, v.
Poplar, Lombardy (*Populus dilatata*), 313.
Potomac River, 90.

Pteris aquilina, 202.
Pupa, 14, 15.

Quahog (*Venus mercenaria*), 228.
Quail (*Ortyx Virginiana*), 292, 382.
Quakers, vii, 45, 47, 293, 369.
Quaker-girls (*Houstonia cærulea*), 68, 102.
Quince (*Cydonia vulgaris*), 142.

Rabbit (*Lepus sylvaticus*), 47, 257, 359, 368.
Raccoon (*Procyon lotor*), 9, 37, 48, 273, 330.
Rail-bird, yellow (*Porzana Novæboracensis*), 21.
Ranatra, 174, 182.
Red-bird, summer (*Pyranga æstiva*), 114.
Reed-birds (see Bobolink).
Reeds—wild rice (*Zizania aquatica*), 343.
Ridgway, R., 128.
Riley, C. V., 200.
Robin (*Turdus migratorius*), 321, 361.
Romanes, Geo. J., 36, 156, 157, 219.
Rose-mallow, swamp (*Hibiscus Moscheutos*), 243.
Ruby-throats (see Humming-birds).
Rue anemone (*Thalictrum anemonoides*), 69.

Sagittaria variabilis, 51.
Salamanders (*Urodela*), 20, 43, 247, 336, 387.
Sandpipers (*Scolopacidæ*), 204, 296.
Sapsucker (*Picus pubescens*), 7.
Sassafras (*Sassafras officinale*), 41.
Saxifrage (*Saxifraga Virginiensis*), 68.
"Science Gossip," Hardwicke's, 127.
Scuttle-bug (see *Gyrinus*).
Seal (*Phoca vitulina*), 56.
Seekonk, Mass., 71.

INDEX.

Sharp-shinned hawk (*Nisus fuscus*), 29.
Shield-ferns (*Aspidium acrostichoides*), 224.
Shrew (*Blarina brevicauda*), 23, 346.
Shrike (*Colluris borealis*), 338.
Shrimp, fairy (*Branchippus vernalis*), 71.
Skunk (*Mephitis mephitica*), 31, 346, 366, 375.
Skunk-cabbage (*Symplocarpus fœtidus*), 43.
Snails (*Helices*), 230.
Snake, garter (*Eutainia saurita et sirtalis*), 217.
Snake, black (*Bascanion constrictor*), 218.
Snake, ring (*Diadophis punctatus*), 305.
Snow-bird (*Junco hyemalis*), 332, 344, 380.
Solomon's seal (*Polygonatum biflorum*), 70.
Song-sparrow (*Melospiza melodia*), 18, 19, 23, 54, 78, 142, 213, 308, 333.
Sparrow, chipping (*Spizella socialis*), 73.
Sparrow, European (*Pyrgita domestica*), 75, 262, 339.
Sparrow, fox-colored (*Passerella iliaca*),
Sparrow, marsh (*Melospiza palustris*), 341.
Sparrow, tree (*Spizella monticola*), 344.
Sparrow, white-throated (*Zonotrichia albicollis*), 377, 380, 384.
Sparrow-hawk (*Tinnunculus sparverius*), 29, 127.
Sphærium, 14, 228.
Spice-wood (*Lindera benzoin*), 102.
Spiders (*Arachnida: Araneina*), 20, 303, 316, 322, 327, 334, 348.
Splatterdock (*Nuphar pumilum*), 162.
Spleenworts (*Asplenium*), 224.
Spring, mineral, 214.

Squirrel (*Sciurus Carolinensis*), 35, 270, 375.
Squirrel, flying (*Sciuropterus volucella*), 40, 331, 346.
Squirrel, red (*Sciurus Hudsonius*), 247.
Star-grass (*Sisyrinchium Bermudiana*), 194.
Stickleback (*Apeltes quadracus*), 151.
St. Lawrence River, 16.
Stockholm, iv.
Stokes, Dr. A. C., 37.
Strawberries (*Fragaria*), 193.
Suckers (*Catostomoidæ*), 51.
Sunfish (*Eupomotis aureus*), 72.
Sunfish, banded (*Mesogonistius chætodon*), 161.
Susquehanna River, 90.
Swallows (*Hirundinidæ*), 20.
Swamp sumac (*Rhus venenata*), 8.
Sweden, New, iv.

Tanager, scarlet (*Pyranga rubra*), 114, 121, 203.
Tarr, Ralph S., 170.
Thoreau, H. D., 206.
Thrips, 137.
Thrush, brown, 78, 91.
Thrush, song (*Turdus mustelinus*), 78, 81, 144, 189.
Thrush, wood (see Song-thrush).
Tiger-beetles (*Cicindelæ*), 15.
Titmouse, common, or Chickadee (*Parus atricapillus*), 270.
Titmouse, crested (*Lophophanes bicolor*), 129, 254.
Toad, common (*Bufo lentiginosus*), 205.
Toad, spade-foot (*Scaphiopus Holbrookii*), 132.
Trakonick, iv, v, vii.
Tree-creeper, brown (*Certhia familiaris*), 53, 283, 295.
Tree-toad, Pickering's (*Hyla Pickeringii*), 271, 328, 345.
Trumpet-creeper (*Tecoma radicans*), 142.
Tulip-tree (*Liriodendron tulipifera*), 339.

Turkey, wild (*Meleagris gallopavo*), 293.
Turtle-dove (*Zenædura Carolinensis*), 83.

Valvata, 242.
Violet, blue (*Viola cucullata*), 44.
Violet, tricolored (*Viola tricolor*), 68.
Vireo, warbling (*Vireo gilvus*), 235.
Vireo, white-eyed (*Vireo Noveboracencis*), 77, 214, 222.
Vireo, yellow-throated (*Vireo flavifrons*), 84.
Virginia-creeper (*Ampelopsis quinquefolia*), 34.

Wagtails (*Siurus*), 20.
Wagtails, golden-crowned (*Siurus auricapillus*), 91.
Warbler, summer (*Dendrœca æstiva*), 77, 91.
Warblers (*Sylvicolidæ*), 294, 386.
Warentapecka, iv.
Washington birds (*Sayornis fuscus*), 63.
Wasp (*Vespa arenaria*), 338.
Water-boatmen (see *Notonecta*).
Watermelon (*Citrullus vulgaris*), 52, 191, 238.
Water-ouzel (*Cinclus Americanus*), 20.

Water-scorpion (*Nepa apiculata*), 175.
Water-tigers (see Dytiscus).
Weasel (*Putorius ermineus*), 49, 346, 348.
Whippoorwill (*Antrostomus vociferus*), 67, 352.
Whitlow-grass (*Draba verna*), 41.
Wildcat (*Lynx rufus*), 12.
Will-o'-the-wisp, 383.
Wilson, Alexander, 91, 115, 119, 124, 351.
Wind-flower (*Anemone nemorosa*), 69, 102.
Witch-hazel (*Hamamelis Virginica*), 41.
Wolf (*Canis lupus*), 7, 47.
Woodpecker, golden-winged (see Flicker).
Woodpecker, hairy (*Picus villosus*), 378.
Woodpecker, red-headed (*Melanerpes erythrocephalus*), 119, 379.
Wren, Carolina (*Thryothorus ludovicianus*), 64, 76, 79, 98, 229, 246, 266, 273, 325, 380.
Wren, house (*Troglodytes œdon*), 22, 73, 83, 210.
Wren, winter (*Anorthura troglodytes*), 19, 54.
Wrens, marsh (*Cistothorus palustris et stellaris*), 88.

THE END.

VALUABLE AND INTERESTING WORKS

FOR

PUBLIC AND PRIVATE LIBRARIES,

PUBLISHED BY

HARPER & BROTHERS, NEW YORK.

☞ *For a full List of Books suitable for Libraries published by* HARPER & BROTHERS, *see* HARPER'S CATALOGUE, *which may be had gratuitously on application to the publishers personally, or by letter enclosing Ten Cents in postage stamps.*
☞ HARPER & BROTHERS *will send their publications by mail, postage prepaid, on receipt of the price.*

HIGGINSON'S LARGER HISTORY OF THE UNITED STATES. A Larger History of the United States of America to the Close of President Jackson's Administration. By THOMAS WENTWORTH HIGGINSON, Author of "Young Folks' History of the United States," &c. Illustrated by Maps, Plans, Portraits, and other Engravings. pp. xii., 470. 8vo, Cloth, $3.50.

WRITINGS AND SPEECHES OF SAMUEL J. TILDEN. Edited by JOHN BIGELOW. pp. xviii., 1202. 2 vols., 8vo, Cloth, Gilt Tops and Uncut Edges, $6.00.

MACAULAY'S ENGLAND. The History of England from the Accession of James II. By THOMAS BABINGTON MACAULAY. New Edition, from New Electrotype Plates. 5 vols., in a Box, 8vo, Cloth, with Paper Labels, Uncut Edges, and Gilt Tops, $10.00; Sheep, $12.50; Half Calf, $21.25. (*Sold only in Sets.*) Cheap Edition, 5 vols., in a Box, 12mo, Cloth, $2.50; Sheep, $5.00.

MACAULAY'S MISCELLANEOUS WORKS. The Miscellaneous Works of Lord Macaulay. From New Electrotype Plates. 5 vols., in a Box, 8vo, Cloth, with Paper Labels, Uncut Edges, and Gilt Tops, $10.00; Sheep, $12.50; Half Calf, $21.25. (*Sold only in Sets.*)

HUME'S ENGLAND. History of England, from the Invasion of Julius Cæsar to the Abdication of James II., 1688. By DAVID HUME. New and Elegant Library Edition, from New Electrotype Plates. 6 vols., in a Box, 8vo, Cloth, with Paper Labels, Uncut Edges, and Gilt Tops, $12.00; Sheep, $15.00; Half Calf, $25.50. (*Sold only in Sets.*) Popular Edition, 6 vols., in a Box, 12mo, Cloth, $3.00.

GEDDES'S JOHN DE WITT. History of the Administration of John De Witt, Grand Pensionary of Holland. By JAMES GEDDES. Vol. I. —1623-1654. With a Portrait. 8vo, Cloth, $2.50.

GIBBON'S ROME. The History of the Decline and Fall of the Roman Empire. By EDWARD GIBBON. With Notes by Dean MILMAN, M. GUIZOT, and Dr. WILLIAM SMITH. New Edition, from New Electrotype Plates. 6 vols., 8vo, Cloth, with Paper Labels, Uncut Edges, and Gilt Tops, $12.00; Sheep, $15.00; Half Calf, $25.50. (*Sold only in Sets.*) Popular Edition, 6 vols., in a Box, 12mo, Cloth, $3.00.

HILDRETH'S UNITED STATES. History of the United States. FIRST SERIES: From the Discovery of the Continent to the Organization of the Government under the Federal Constitution. SECOND SERIES: From the Adoption of the Federal Constitution to the End of the Sixteenth Congress. By RICHARD HILDRETH. Popular Edition, 6 vols., in a Box, 8vo, Cloth, with Paper Labels, Uncut Edges, and Gilt Tops, $12.00; Sheep, $15.00; Half Calf, $25.50. (*Sold only in Sets.*)

MOTLEY'S DUTCH REPUBLIC. The Rise of the Dutch Republic. A History. By JOHN LOTHROP MOTLEY, LL.D., D.C.L. With a Portrait of William of Orange. New Library Edition, 3 vols., in a Box 8vo, Cloth, with Paper Labels, Uncut Edges, and Gilt Tops, $6.00; Sheep, $7.50; Half Calf, $12.75. (*Sold only in Sets.*) Original Library Edition, 3 vols., 8vo, Cloth, $10.50.

MOTLEY'S UNITED NETHERLANDS. History of the United Netherlands: From the Death of William the Silent to the Twelve Years' Truce—1584–1609. With a full View of the English-Dutch Struggle against Spain, and of the Origin and Destruction of the Spanish Armada. By JOHN LOTHROP MOTLEY, LL.D., D.C.L. Portraits. New Library Edition, 4 vols., in a Box, 8vo, Cloth, with Paper Labels, Uncut Edges, and Gilt Tops, $8.00; Sheep, $10.00; Half Calf, $17.00. (*Sold only in Sets.*) Original Library Edition, 4 vols., 8vo, Cloth, $14.00.

MOTLEY'S JOHN OF BARNEVELD. The Life and Death of John of Barneveld, Advocate of Holland. With a View of the Primary Causes and Movements of the "Thirty Years' War." By JOHN LOTHROP MOTLEY, LL.D., D.C.L. Illustrated. New Library Edition, 2 vols., in a Box, 8vo, Cloth, with Paper Labels, Uncut Edges, and Gilt Tops, $4.00; Sheep, $5.00; Half Calf, $8.50. (*Sold only in Sets.*) Original Library Edition, 2 vols., 8vo, Cloth, $7.00.

THE FALL OF CONSTANTINOPLE. Being the Story of the Fourth Crusade. By EDWIN PEARS, LL.B. pp. xvi., 422. 8vo, Cloth, $2.50.

GOLDSMITH'S WORKS. The Works of Oliver Goldsmith. Edited by PETER CUNNINGHAM, F.S.A. From New Electrotype Plates. 4 vols., 8vo, Cloth, Paper Labels, Uncut Edges, and Gilt Tops, $8.00; Sheep, $10.00; Half Calf, $17.00. Uniform with the New Library Editions of Macaulay, Hume, Gibbon, Motley, and Hildreth.

HUDSON'S HISTORY OF JOURNALISM. Journalism in the United States, from 1690 to 1872. By FREDERIC HUDSON. 8vo, Cloth, $5.00.

SYMONDS'S SKETCHES AND STUDIES IN SOUTHERN EUROPE. By JOHN ADDINGTON SYMONDS. 2 vols., Post 8vo, Cloth, $4.00; Half Calf, $7.50.

SYMONDS'S GREEK POETS. Studies of the Greek Poets. By JOHN ADDINGTON SYMONDS. 2 vols., Square 16mo, Cloth, $3.50; Half Calf, $7.00

GEORGE ELIOT'S LIFE, as Related in her Letters and Journals. Arranged and Edited by her Husband, J. W. CROSS. Portrait and Illustrations. Library Edition, 3 vols., 12mo, Cloth, $3.75; Half Calf, $9.00.

TREVELYAN'S LIFE OF MACAULAY. The Life and Letters of Lord Macaulay. By his Nephew, G. OTTO TREVELYAN, M.P. With Portrait on Steel. 2 vols., 8vo, Cloth, Uncut Edges and Gilt Tops, $5.00; Sheep, $6.00; Half Calf, $9.50. Popular Edition, 2 vols. in one, 12mo, Cloth, $1.75.

TREVELYAN'S LIFE OF FOX. The Early History of Charles James Fox. By GEORGE OTTO TREVELYAN. 8vo, Cloth, Uncut Edges and Gilt Tops, $2.50; Half Calf, $4.75.

MÜLLER'S POLITICAL HISTORY OF RECENT TIMES (1816–1875). With Special Reference to Germany. By WILLIAM MÜLLER. Translated, with an Appendix covering the Period from 1876 to 1881, by the Rev. JOHN P. PETERS, Ph.D. 12mo, Cloth, $3.00.

LOSSING'S CYCLOPÆDIA OF UNITED STATES HISTORY. From the Aboriginal Period to 1876. By B. J. LOSSING, LL.D. Illustrated by 2 Steel Portraits and over 1000 Engravings. 2 vols., Royal 8vo, Cloth, $10.00; Sheep, $12.00; Half Morocco, $15.00. (*Sold by Subscription only.*)

LOSSING'S FIELD-BOOK OF THE REVOLUTION. Pictorial Field-Book of the Revolution; or, Illustrations by Pen and Pencil of the History, Biography, Scenery, Relics, and Traditions of the War for Independence. By BENSON J. LOSSING. 2 vols., 8vo, Cloth, $14.00; Sheep or Roan, $15.00; Half Calf, $18.00.

LOSSING'S FIELD-BOOK OF THE WAR OF 1812. Pictorial Field-Book of the War of 1812; or, Illustrations by Pen and Pencil of the History, Biography, Scenery, Relics, and Traditions of the Last War for American Independence. By BENSON J. LOSSING. With several hundred Engravings. 1088 pages, 8vo, Cloth, $7.00; Sheep, $8.50; Half Calf, $10.00.

PARTON'S CARICATURE. Caricature and Other Comic Art, in All Times and Many Lands. By JAMES PARTON. 203 Illustrations. 8vo, Cloth, Uncut Edges and Gilt Tops, $5.00; Half Calf, $7.25.

MAHAFFY'S GREEK LITERATURE. A History of Classical Greek Literature. By J. P. MAHAFFY. 2 vols., 12mo, Cloth, $4.00; Half Calf, $7.50.

SIMCOX'S LATIN LITERATURE. A History of Latin Literature, from Ennius to Boethius. By GEORGE AUGUSTUS SIMCOX, M.A. 2 vols., 12mo, Cloth, $4.00.

DU CHAILLU'S LAND OF THE MIDNIGHT SUN. Summer and Winter Journeys in Sweden, Norway, and Lapland, and Northern Finland. By PAUL B. DU CHAILLU. Illustrated. 2 vols., 8vo, Cloth, $7.50; Half Calf, $12.00.

DU CHAILLU'S ASHANGO LAND. A Journey to Ashango Land, and Further Penetration into Equatorial Africa. By P. B. DU CHAILLU. Illustrated. 8vo, Cloth, $5.00; Half Calf, $7.25.

FORBES'S NATURALIST'S WANDERINGS IN THE EASTERN ARCHIPELAGO. A Narrative of Travel and Exploration from 1878 to 1883. By HENRY O. FORBES, F.R.G.S., &c. With many Illustrations and Maps. pp. xx. 536. 8vo, Ornamental Cloth $5.00.

DEXTER'S CONGREGATIONALISM. The Congregationalism of the Last Three Hundred Years. as Seen in its Literature: with Special Reference to certain Recondite, Neglected, or Disputed Passages. With a Bibliographical Appendix. By H. M. DEXTER. Large 8vo, Cloth, $6.00.

STANLEY'S CONGO. The Congo, and the Founding of its Free State: A Story of Work and Exploration. By H. M. STANLEY. With over One Hundred Illustrations and two Large Maps in Pockets and Smaller Maps. 2 vols., pp. 1130. 8vo, Ornamental Cloth, $10.00; Sheep, $12.00; Half Morocco, $15.00.

STANLEY'S THROUGH THE DARK CONTINENT. Through the Dark Continent; or, The Sources of the Nile, Around the Great Lakes of Equatorial Africa, and Down the Livingstone River to the Atlantic Ocean. 149 Illustrations and 10 Maps. By H. M. STANLEY. 2 vols., 8vo, Cloth. $10.00; Sheep, $12.00; Half Morocco, $15.00.

BARTLETT'S FROM EGYPT TO PALESTINE. Through Sinai, the Wilderness, and the South Country. Observations of a Journey made with Special Reference to the History of the Israelites. By S. C. BARTLETT, D.D. Maps and Illustrations. 8vo, Cloth, $3.50.

FORSTER'S LIFE OF DEAN SWIFT. The Early Life of Jonathan Swift (1667–1711). By JOHN FORSTER. With Portrait. 8vo, Cloth, Uncut Edges and Gilt Tops. $2.50.

GREEN'S ENGLISH PEOPLE. History of the English People. By JOHN RICHARD GREEN, M.A. With Maps. 4 vols., 8vo, Cloth, $10.00; Sheep, $12.00; Half Calf, $19.00.

GREEN'S MAKING OF ENGLAND. The Making of England. By J. R. GREEN. With Maps. 8vo, Cloth, $2.50; Sheep, $3.00; Half Calf, $4.75.

GREEN'S CONQUEST OF ENGLAND. The Conquest of England. By J. R. GREEN. With Maps. 8vo, Cloth, $2.50; Sheep, $3.00; Half Calf, $4.75.

BENJAMIN'S CONTEMPORARY ART. Contemporary Art in Europe. By S. G. W. BENJAMIN. Illustrated. 8vo, Cloth, $3.50; Half Calf, $5.75.

BENJAMIN'S ART IN AMERICA. Art in America. By S. G. W. BENJAMIN. Illustrated. 8vo, Cloth, $4.00.

REBER'S HISTORY OF ANCIENT ART. History of Ancient Art. By Dr. FRANZ VON REBER. Revised by the Author. Translated and Augmented by JOSEPH THACHER CLARKE. With 310 Illustrations and a Glossary of Technical Terms. 8vo, Cloth, $3.50.

REBER'S HISTORY OF MEDIÆVAL ART. History of Mediæval Art. By Dr. FRANZ VON REBER. (*In Press.*)

ADAMS'S MANUAL OF HISTORICAL LITERATURE. Comprising Brief Descriptions of the Most Important Histories in English, French, and German. By Professor C. K. ADAMS. 8vo, Cloth, $2.50.

KINGLAKE'S CRIMEAN WAR. The Invasion of the Crimea: its Origin, and an Account of its Progress down to the Death of Lord Raglan. By ALEXANDER WILLIAM KINGLAKE. With Maps and Plans. Four Volumes now ready. 12mo, Cloth, $2.00 per vol. 4 vols., Half Calf, $15.'0.

HALLAM'S MIDDLE AGES. View of the State of Europe during the Middle Ages. By HENRY HALLAM. 8vo, Cloth, $2.00.

HALLAM'S CONSTITUTIONAL HISTORY OF ENGLAND. The Constitutional History of England, from the Accession of Henry VII. to the Death of George II. By HENRY HALLAM. 8vo, Cloth, $2.00.

PRIME'S POTTERY AND PORCELAIN. Pottery and Porcelain of All Times and Nations. With Tables of Factory and Artists' Marks, for the Use of Collectors. By WILLIAM C. PRIME, LL.D. Illustrated. 8vo, Cloth, Uncut Edges and Gilt Tops, $7.00; Half Calf, $9.25. (In a Box.)

ENGLISH MEN OF LETTERS. Edited by JOHN MORLEY. The following volumes are now ready. Others will follow:
JOHNSON. By L. Stephen.—GIBBON. By J. C. Morison.—SCOTT. By R. H. Hutton.—SHELLEY. By J. A. Symonds.—GOLDSMITH. By W. Black.—HUME. By Professor Huxley.—DEFOE. By W. Minto.—BURNS. By Principal Shairp.—SPENSER. By R. W. Church.—THACKERAY. By A. Trollope.—BURKE. By J. Morley.—MILTON. By M. Pattison.—SOUTHEY. By E. Dowden.—CHAUCER. By A. W. Ward.—BUNYAN. By J. A. Froude.—COWPER. By G. Smith.—POPE. By L. Stephen.—BYRON. By J. Nichols.—LOCKE. By T. Fowler.—WORDSWORTH. By F. W. H. Myers.—HAWTHORNE. By Henry James, Jr.—DRYDEN. By G. Saintsbury.—LANDOR. By S. Colvin.—DE QUINCEY. By D. Masson.—LAMB. By A. Ainger.—BENTLEY. By R. C. Jebb.—DICKENS. By A. W. Ward.—GRAY. By E. W. Gosse.—SWIFT. By L. Stephen.—STERNE. By H. D. Traill.—MACAULAY. By J. C. Morison.—FIELDING. By Austin Dobson.—SHERIDAN. By Mrs. Oliphant.—ADDISON. By W. J. Courthope.—BACON. By R. W. Church.—COLERIDGE. By H. D. Traill. 12mo, Cloth, 75 cents per volume.

STORMONTH'S ENGLISH DICTIONARY. A Dictionary of the English Language, Pronouncing, Etymological, and Explanatory: embracing Scientific and other Terms, Numerous Familiar Terms, and a Copious Selection of Old English Words. By the Rev. JAMES STORMONTH. The Pronunciation Carefully Revised by the Rev. P. H. PHELP, M.A. pp. xiv., 1234. Imperial 8vo, Cloth, $6.00; Half Roan, $7.00; Full Sheep, $7.50.

NEWCOMB'S POLITICAL ECONOMY. Principles of Political Economy. By SIMON NEWCOMB, LL.D., Professor of Mathematics, U. S. Navy. pp. xvi., 548. 8vo, Cloth, $2.50.

NEWCOMB'S ASTRONOMY. Popular Astronomy. By SIMON NEWCOMB, LL.D. With 112 Engravings, and 5 Maps of the Stars. 8vo, Cloth, $2.50.

MAURY'S PHYSICAL GEOGRAPHY OF THE SEA. The Physical Geography of the Sea, and its Meteorology. By M. F. MAURY, LL.D. 8vo, Cloth, $4.00.

CESNOLA'S CYPRUS. Cyprus: its Ancient Cities, Tombs, and Temples. A Narrative of Researches and Excavations during Ten Years' Residence in that Island. By L. P. DI CESNOLA. With Portrait, Maps, and 400 Illustrations. 8vo, Cloth, Extra, Uncut Edges and Gilt Tops, $7.50; Half Calf, $10.00.

GROTE'S HISTORY OF GREECE. 12 vols., 12mo, Cloth, $18.00; Sheep, $22.80; Half Calf, $39.00.

COMPLETE WORKS OF ALFRED, LORD TENNYSON. With an Introductory Sketch by ANNE THACKERAY RITCHIE. With Portraits and Illustrations. pp. 430. 8vo, Cloth, $2.00; Gilt Edges, $2.50.

VAN-LENNEP'S BIBLE LANDS. Bible Lands: their Modern Customs and Manners Illustrative of Scripture. By HENRY J. VAN-LENNEP, D.D. 350 Engravings and 2 Colored Maps. 8vo, Cloth, $5.00; Sheep, $6.00; Half Morocco, $8.00.

FLAMMARION'S ATMOSPHERE. Translated from the French of CAMILLE FLAMMARION. With 10 Chromo-Lithographs and 86 Woodcuts. 8vo, Cloth, $6.00; Half Calf, $8.25.

STRICKLAND'S (MISS) QUEENS OF SCOTLAND. Lives of the Queens of Scotland and English Princesses connected with the Regal Succession of Great Britain. By AGNES STRICKLAND. 8 vols., 12mo, Cloth, $12.00; Half Calf, $26.00.

BAKER'S ISMAÏLIA: a Narrative of the Expedition to Central Africa for the Suppression of the Slave-trade, organized by Ismaïl, Khedive of Egypt. By Sir SAMUEL W. BAKER. With Maps, Portraits, and Illustrations. 8vo, Cloth, $5.00; Half Calf, $7.25.

LIVINGSTONE'S LAST JOURNALS. The Last Journals of David Livingstone, in Central Africa, from 1865 to his Death. Continued by a Narrative of his Last Moments. By HORACE WALLER. With Portrait, Maps, and Illustrations. 8vo, Cloth, $5.00; Sheep, $6.00. Cheap Popular Edition, $2.50.

BLAIKIE'S LIFE OF DAVID LIVINGSTONE. Memoir of his Personal Life, from his Unpublished Journals and Correspondence. By W. G. BLAIKIE, D.D. With Portrait and Map. 8vo, Cloth, $2.25.

"THE FRIENDLY EDITION" OF SHAKESPEARE'S WORKS. Edited by W. J. ROLFE. In 20 Volumes. Illustrated. 16mo, Cloth, Uncut Edges and Gilt Tops, $30.00; Half Calf, $60.00 per Set.

GIESELER'S ECCLESIASTICAL HISTORY. A Text-Book of Church History. By Dr. JOHN C. L. GIESELER. Translated from the German. Revised and Edited by Rev. HENRY B. SMITH, D.D. Vols. I., II., III., and IV., 8vo, Cloth, $2.25; Vol. V., 8vo, Cloth, $3.00. Complete Sets, 5 vols., Sheep, $14.50; Half Calf, $23.25.

NORDHOFF'S COMMUNISTIC SOCIETIES OF THE UNITED STATES; including Detailed Accounts of the Economists, Zoarites, Shakers, the Amana, Oneida, Bethel, Aurora, Icarian, and other existing Societies. By CHARLES NORDHOFF. Illustrations. 8vo, Cloth, $4.00.

GENERAL BEAUREGARD'S MILITARY OPERATIONS. The Military Operations of General Beauregard in the War between the States, 1861 to 1865; including a brief Personal Sketch, and a Narrative of his Services in the War with Mexico, 1846 to 1848. By ALFRED ROMAN, formerly Aide-de-Camp on the Staff of General Beauregard. With Portraits, &c. 2 vols., 8vo, Cloth, $3.50; Sheep, $4.50; Half Morocco, $5.50; Full Morocco, $7.50. (*Sold only by Subscription.*)

CURTIS'S LIFE OF BUCHANAN. Life of James Buchanan, Fifteenth President of the United States. By GEORGE TICKNOR CURTIS. With Portraits. 2 vols., 8vo, Cloth, Uncut Edges and Gilt Tops, $6.00.

GRIFFIS'S MIKADO'S EMPIRE: Book I. History of Japan, from 660 B.C. to 1872 A.D. Book II. Personal Experiences, Observations, and Studies in Japan, from 1870 to 1874. By W. E. GRIFFIS. Copiously Illustrated. 8vo, Cloth, $4.00; Half Calf, $6.25.

SMILES'S HISTORY OF THE HUGUENOTS: their Settlements, Churches, and Industries in England and Ireland. By SAMUEL SMILES. With an Appendix relating to the Huguenots in America. Crown 8vo, Cloth, $2.00.

SMILES'S HUGUENOTS AFTER THE REVOCATION. The Huguenots in France after the Revocation of the Edict of Nantes; with a Visit to the Country of the Vaudois. By SAMUEL SMILES. Crown 8vo, Cloth, $2.00.

SMILES'S LIFE OF THE STEPHENSONS. The Life of George Stephenson, and of his Son, Robert Stephenson; comprising, also, a History of the Invention and Introduction of the Railway Locomotive. By SAMUEL SMILES. Illustrated. 8vo, Cloth, $3.00.

SCHLIEMANN'S ILIOS. The City and Country of the Trojans. A Narrative of the Most Recent Discoveries and Researches made on the Plain of Troy. By Dr. HENRY SCHLIEMANN. Maps, Plans, and Illustrations. Imperial 8vo, Illuminated Cloth, $12.00; Half Morocco, $15.00.

SCHLIEMANN'S TROJA. Results of the Latest Researches and Discoveries on the Site of Homer's Troy, made in the Year 1882, and a Narrative of a Journey in the Troad in 1881. By Dr. HENRY SCHLIEMANN. With Woodcuts, Maps, and Plans. 8vo, Cloth, $7.50; Half Calf, $10.00.

NORTON'S STUDIES OF CHURCH-BUILDING. Historical Studies of Church-Building in the Middle Ages. Venice, Siena, Florence. By CHARLES ELIOT NORTON. 8vo, Cloth, $3.00.

"THE VOYAGE OF THE "CHALLENGER." An Account of the General Results of the Voyage during 1873 and the Early Part of 1876. By Sir WYVILLE THOMSON, K.C.B. Ill'd. 2 vols., 8vo, Cloth, $12.00.

BOSWELL'S JOHNSON. The Life of Samuel Johnson, LL.D., including a Journal of a Tour to the Hebrides. By JAMES BOSWELL. Edited by J. W. CROKER, LL.D., F.R.S. With a Portrait of Boswell. 2 vols., 8vo, Cloth, $4.00; Sheep, $5.00.

OUTLINES OF ANCIENT HISTORY. From the Earliest Times to the Fall of the Western Roman Empire, A.D. 476. By P. V. N. MYERS, A.M. 12mo, Cloth, $1.75.

BROUGHAM'S AUTOBIOGRAPHY. Life and Times of Henry, Lord Brougham. Written by Himself. 3 vols., 12mo, Cloth, $6.00.

THE BEDOUIN TRIBES OF THE EUPHRATES. By LADY ANNE BLUNT. Edited, with a Preface and some Account of the Arabs and their Horses, by W. S. B. Map and Sketches by the Author. 8vo, Cloth, $2.50.

THE PAPACY AND THE CIVIL POWER. By the Hon. R. W. THOMPSON. Crown 8vo, Cloth, $3.00.

FOUR CENTURIES OF ENGLISH LETTERS. Selections from the Correspondence of One Hundred and Fifty Writers, from the Period of the Paston Letters to the Present Day. Edited by W. BAPTISTE SCOONES. 12mo, Cloth, $2.00.

THE POETS AND POETRY OF SCOTLAND. Comprising Characteristic Selections from the Works of the more Noteworthy Scottish Poets, with Biographical and Critical Notices. By JAMES GRANT WILSON. With Portraits. 2 vols., 8vo, Cloth $10.00; Gilt Edges, $11.00.

THE STUDENT'S SERIES. Maps and Illustrations. 12mo, Cloth:
  FRANCE.—GIBBON.—GREECE.—ROME (by LIDDELL).—OLD TESTAMENT HISTORY.—NEW TESTAMENT HISTORY.—STRICKLAND'S QUEENS OF ENGLAND.—ANCIENT HISTORY OF THE EAST.—HALLAM'S MIDDLE AGES.—HALLAM'S CONSTITUTIONAL HISTORY OF ENGLAND.—LYELL'S ELEMENTS OF GEOLOGY.—MERIVALE'S GENERAL HISTORY OF ROME. —COX'S GENERAL HISTORY OF GREECE.—CLASSICAL DICTIONARY.— SKEAT'S ETYMOLOGICAL DICTIONARY. $1.25 per volume.

  LEWIS'S HISTORY OF GERMANY. — ECCLESIASTICAL HISTORY. 2 vols.—HUME'S ENGLAND. $1.50 per volume.

BOURNE'S LOCKE. The Life of John Locke. By H. R. FOX BOURNE. 2 vols., 8vo, Cloth, $5.00.

COLERIDGE'S WORKS. The Complete Works of Samuel Taylor Coleridge. With Introductory Essay upon his Philosophical and Theological Opinions. Edited by Prof. W. G. T. SHEDD. With Portrait and Index. 7 vols., 12mo, Cloth, $2.00 per vol.; $12.00 per Set.

CAMERON'S ACROSS AFRICA. Across Africa. By VERNEY LOVETT CAMERON. Map and Illustrations. 8vo, Cloth, $5.00.

THE LAND AND THE BOOK. By WILLIAM M. THOMSON, D.D., Forty-five Years a Missionary in Syria and Palestine. In Three Volumes Copiously Illustrated. Square 8vo, Ornamental Cloth, $6.00; Sheep, $7.00; Half Morocco, $8.50; Full Morocco, Gilt Edges, $10.00 per Vol. (*The Volumes sold separately.*)

 Volume I. SOUTHERN PALESTINE AND JERUSALEM. (140 Illustrations and Maps.)
 Volume II. CENTRAL PALESTINE AND PHŒNICIA. (130 Illustrations and Maps.)
 Volume III. LEBANON, DAMASCUS, AND BEYOND JORDAN. (147 Illustrations and Maps.)

CYCLOPÆDIA OF BRITISH AND AMERICAN POETRY. Edited by EPES SARGENT. Royal 8vo, Ill'd Cloth, Colored Edges, $4.50.

NICHOLS'S ART EDUCATION. Art Education Applied to Industry. By G. W. NICHOLS. Illustrated. 8vo, Cloth, $4.00; Half Calf, $6.25.

CARLYLE'S WORKS:
 FREDERICK THE GREAT. History of Friedrich II., called Frederick the Great. Portraits, Maps, Plans, &c. 6 vols., 12mo, Cloth, $7.50.
 THE FRENCH REVOLUTION: a History. 2 vols., 12mo, Cloth, $2.50.
 OLIVER CROMWELL'S LETTERS AND SPEECHES. With Elucidations. 2 vols., 12mo, Cloth, $2.50.
 PAST AND PRESENT, CHARTISM, AND SARTOR RESARTUS. 12mo, Cloth, $1.25.
 EARLY KINGS OF NORWAY, AND THE PORTRAITS OF JOHN KNOX. 12mo, Cloth, $1.25.
 TOUR IN IRELAND IN 1849. With Portrait. 12mo. Cloth, $1.00.
 REMINISCENCES. 12mo, Cloth, 50 cents.

FROUDE'S LIFE OF THOMAS CARLYLE. Part I. A History of the First Forty Years of Carlyle's Life (1795–1835). Part II. A History of Carlyle's Life in London (1834–1881). By JAMES ANTHONY FROUDE, M.A. With Portraits and Illustrations. 2 vols., 12mo, Cloth, $1.00 per volume.

RANKE'S UNIVERSAL HISTORY. The Oldest Historical Group of Nations and the Greeks. By LEOPOLD VON RANKE. Edited by G. W. PROTHERO, Fellow and Tutor of King's College, Cambridge. pp. xvi., 494. 8vo, Cloth, $2.50.

www.ingramcontent.com/pod-product-compliance
Lightning Source LLC
Chambersburg PA
CBHW030558300426
44111CB00009B/1025